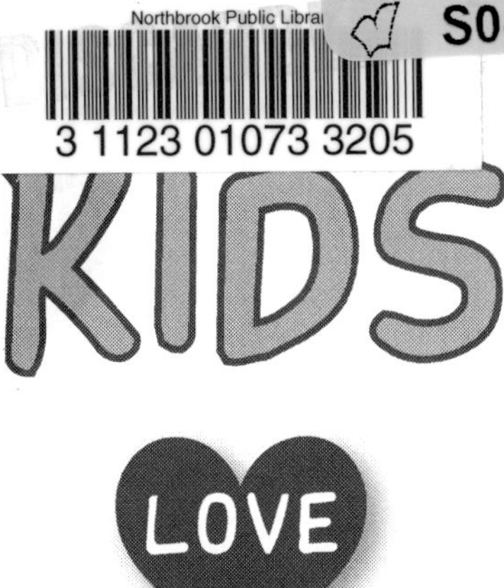

KIDS LOVE GEORGIA

3rd Edition

Your Family Travel Guide to Exploring Kid-Friendly Georgia
400 Fun Stops & Unique Spots

Michele Darrall Zavatsky

Dedicated to the Families of Georgia

In a Hundred Years...It will not matter, The size of my bank account...The kind of house that I lived in, the kind of car that I drove...But what will matter is...That the world may be different Because I was important in the life of a child.

- author unknown

For the latest major updates corresponding to the pages in this book visit our website:

www.KidsLoveTravel.com

- ***REMEMBER:*** *Museum exhibits change frequently. Check the site's website before you visit to note any changes. Also, HOURS and ADMISSIONS are subject to change at the owner's discretion. If you are tight on time or money, check the attraction's website or call before you visit.*
- ***INTERNET PRECAUTION:*** *All websites mentioned in KIDS LOVE GEORGIA have been checked for appropriate content. However, due to the fast-changing nature of the Internet, we strongly urge parents to preview any recommended sites and to always supervise their children when on-line.*
- ***EDUCATORS:*** *There are suggestions for finding FREE lessons plans embedded in many listings as helpful notes for educators.*

ISBN-13: 978-0-615926049

KIDS ♥ Georgia ™ Kids Love Publications, LLC

TABLE OF CONTENTS

State Detail Map

(With Major Routes and Cities Marked)

Chapter Area Map

(Chapters arranged alphabetically by chapter name)

HOW TO USE THIS BOOK

(a few hints to make your adventures run smoothly:)

BEFORE YOU LEAVE:

- Each chapter represents a two hour radius area of the state or a Day Trip. The chapter begins with an introduction and Quick Tour of favorites within the chapter. The listings are by City and then alphabetical by name, numeric by zip code. Each listing has tons of important details (pricing, hours, website, etc.) and a review noting the most engaging aspects of the place. Our popular Activity Index in back is helpful if you want to focus on a particular type of attraction (i.e. History, Tours, Outdoor Exploring, Animals & Farms, etc.).
- Begin by assigning each family member a different colored highlighter (for example: Daniel gets blue, Jenny gets pink, Mommy gets yellow and Daddy gets green). At your leisure, begin to read each review and put a highlighter "check" mark next to the sites that most interest each family member or highlight the features you most want to see. Now, when you go to plan a quick trip - or a long van ride - you can easily choose different stops in one day to please everyone.
- Know directions and parking. Use a GPS system or print off directions from websites.
- Most attractions are closed major holidays unless noted.
- When children are in tow, it is better to make your lodging reservations ahead of time. Every time we've tried to "wing it", we've always ended up at a place that was overpriced, in a unsafe area, or not super clean. We've never been satisfied when we didn't make a reservation ahead of time.
- If you have a large family, or are traveling with extended family or friends, most places offer group discounts. Check out the company's website for details.
- For the latest critical updates corresponding to the pages in this book, visit our website: www.kidslovetravel.com. Click on *Updates*.

ON THE ROAD:

- Consider the child's age before you stop at an exit. Some attractions and restaurants, even hotels, are too formal for young ones or not enough adventure for teens. Read our trusted reviews first.
- Estimate the duration of the trip and how many stops you can afford to make. From our experience, it is best to stop every two hours to stretch your legs or eat/snack or maybe visit an inexpensive attraction.
- Bring along travel books and games for "quiet time" in the van. (see tested travel products on www.kidslovetravel.com) As an added bonus, these "enriching" games also stimulate conversation - you may get to know your family better and create memorable life lessons.

ON THE ROAD: *(cont.)*

- In between meals, we offer the family snacks like: pretzels, whole grain chips, nuts, water bottles, bite-size (dark) chocolates, grapes and apples. None of these are messy and all are healthy.
- Plan picnics along the way. Many Historical sites and State Parks are scattered along the highway. Allow time for a rest stop or a scenic byway to take advantage of these free picnic facilities.

WHEN YOU GET HOME:

- Make a family "treasure chest". Decorate a big box or use an old popcorn tin. Store memorabilia from a fun outing, journals, pictures, brochures and souvenirs. Once a year, look through the "treasure chest" and reminisce. "Kids Love Travel Memories!" is an excellent travel journal and scrapbook template that your family can create (available on www.kidslovetravel.com).

WAYS TO SAVE MONEY:

- Memberships - many children's museums, science centers, zoos and aquariums are members of associations that provide FREE or Discounted reciprocity to other such museums across the country. AAA Auto Club cards offer discounts to many of the activities and hotels in this book. If grandparents are along for the ride, they can use their AARP card and get discounts. Be sure to carry your member cards with you as proof to receive the discounts.
- Supermarket Customer Cards - national and local supermarkets often offer good discounted tickets to major attractions in the area.
- Internet Hotel Reservations - if you're traveling with kids, don't take the risk of being spontaneous with lodging. Make reservations ahead of time. We don't use non-refundable, deep discount hotel "scouting" websites (ex. Hotwire) unless we're traveling on business - just adults. You can't cancel your reservation, or change them, and you can't be guaranteed the type of room you want (ex. non-smoking, two beds). Instead, stick with a national hotel chain you trust and join their rewards program (ex. Choice Privileges) to accumulate points towards FREE night stays.
- State Travel Centers - as you enter a new state, their welcome centers offer many current promotions.
- Hotel Lobbies - often have a display of discount coupons to area shops and restaurants. When you check in, ask the clerk for discount pizza coupons they may have at the front desk.
- Attraction Online Coupons - check the websites listed with each review for possible printable coupons or discounted online tickets good towards the attraction.

MISSION STATEMENT

At first glance, you may think that this is a book that just lists hundreds of places to travel. While it is true that we've invested thousands of hours of exhaustive research (*and drove over 3000 miles in Georgia*) to prepare this travel resource…just listing places to travel is not the mission statement of these projects.

As a child, I was able to travel throughout the United States. I consider these family times some of the greatest memories I cherish today. Quite frankly, I felt that most children had this opportunity to travel with their family. However, as we started our own family, we found that wasn't necessarily the case. We continually heard friends express several concerns when deciding how to spend "quality" and "quantity" family time. 1) What to do? 2) Where to do it? 3) How much will it cost? 4) How do I know that my kids will enjoy it?

Interestingly enough, as I reflect on experiences with my family trips, many of the fondest memories were not made at an expensive attraction, but rather when it was least expected.

It is my belief and mission statement that if you as a family will study and use the contained information to create family memories, these memories will grow more well-rounded children. Our ultimate mission statement is, that your children will develop a love and a passion for quality family experiences that they can pass to another generation of family travelers.

We thank you for purchasing this book, and we hope to see you on the road (*and hear your travel stories!*) God bless your journeys!

Happy Exploring, Michele

General State Agency & Recreational Information

Call *(or visit websites)* for the services of interest. Request to be added to their mailing lists.

- ❑ Georgia State Parks (800) 864-7275 www.gastateparks.org
- ❑ Georgia Travel Information (800) VISIT GA or www.exploregeorgia.org
- ❑ **MW** - Columbus Area Convention & Visitors Bureau - www.columbusgeorgiaonline.com
- ❑ **MW** - Macon-Bibb County Convention & Visitors Bureau - www.maconga.org
- ❑ **ME** - Augusta Metro Convention & Visitors Bureau - www.AugustaGA.org
- ❑ **NE** - Georgia Mountains Regional Tourism - www.georgiamountains.org

- ❑ **NW** - Atlanta Convention & Visitors Bureau - (800) ATLANTA or www.atlanta.net
- ❑ **NW** - Cartersville area Tourism - www.notatlantaga.org
- ❑ **SE** - Brunswick and the Golden Isles (St. Simons, Sea Island, Jekyll Island) CVB - (800) 933-COAST or www.bgivb.com
- ❑ **SE** - Savannah Area Convention & Visitors Bureau - www.savannahvisit.com.
- ❑ **SE** - Tybee Island - www.tybeevisit.com

Check out these businesses / services in your area for tour ideas:

AIRPORTS - All children love to visit the airport! Why not take a tour and understand all the jobs it takes to run an airport? Tour the terminal, baggage claim, gates and security / currency exchange. Maybe you'll even get to board a plane.

ANIMAL SHELTERS - Great for the would-be pet owner. Not only will you see many cats and dogs available for adoption, but a guide will show you the clinic and explain the needs of a pet. Be prepared to have the children "fall in love" with one of the animals while they are there!

BANKS - Take a "behind the scenes" look at automated teller machines, bank vaults and drive-thru window chutes. You may want to take this tour and then open a savings account for your child.

CITY HALLS - Halls of Fame, City Council Chambers & Meeting Room, Mayor's Office and famous statues.

ELECTRIC COMPANY / POWER PLANTS - Modern science has created many ways to generate electricity today, but what really goes on with the "flip of a switch". Because coal can be dirty, wear old, comfortable clothes. Coal furnaces heat water, which produces steam, that propels turbines, that drives generators, that make electricity.

FIRE STATIONS - Many Open Houses in October, Fire Prevention Month. Take a look into the life of the firefighters servicing your area and try on their gear. See where they hang out, sleep and eat. Hop aboard a real-life fire engine truck and learn fire safety too.

HOSPITALS - Some Children's Hospitals offer pre-surgery and general tours.

NEWSPAPERS - You'll be amazed at all the new technology. See monster printers and robotics. See samples in the layout department and maybe try to put together your own page. After seeing a newspaper made, most companies give you a free copy (dated that day) as your souvenir. National Newspaper Week is in October.

PETCO - Various stores. Contact each store manager to see if they participate. The Fur, Feathers & Fins™ program allows children to learn about the characteristics and habitats of fish, reptiles, birds, and small animals. At your local Petco, lessons in science, math and geography come to life through this hands-on field trip. As students develop a respect for animals, they will also develop a greater sense of responsibility.

PIZZA HUT & PAPA JOHN'S - Participating locations. Telephone the store manager. Best days are Monday, Tuesday and Wednesday mid-afternoon. Minimum of 10 people. Small charge per person. All children love pizza – especially when they can create their own! As the children tour the kitchen, they learn how to make a pizza, bake it, and then eat it. The admission charge generally includes lots of creatively made pizzas, beverage and coloring book.

KRISPY KREME DONUTS - Participating locations. Get an "inside look" and learn the techniques that make these donuts some of our favorites! Watch the dough being made in "giant" mixers, being formed into donuts and taking a "trip" through the fryer. Seeing them being iced and topped with colorful sprinkles is always a favorite with the kids. Contact your local store manager. They prefer Monday or Tuesday. Free.

SUPERMARKETS - Kids are fascinated to go behind the scenes of the same store where Mom and Dad shop. Usually you will see them grind meat, walk into large freezer rooms, watch cakes and bread bake and receive free samples along the way. Maybe you'll even get to pet a live lobster!

TV / RADIO STATIONS - Studios, newsrooms, Fox kids clubs. Why do weathermen never wear blue/green clothes on TV? What makes a "DJ's" voice sound so deep and smooth?

WATER TREATMENT PLANTS - A giant science experiment! You can watch seven stages of water treatment. The favorite is usually the wall of bright buttons flashing as workers monitor the different processes.

U.S. MAIN POST OFFICES - Did you know Ben Franklin was the first Postmaster General (over 200 years ago)? Most interesting is the high-speed automated mail processing equipment. Learn how to address envelopes so they will be sent quicker (there are secrets). To make your tour more interesting, have your children write a letter to themselves and address it with colorful markers. Mail it earlier that day and they will stay interested trying to locate their letter in all the high-speed machinery.

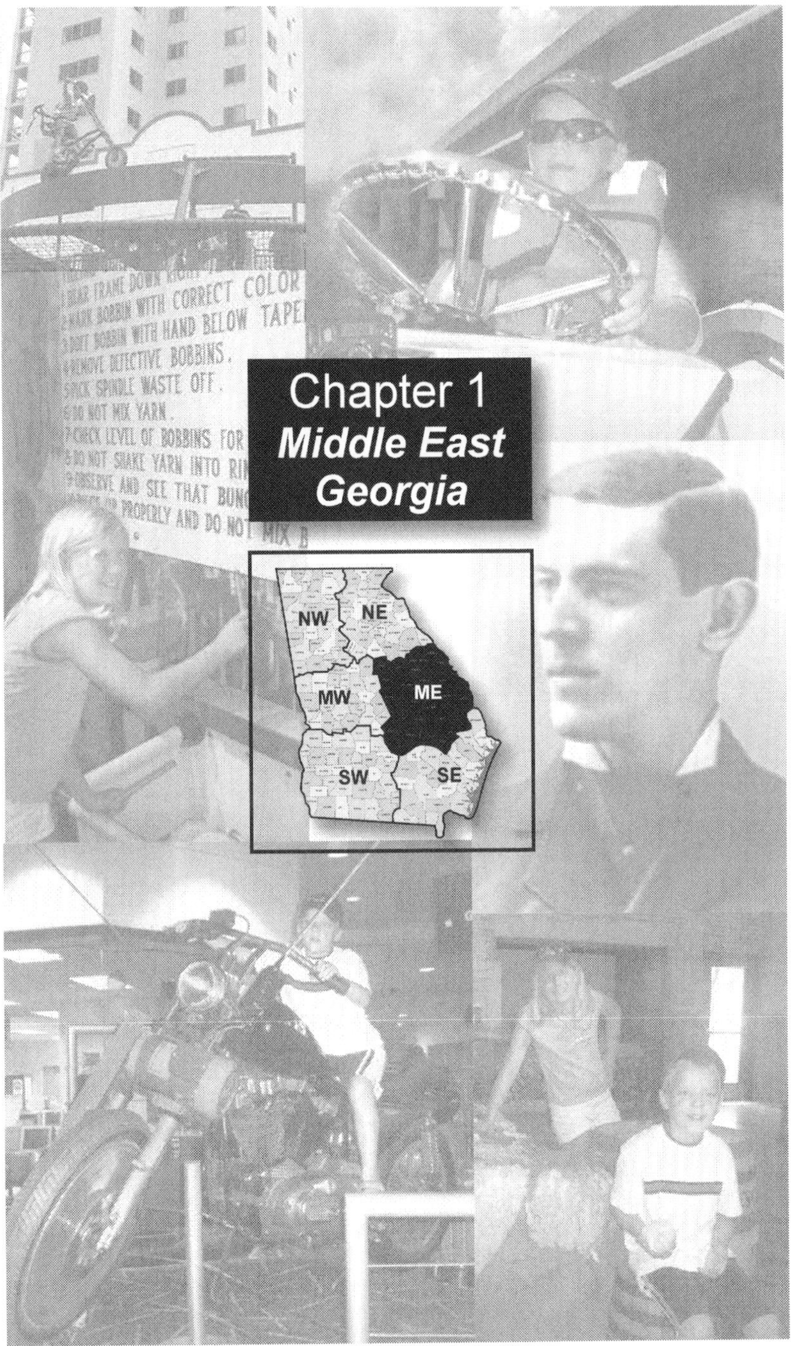

Chapter 1
Middle East Georgia

Appling

- Mistletoe State Park

Augusta

- Augusta Canal
- Augusta Museum Of History
- Fort Discovery, National Science Center's
- Phinizy Swamp Nature Park
- President Woodrow Wilson Boyhood Home
- July 4th Celebration - River Blast

Eatonton

- Oconee National Forest

Harlem

- Laurel And Hardy Museum

Helena

- Little Ocmulgee State Park And Lodge

Metter

- Christmas In The Gardens

Millen

- Magnolia Springs State Park

Mitchell

- Hamburg State Park

Reidsville

- Gordonia-Alatamaha State Park

Statesboro

- Georgia Southern University Nature Centers

Twin City

- George L. Smith State Park

Vidalia

- Vidalia Onion Factory
- Vidalia Onion Festival

Warrenton

- Ogeechee River Mill

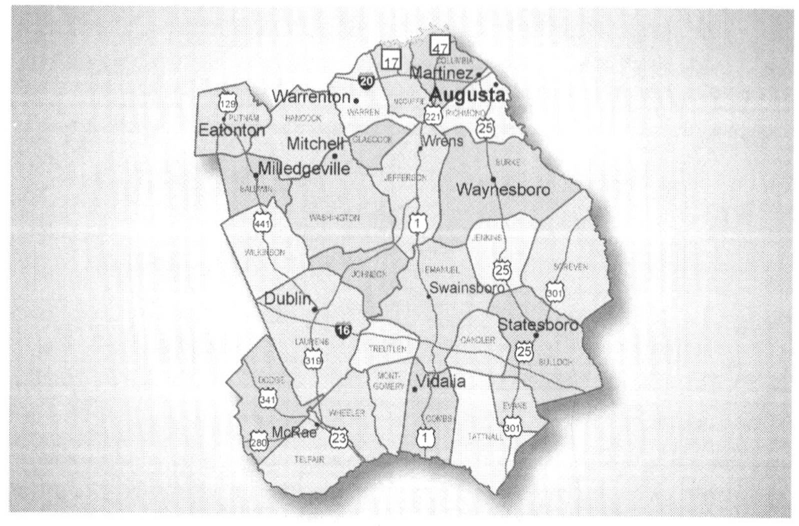

A Quick Tour of our Hand-Picked Favorites Around...

Middle East Georgia

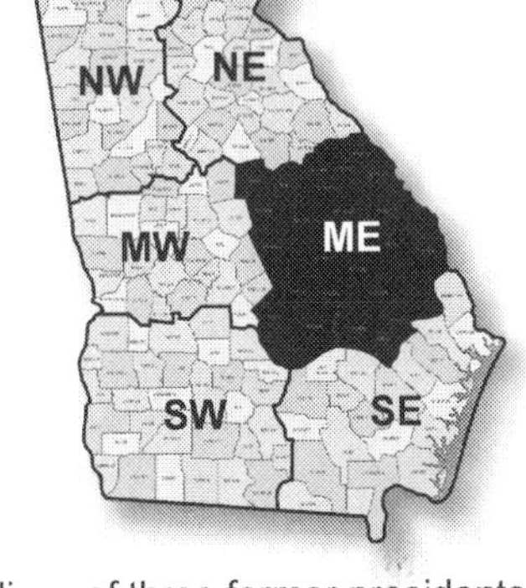

Southern people, culture, heritage and events have had an impact on American and World history through the lives of three former presidents. One of them was **Woodrow Wilson**. Walk the halls of the Augusta home where President Woodrow Wilson lived as boy and hear how some of his childhood experiences helped shape him as the Nation's 28th President. Listen for stories of some of the pranks he liked to play.

Nearby, meander along the banks of the Savannah River as you stroll Riverwalk Augusta. Canoe the river or the adjacent **Augusta Canal**. The Canal Heritage Corridor is the place to relive the Industrial Revolution. Kids can steer a canal boat, pick cotton, or play the lightning speed round of the Bobbin Game. The exhibit spaces aren't roped off but rather "invite in."

The National Science Center's **Fort Discovery** location along another part of the Riverwalk is not to be missed – especially if you have 8 year olds to teens in tow. If Science could be completely taught in one classroom setting – this would be the place. Exhibits range from indoor lightning to pendulum swings, "chopping up" sound into bits, and thermal imaging technology. Slide around and down the two-story Martian Tower or witness Morse code via a water fountain, super soaker display. Play virtual sports, ride a motorcycle or a magnetic car - all using principles of math and motion to operate.

The rest of this area is blessed with dozens of state parks and nature centers. See otters, egrets and alligators in **Phinizy Swamp Nature Park**, over 1150 acres of wild lands in an urban Nature Park via trails, boardwalks, and observation decks. Another easy to manage family outdoor adventure is found at **Georgia Southern University Nature Centers**. Their Raptor Center and elevated walkways eliminate the challenge of having to trudge through muck to see the good stuff.

Sites and attractions are listed in order by City, Zip Code, and Name. Symbols indicated represent:

Festivals Restaurants Lodging

Appling

MISTLETOE STATE PARK

Appling - *3723 Mistletoe Road (I-20 exit 175 north 8 miles) 30802. Phone: (706) 541-0321. http://gastateparks.org/info/mistletoe/. Hours: Daily 7:00am-10:00pm. Admission: $5.00 daily vehicle parking fee. **NOTICE: When there is lengthening drought the fishing dock and ALL boat ramps at the Park are unusable until further notice.***

Located on Clarks Hill Lake near Augusta, this park is known as one of the finest bass fishing spots in the nation. Summer guests can cool down at the beach or on miles of shaded nature trails. Canoes and fishing boats may be rented, and a wildlife observation area is available. The park has several fully equipped cottages on the lake, five of which are log cabins. The campground is on a peninsula, offering wonderful views of sunsets over the open water. A multi-camper cabin with electricity and water faces the lake.

Augusta

AUGUSTA CANAL

Augusta - *1450 Greene Street (3/4 mile from Riverwalk Downtown, Enterprise Mill complex, I-20 exit 200) 30901. www.augustacanal.com. Phone: (706) 823-7089. Hours: Monday-Saturday 9:30am-5:30pm, Sunday 1:00-5:30pm. Closed winter Mondays. Admission: Center: $6.00 adult, $5.00 senior (55+) & Military, $4.00 youth (6-18). Boat (includes admission to center): $12.50 adult, $10.50 senior, military & students. Purchase tickets inside the Interpretive Center. Tours: One-hour boat tour: Monday-Saturday departures: 10:00am, 11:30am, 1:30pm. Saturday also 3:00pm. Passengers may bring beverages*

Huge bales of the cotton crop

on board. Note: Canoe, walk or bike the historic Canal and its towpath and trails. Pass restored lockkeepers, cottage, dance pavilion and barbeque pit. Educators: a wealth of thorough Lesson Plans & simple Worksheets online under School/ Field Trips links.

Capt. Daniel piloting the canal boat

Learn the history of the nation's only industrial power canal still in use for its original purposes (the canal is still used for supply water and water power to the city). Visit the interactive Canal Interpretive Center, located in a reclaimed 19th century textile mill where models, machinery, and movies tell the story of the Industrial Revolution in the New South. The Canal was built to control water from the Savannah River for the textile industry in 1845. Exhibits illustrate how waterpower was harnessed, creating electricity to run the factories (try generating power yourself operating a flywheel), provide lighting and the streetcar system. Gaze through the mill floor itself to view the huge mill-race as canal water surges beneath your feet on its way to and from turbines. Hands-on activities such as the "Bobbin game" encourage motor skills and speed as kids must beat the clock to spool bobbins, much like the original mill operation. Handwritten letters and oral histories tell stories of mill families. A walk-in mill house display is complete with furniture demonstrating the living conditions in those days. Lots of "Oh, look at this!" here.

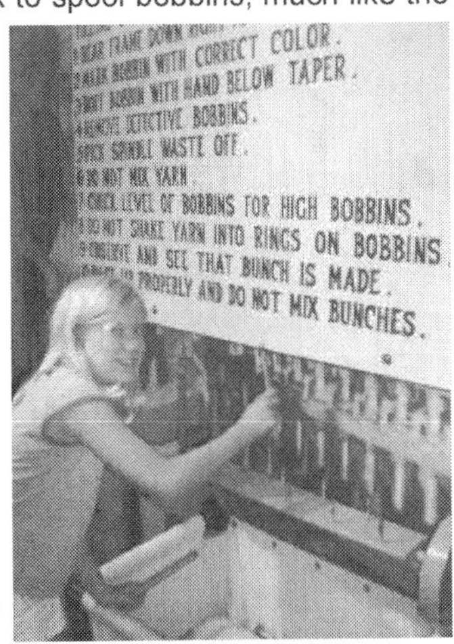

Jenny tries to beat the clock in the "Bobbin Game"...

The PETERSBURG BOATS were utilized to transport cotton and other goods to and from the mills. You can now ride part of the original canal path. Shallow tour boats take passengers (vs. cargo) along half the length of the canal. Pass old mill factories still in use, historic mill homes, several bridges or overpasses and look for yellow-bellied slider turtles. The kids even get to captain the boat on the way back. Well done!

AUGUSTA MUSEUM OF HISTORY

Augusta - *560 Reynolds Street (I-20 exit 200 onto Riverwatch Pkwy., between 5th and 6th Street, downtown) 30901. www.augustamuseum.org. Phone: (706) 722-8454. Hours: Tuesday-Saturday 10:00am-5:00pm, Sunday 1:00-5:00pm. Closed Mondays and legal holidays. Admission: $4.00 adult, $3.00 senior, $2.00 student (6-18). Note: The Hunt for History Scavenger Hunt with Time Travelers Mr. Peabody & Sherman is free with Museum admission, just ask. Educators: specific Hunt for History Worksheets on 5 different topics: www.augustamuseum.org/TeacherResources.*

This museum's multi-media permanent exhibit, "Augusta's Story", traces 12,000 years of local history from a 10,000 year old projectile point to a 1914 locomotive. The site presents the events, people and forces that shaped the community. Climb aboard the passenger car of a 1914 train, see James Brown Memorabilia and view a photo collection of past Masters® Champions. Children can participate in hands-on history in the Children's Discovery Gallery. Fly a plane... Command a space shuttle mission... Canoe the Savannah River. Find out about the important role of local medicine to the community.

PHINIZY SWAMP NATURE PARK

Augusta - *1858 Lock & Dam Road (Lock & Dam Road, near the airport) 30901. Phone: (706) 828-2109. http://naturalsciencesacademy.org/. Hours: Open dawn to dusk. Visitors Center open weekends 9:00am-5:00pm.*

See otters, egrets and alligators in Phinizy Swamp Nature Park, over 1150 acres of wild lands in an urban Nature Park. Visitors can enjoy the natural resources of the swamp and its wildlands at this park via trails, boardwalks, observation decks. A newer boardwalk enables visitors to "walk across the swamp". Look for blue heron, too. The Visitor Center includes a breathtaking view of the swamp, a sneak peak at the "Look Outside at Phinizy Swamp" video, species lists, and park maps. Staffed entirely by volunteers, the Center is soon to be complete with educational displays on area history, wetland wildlife and habitats, and restoration ecology.

PRESIDENT WOODROW WILSON BOYHOOD HOME

Augusta - *419 Seventh Street 30901. www.wilsonboyhoodhome.org. Phone: (706) 722-9828. Hours: Monday - Saturday 10:00am-5:00pm. Last tour departs at 4:00pm. Admission: $5.00 adult, $4.00 senior (60+), $3.00 student (K-12). Note: Parking is available adjacent to the Lamar House at 415 Seventh Street and along Telfair Street. Educators: Click on Learn for Biography pages.*

Thomas Woodrow Wilson was inaugurated as the 28th President of the United States on March 4, 1913. In 1917, during his second term, the United States entered the First World War and Wilson played an international role in the negotiation of the Treaty of Versailles and the organization of the League of Nations. Walk the halls of the home where President Woodrow Wilson lived as boy and hear how some of his childhood experiences helped shape him as the Nation's 28th President. "Tommy" lived in this house for 10 years of his childhood in Augusta. Hear stories of the hardships of the Civil War and Reconstruction, baseball clubs and being raised in a minister's home. Do you think he was a Mamma's Boy? Who put the scuff marks in the dining room table? How do we know Woodrow "borrowed" his mother's diamond ring? (clue: what about the etchings on the window?). You'll see many original furnishings of the Wilson family within the home.

A look at a younger Woodrow Wilson

JULY 4TH CELEBRATION - RIVER BLAST

Augusta - *River Walk / Augusta Common. www.augustaga.org. Activities include musical entertainment, dance, patriotic concert, cannon firing and fireworks display.*

Eatonton

OCONEE NATIONAL FOREST

Eatonton - ***1199 Madison Road 31024. www.fs.usda.gov/conf/. Phone: (706) 485-7110.***

Many visitors enjoy Oconee's recreation facilities - daily, for FREE. There are camping areas; trails for horses, hikers, and all-terrain vehicles; boat launches, picnic areas; and wildlife viewing areas. Annually, the Oconee hosts a Kid's Fishing Rodeo to promote outdoor activities for young people. Come and visit some of the more popular sites, such as Skull Shoals Historic Area, Dyar Pasture waterfowl habitat, Falling Creek beaver pond, and the newly restored Miller Lake.

Harlem

LAUREL AND HARDY MUSEUM

Harlem - *250 N Louisville Street (I-20 exit 183 south, follow signs) 30814. Phone: (706) 556-0401. www.laurelandhardymuseum.com. Hours: Tuesday-Saturday 10:00am-4:00pm. Admission: Donations. Note: Hardy's mustachioed face is everywhere, from the water tower looming overhead to the sign welcoming visitors on the outskirts of town.*

Looking for another nice mess to get into? Head to Harlem, birthplace of Oliver Hardy and home of the Laurel and Hardy Museum. The museum is the only one in the United States for the "rotund member" of one of Hollywood's greatest comedy teams. Oliver Hardy was born in Harlem in 1892. The museum is filled with memorabilia items donated from all over the world. The museum even has two hats worn by Laurel and Hardy in movies — a pith helmet from 1935's "Bonnie Scotland" and a fez from 1933's "Sons of the Desert." Everyone knows hats where a big part of their act. The kids will really get a kick out of watching the Laurel & Hardy movies shown continuously. Children drop by after school and join tourists in the museum's back room, munching on homemade cookies as they watch one of Laurel and Hardy's 106 movies - they even request favorites.

Helena

LITTLE OCMULGEE STATE PARK & LODGE

Helena - *80 Live Oak Trail (I-16 exit 51 south, 2 miles north of town via US 319 and 441) 31037. Phone: (229) 868-6651. http://gastateparks.org/info/liocmulgee/. Hours: Daily 7:00am-10:00pm. Lodge hours 6:00am-midnight. Admission: $5.00 daily vehicle parking fee.*

Boaters and anglers will enjoy the park's 265-acre lake that includes a swimming beach. Hikers enjoy the Oak Ridge Trail winding through scrub oaks and pines towards a buzzard roost and boardwalk (2.5 mile trail). The renovated lodge offers hotel-style guest rooms, a restaurant with golf course view, and a swimming pool and tennis courts. There are campsite, cottage and canoe/pedal boat rentals and a mini-golf course within the park, too.

Metter

CHRISTMAS IN THE GARDENS

Metter - *Guido Gardens, 600 N. Lewis Street (GA 121 North).* ***www.n-georgia.com/guido-gardens.html*** *One million lights burning bright. Flying angels over the manger scene, animated Fishermen and Butterflies, and Noah and the ark. Enjoy this walk-through experience celebrating the beauty and wonder of Christmas. (nightly, entire month of December)*

Millen

MAGNOLIA SPRINGS STATE PARK

Millen - ***1053 Magnolia Springs Drive (5 miles north of Millen on US 25) 30442. Phone: (478) 982-1660. http://gastateparks.org/info/magspr/. Hours: Daily 7:00am-10:00pm. Aquarium: Daily 9:00am-4:00pm. Admission: $5.00 daily vehicle parking fee.***

The park is known for its crystal clear springs flowing 7 million gallons of water per day and the beautiful boardwalk which spans the cool water. Visitors may watch for alligators, turtles and other wildlife near the springs. A free, freshwater aquarium features native species to the area. The 28-acre lake is available for fishing and boating. Historically, during the Civil War, the site was called Camp Lawton and served as "the world's largest prison." Today, little remains of the prison stockade except some earthen breastworks. Hikers and bikers can enjoy the 10 miles of trails. A pool is open seasonally.

Mitchell

HAMBURG STATE PARK

Mitchell - ***6071 Hamburg State Park Road (I-20 exit 54 south or off GA 102, 20 miles north of Sandersville) 30820. http://gastateparks.org/info/hamburg/. Phone: (478) 552-2393. Hours: Daily 7:00am-10:00pm. Admission: $5.00 daily vehicle parking fee.***

Hamburg State Park offers a wonderful mix of history and outdoor recreation. Anglers can enjoy great lake fishing for largemouth bass, crappie and bream, as well as boat ramps and a fishing pier. Campers find shaded campsites along the edge of the lake.

See the insides of a working gristmill

The restored 1921 water-powered grist mill is still operational and beckons visitors to buy a bag of corn meal at the country store (call ahead to ask when it will be operating - every other Saturday from March thru October). The mill museum displays old agricultural tools and appliances used in rural Georgia.

Reidsville

GORDONIA-ALATAMAHA STATE PARK

Reidsville - *322 Park Lane, HWY 280 West (just off US 280, I-16 exit 98) 30453. Phone: (912) 557-7744. http://gastateparks.org/info/gordonalt/. Hours: Daily 7:00am-10:00pm. Admission: $5.00 daily vehicle parking fee.*

Gordonia-Alatamaha's unusual name comes from the rare Gordonia tree - a member of the bay family - and the original spelling of the nearby Altamaha River. This park is a favorite for picnicking, family reunions and golf. Picnic tables and shelters surround a small lake, where visitors can swim or rent pedal boats and fishing boats during warmer months (no private boats allowed). Docks are available for anglers and children enjoy looking for beaver dams from the observation deck.

Statesboro

GEORGIA SOUTHERN UNIVERSITY NATURE CENTERS

Statesboro - *(GA 25 to US 301, North Mail Street. Follow signs) 30460. Admission: FREE. www.georgiasouthern.edu/public.php. Educators: Teaching Tool Kits are available to rent and include many curriculum and hands-on activities to do.*

The University has three great areas for family learning and adventure:

CENTER FOR WILDLIFE EDUCATION AND THE RAPTOR CENTER - Five acres in the heart of campus provide a center including a self-guided nature walk through six habitat displays, housing eleven species of live birds of prey. Within these habitats, wetlands, mountains, and forest you have an opportunity to view native raptors in their natural environments. An elevated walkway allows visitors an unobstructed and up-close encounter with a Bald

Eagle nest, complete with a live Eagle!

The Children's Discovery Trail has 17 exploratory stations and an eagle nest "fly-in" area. The Pavilion or Amphitheater hold flighted raptor demonstrations (rain or shine). Falconers fly several species of birds of prey while explaining the various adaptations the wounded birds must make. Take the field guide challenge indoors through the Center's hands-on encounter displays. Try to locate and identify the 50+ animals inhabiting the exhibit. Also indoors, you will find the reptile program including hands-on reptiles and amphibians. (912-681-0831, Weekdays 9:00am-5:00pm, School Year Saturdays 1:00-5:00pm. Public demos on weekends. Group tours, weekdays. Closed summer Sundays.)

BOTANICAL GARDENS - The native Southern and coastal gardens surround an old cottage. Volunteer for the Children's Vegetable Garden where you'll learn to cultivate the soil, nurture seeds and finally harvest vegetables. Each Wednesday, you'll work in the garden with staff and volunteers to grow produce to donate to the Statesboro Food Bank. (1505 Bland Avenue. 912-871-1149, open 9:00am-dusk. Tours by appointment.)

MUSEUM - Traveling natural history displays might have you reconstruct ancient structures or dig for dino eggs. A 25-foot fossil of a prehistoric Mosasaur greets visitors along with the oldest whale fossil found in North America. (Southern Drive, Rosenwald Bldg., 912-681-5444. Weekdays 9:00am-5:00pm, weekends 2:00-5:00pm.)

Twin City

GEORGE L. SMITH STATE PARK

Twin City - ***371 George L. Smith State Park Road (I-16 exit 104, off GA 23) 30471. Phone: (478) 763-2759. http://gastateparks.org/info/georgels/. Hours: Daily 7:00am-10:00pm. Admission: $5.00 daily vehicle parking fee.***

The park is named after one of Georgia's great legislators. With lakeside camping and cozy cottages, this secluded park is the perfect south Georgia retreat. It is best known for the Parrish Mill, a combination grist mill, sawmill, covered bridge and dam built in 1880 and still open for tours.

Anglers and canoeists can explore the mill pond dotted with Spanish moss-draped trees and home to blue heron and gopher tortoises. There are 11 miles of walking and biking trails. Look for the Annual Cane Grinding event each November as they turn cane into syrup.

Vidalia

VIDALIA ONION FACTORY

Vidalia - ***US Hwy 280E, 3309 East First Street (I-16 south to US 1 east to Lyons. Turn right on Hwy 280, straight about 3 miles) 30474. Phone: (912) 526-3466. www.vidaliaonionfactory.com. Tours: Pre-arranged through Vidalia Area CVB at (912) 538-8687. Note: A small sandwich shop is within the store.***

Do you love Vidalia Onions? A visit to the Vidalia Onion Factory is a perfect way to make your trip yummy (free samples) and fun (interesting onion facts). You'll see it on the left side of the highway - in the middle of an onion field! The Vidalia sweet onion was first grown back in 1931. It is a family business, owned and operated by Stanley Farms. Several hundred acres are devoted to Georgia's Official State Vegetable - the sweet Vidalia Onion. Farmers and scientists have concluded that the loamy soil and mild temperatures combine to give the Vidalia Onion its sweet taste. In fact, the Vidalia Onion can only be grown in 14 southeast Georgia counties and parts of six others. Free seasonal factory tours are available with advanced scheduling. Harvesting and processing begins in mid-April and continues through mid-June.

VIDALIA ONION FESTIVAL

Vidalia - *Downtown 99905. Phone: (912) 538-8687. www.vidaliaga.com. Festival events include an air show, fireworks, a street dance, rodeo, onion-eating contest, etc. (first long weekend in May)*

Warrenton

OGEECHEE RIVER MILL

Warrenton - ***262 Reynolds Road (I-20 exit 154 east on US 278) 30828. Phone: (706) 465-9683. Admission: FREE. Tours: Mondays & Wednesdays at 8:30am. Call in advance for confirmation.***

Not many things are done as they were 150-200 years ago but Alvester "Cabbage" Allen grinds corn meal just like they did centuries ago. See how good, old-fashioned ground Georgia corn meal is milled.

He starts by lifting the gates impounding the Ogeechee River, allowing tons of water to flow through the turbine. A wheel in the mill house is turned, activating a shaft and the mill rumbles into action. The millstones are made of a special kind of granite. One stone is about 6" thick and is stationary. The other, is two tons, and is rotated by waterpower. As the cracked corn is slowly fed into the hole, out below comes a small stream of fine corn meal, which is warm when it comes from the stones. You'll love the smell! Try the "Ogeechee Hush Puppy Mix".

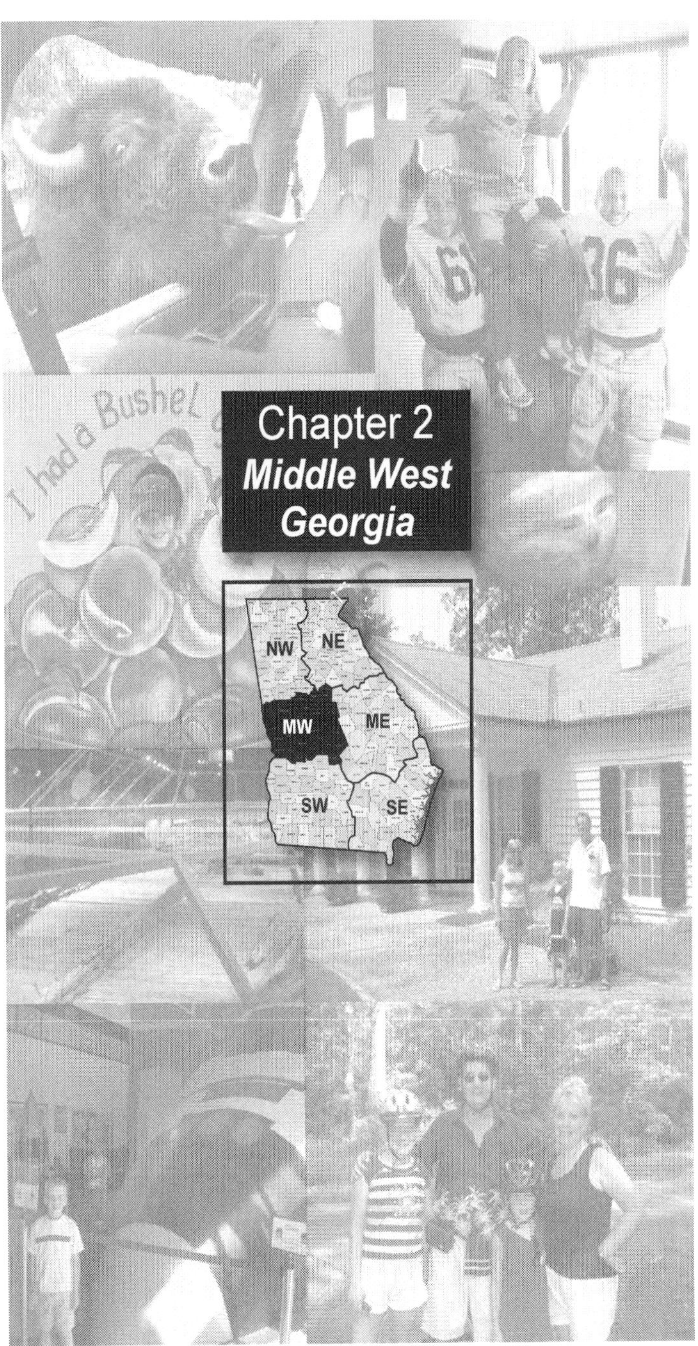

Chapter 2 *Middle West Georgia*

Andersonville

- Andersonville National Historic Site/ National Pow Museum

Barnesville

- Barnesville Buggy Days

Columbus

- Coca-Cola Space Science Center
- Columbus Symphony Orchestra
- Oxbow Meadows Environmental Learning Center
- Port Columbus National Civil War Naval Museum
- Port Columbus National Civil War Naval Museum - River Blast
- Port Columbus National Civil War Naval Museum - Southern Pirate Festival
- Port Columbus National Civil War Naval Museum - Victorian Holiday House
- Country Inn & Suites, ColumBus
- Columbus Museum
- Dinglewood Pharmacy Lunch Counter
- Country's Barbeque

Flovilla

- Indian Springs State Park

Fort Valley

- Lane Southern Orchards
- Lane Southern Orchards - Corn Maze Days

Gay

- Cotton Pickin' Fair

Hamilton

- Ossahatchee Indian Festival And Pow-Wow

Jackson

- High Falls State Park

Juliette

- Jarrell Plantation Historic Site
- Jarrell Plantation Historic Site - Old Fashioned July 4th
- Jarrell Plantation Historic Site - Syrup Makin' & Storytellin'
- Jarrell Plantation Historic Site - Plantation Christmas
- Whistle Stop Café - Fried Green Tomatoes

LaGrange

- Explorations Antiquity Center
- Azalea Storytelling Festival

Macon

- Around Town Tours – Macon
- Around Town Tours - Macon - Christmas Open House
- Georgia Music Hall Of Fame
- Georgia Sports Hall Of Fame
- Nu-Way Weiners
- Sidney Lanier Cottage
- Tubman African American Museum
- Tubman African American Museum - Pan African Festival
- Courtyard By Marriott, Macon
- Macon Little Theatre
- Museum Of Arts And Sciences
- Ocmulgee National Monument Indian Mounds
- Ocmulgee National Monument Indian Mounds - Ocmulgee Indian Celebration

Macon (cont.)

- Cherry Blossom Festival
- Georgia State Fair
- First Night Macon

Omaha

- Florence Marina State Park

Perry-Warner Robins

- Mossy Creek Barnyard Festival (s)

Pine Mountain

- Butts Mill Farm
- Callaway Gardens
- Callaway Gardens - Sky High Hot Air Balloon Festival
- Callaway Gardens - Autumnfest
- Callaway Gardens - Fantasy In Lights
- Callaway Gardens Resort
- F. D. Roosevelt State Park
- Wild Animal Safari

Thomaston

- Sprewell Bluff State Park
- Rock Ranch
- Rock Ranch - Fall Family Fun Days Corn Maze

Warm Springs

- Best Western White House Inn
- Bulloch House
- Roosevelt's Little White HousE Historic Site
- Roosevelt's Little White House Historic Site - Fala Day Tribute

Warner Robins

- Museum Of Aviation

West Point

- Battle Of West Point Reenactment

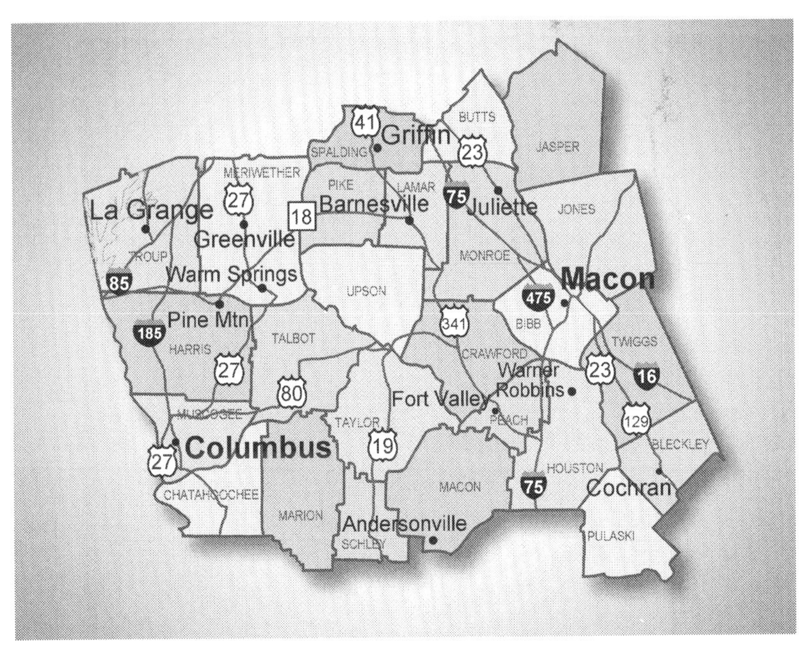

A Quick Tour of our Hand-Picked Favorites Around...

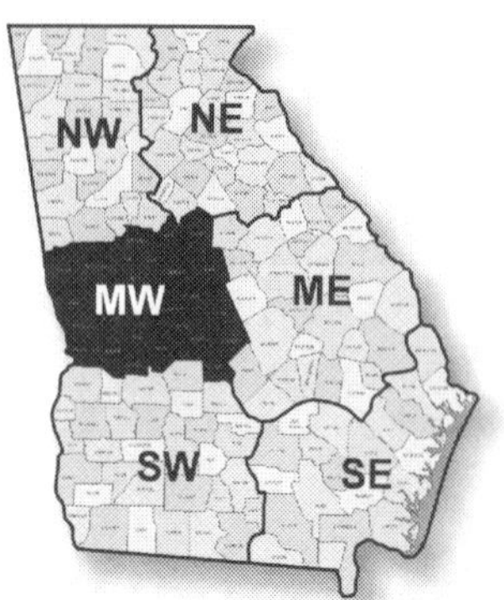

Middle West Georgia

Let's retreat to some hidden gems first...a Pine Mountain/Warm Springs getaway. **Callaway Gardens** reminds us of resort properties from the 50s – hundreds of cottages and a massive inn complete with daily activities for each family member – even the grandparents. Here you can go to a circus, watch butterflies flutter or parrots sing, discover history, ride a mini-train, and paddleboat. Don't forget the sandy beach and the famous Robin Lake, the floating water park, water ski lessons, premier hiking or biking trails, and a nationally acclaimed family golf program.

Still want more adventure? Try a safari ride in **Wild Animal Safari**. It's recommended to go on a safari bus/van tour vs. riding your own vehicle. It will be covered with slobber from the dozens of large animals you'll encounter! This is one of those "you have to be there" experiences.

On a more historical note, be sure to visit **Roosevelt's Little White House State Historic Site.** Begin with the orientation video and preview the time line. What is polio? Feel the temperature difference of warm vs. cold springs. How do you drive a vehicle without use of your legs? So much to learn about times of Depression and War and the American spirit lead by a compassionate man.

For the next part of the trip head south on I-85 towards the Georgia/Alabama border. Start your morning by visiting the **Columbus Museum**. The museum is FREE and a wonderful representation of local history. See an archeological dig site and then watch for the giant alligator – many dioramas have sound effects, too. Their Chihuly artwork on display will capture your child's eye with its rainbow of spun color. For some of the best display of Civil War Naval history, you absolutely must visit **Port Columbus National Civil War Naval Museum**. Listen in on an orientation – then, gasp as you have full view of the ships hull of a real Confederate ironclad warship. Fitted with a "ghost" metal outline, this is truly unbelievable. Hungry? Columbus, Georgia has a place where you can eat Scrambled Hot Dogs or dine in a real bus.

Head east on SR 96 to Georgia Grown **Lane Southern Orchards** in Fort Valley - a family farm featuring Georgia's seasonal produce in a giant Peachy gift shop and Café (guess what flavor they serve most?). Summertime, sweet Georgia peaches are in season. This is the best chance to see those little peaches line up like soldiers and get washed, dried and pruned as you watch the colorful packing lines. Plus, you can visit the five acre "you pick or we pick" strawberry patch each spring. It's all about pecans from October through January.

Next, head further northeast back to I-75 and into Macon. Start your adventure at the beginning—**Ocmulgee National Monument** is one of the nation's most important archaeological sites. Survey the landscape from atop ancient Indian mounds, step inside a 1,000 year-old ceremonial earthlodge, hike along mysterious river trails and study artifacts dating back 10,000 years! Then, shoot baskets and kick field goals at the **Georgia Sports Hall of Fame** in Macon. See how Georgia geography, mathematics, science and history relate to sports on themed computer programs, and watch Georgia sports greats on a huge screen! Pretty much every exhibit here is visitor interactive so plan on being active. Dance to your favorite music videos at the **Georgia Music Hall of Fame** & The Music Factory. Here, you can compose your own music, explore Georgia geography, learn how instruments are made, slide down the giant fiddle, play with your feet on the in-floor piano keyboard and much more!

Finally, just a few exits north on I-75, end your tour of Middle West Georgia at a truly Southern place – the **Whistle Stop Café** in Juliette. A national forest, wildlife refuge and state parks surround this sleepy little town and this famous little café. Get out and stretch your legs or sit on the porch and rock awhile before you try some old-fashioned specialties like homemade Fried Green Tomatoes. Remember, the secret's in the sauce...

Sites and attractions are listed in order by City, Zip Code, and Name. Symbols indicated represent:

 Festivals  Restaurants  Lodging

Andersonville

ANDERSONVILLE NATIONAL HISTORIC SITE / NATIONAL POW MUSEUM

Andersonville - *496 Cemetery Road (I-75 exit Hwy 26 or 27 heading west, follow signs) 31711. Phone: (229) 924-0343. www.nps.gov/ande/. Hours: Daily 9am-4:30pm. Admission: FREE. Tours: Walking and/or driving through the National Cemetery and prison site are recommended. An audio driving tour is available for a $1.00 rental fee. Educators: Lesson Plans-www.nps.gov/ande/forteachers/classrooms/curriculummaterials.htm Note: A picnic area is located within the park. Interpretive Programs are presented at the historic prison site daily at 11:00am and 2:00pm. Special events here include a Memorial Day Observance and Luminary Event.*

Andersonville, or Camp Sumter as it was officially known, was one of the largest Confederate military prisons established during the Civil War. During the 14 months the prison existed, more than 45,000 Union soldiers were confined here. Of these, almost 13,000 died from disease, poor sanitation, malnutrition, overcrowding, or exposure to the elements.

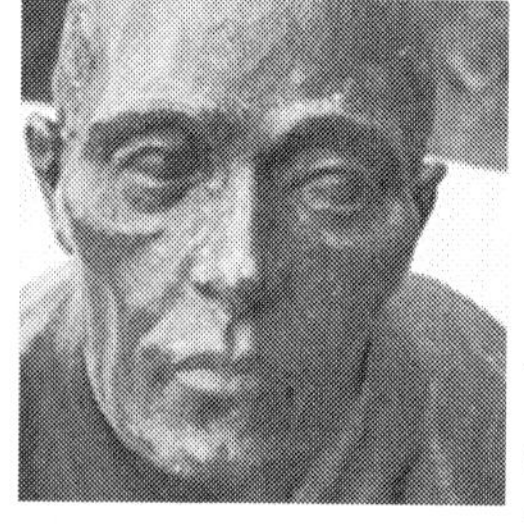

The only park in the National Park System to serve as a memorial to all American prisoners of war throughout the nation's history, this 515 acre park consists of the original historic prison site complete with rebuilt stockade wall sections and remnants of escape tunnels, as well as the National Cemetery and the Civil War cemetery. A 27-minute audio-visual program entitled "Echoes of Captivity" provides an orientation to the overall prisoner of war story. We would suggest families participate in the Prison Historical Hike - a 3-mile walking historic hike designed to acquaint young hikers with the story of Andersonville and American prisoners of war. The hike is not along a physical trail, but allows an exploration of the park through the use of a questionnaire to direct your visit.

Nearby is **DRUMMER BOY CIVIL WAR MUSEUM**, a small museum with full uniform displays and a large diorama depicting Andersonville confederate Prison and the village in 1864 (114 Church St, 229-924-2558, open Thursday-Sunday afternoons. www.andersonvillegeorgia.com/Drummer_Boy_Museum.htm. Admission charged).

Barnesville

BARNESVILLE BUGGY DAYS

Barnesville - *Main Street, downtown. www.barnesville.org/pages/Buggy_Days.php. Phone: (770) 358-5884. The annual festival features a parade of buggies, equestrian units, antique cars and floats. Entertainment includes old-fashioned games, a car show, a military band, fireworks, music and dancers. In Buggy Blast Fun Park, kids can try a variety of fun activities. (third full weekend in September)*

Columbus

COCA-COLA SPACE SCIENCE CENTER

Columbus - *701 Front Avenue, GA 133/91 (Columbus State University) 31901. Phone: (706) 649-1470. www.ccssc.org. Hours: Monday-Friday 10:00am-4:00pm, Saturday 10:30am-8:00pm. Closed Sunday. Admission: Charged for exhibits and planetarium shows ($4.00-$6.00) and Challenger Learning Center missions.*

First, visitors enjoy the dynamic experience of the many interactive lobby displays. The Exhibit Hall includes: Space Suit and Apollo Capsule replicas, seven flight simulators (four are motion bases), and the Planetarium.

The Space Shuttle Orbiter is a full size replica of the first 50 feet of the NASA space shuttle orbiter. Inside there is a mini theater, comprising of 26 seats and a video screen. The Telescopes Exhibit looks at various large telescopes located around the world and displays some of the images taken with them. The Coca-Cola drink dispenser is a replica of the first such beverage machine taken into space.

Daniel, up close with the Space Shuttle

The Orbiter is used as part of the Challenger Learning Center to launch the students into space and from there, they proceed through an air lock into the Space Station. Test your talent to be an astronaut as you master the controls of the Shuttle or take the helm of the controls in the launch pad. Remember, not all space flights are problem-free! Groups of 20-30 can experience a simulated mission in the Challenger Learning Center on an appointment basis. The Mead Observatory is open to the public once a month for astronomical viewing.

COLUMBUS SYMPHONY ORCHESTRA

Columbus - ***900 Broadway (RiverCenter for the Performing Arts, downtown) 31901. Phone: (706) 323-5059 or (888) 332-5200. www.csoga.org.***

Founded in 1855 by Mendelssohn's student, Herman S. Saroni, the Columbus Symphony Orchestra became the third orchestra formed in the United States. Kids under eight will most enjoy CSO Family Concerts. Activities include an instrument petting zoo; a chance to meet the musicians and hear them play close-up; musical games (complete with prizes); and a special concert including musical stories.

OXBOW MEADOWS ENVIRONMENTAL LEARNING CENTER

Columbus - ***3535 S. Lumpkin Road (I-185; take exit 1B, traveling north on Victory Drive (U.S. Hwy 27/280). Drive approximately 2.3 miles to South Lumpkin Road) 31901. Phone: (706) 687-4090. www.oxbow.columbusstate.edu. Hours: Tuesday-Friday 9:00am-4:00pm, Saturday 10am-6pm. Admission: $2.00 adult, $1.00 child (10 & younger). Note: the Treetop Trail closes occasionally for maintenance and upgrades. Check website for current status. Usually only open weekends.***

If it's a nice day, venture outdoors to Oxbow Meadows Center where nature is explored in a wetland habitat (along the bike trail). Nestled in a bend of the Chattahoochee River, the center has an indoor facility with live owl and hawk on perches! They'll check you out. Meet an alligator named Wally. For the nature lover, butterflies, birds, turtles, and dragonflies can be found in abundance.

TreeTop Canopy Trail: Go up 80 feet (must be over 8 years old for this) along the forest canopy walkway through the treetops outside - the first phase in a system of suspended canopy trails that will allow visitors to literally walk among the treetops! Two walking trails wind between ponds taking hikers around native flora and fauna. Walk along suspended bridges and stop at a viewing platform designed for observation. ($5.00 per person for 30 minute tour)

PORT COLUMBUS NATIONAL CIVIL WAR NAVAL MUSEUM

Columbus - ***1002 Victory Drive (off Rte. 27/280, downtown. South Commons near the Civic Center) 31901. Phone: (706) 327-9798. www.portcolumbus.org. Hours: Tuesday-Saturday 10am-4:30pm, Sunday-Monday 12:30pm-4:30pm. Closed Christmas Day. Admission: $6.00-$7.50 (age 7+). Educators: Civil War Navy***

Activity Book - http://portcolumbus.org/tours/wp-content/uploads/2011/07/Civil-War-Naval-History-Activity-Book.pdf

For some of the best display of Civil War Naval history, this museum is absolutely a must visit. Columbus, Georgia was the site of a Confederate Naval Shipyard. The largest product of this facility was the CSS Jackson, one of the largest of the ironclads built in the south. The Jackson was nearly 225 feet long, 54 feet wide and weighed 2000 tons.

It was surreal to see the actual timbers and the metal "ghost ship". Nearly the size of a football field...

The Jackson's remains are displayed in an elevated form. Listen in on an orientation – then, gasp as you have full view of the ships hull of a real Confederate ironclad warship. Fitted with a "ghost" metal outline of the top of the ship, this is truly unbelievable!

Now, look at a regular ship to compare and models of other famous ironclads. This 40,000 square foot facility also features the remains of two original Civil War Confederate Navy ships and full-size sectional reconstructions of the U.S.S. Monitor. Look at vessels, uniforms, equipment and weapons used by the Union and Confederate navies. Who were Powder Monkeys? Interactive exhibits, including a Confederate ironclad ship simulator, offer the visitor an opportunity to experience 19th century naval combat first hand.

Actual Timbers - upclose

PORT COLUMBUS NATIONAL CIVIL WAR NAVAL MUSEUM - RIVER BLAST

Columbus - 1002 Victory Drive, 31901. Phone: (706) 327-9798. www.portcolumbus.org. In 2004, the museum rolled out its newly restored scale model of the USS Monitor and let it fight a Confederate type ironclad ship in the Chattahoochee River. Sailors and marines from around the south show up to get combat training ala 1863, including serving on the big Brooke Rifled cannon over looking the river. (second weekend in March)

PORT COLUMBUS NATIONAL CIVIL WAR NAVAL MUSEUM - SOUTHERN PIRATE FESTIVAL

Columbus - *1002 Victory Drive, 31901. Phone: (706) 327-9798. www.portcolumbus.org. The Pirates of the Chattahoochee invade the Southern Pirate Festival with a fun-filled day of pirate activities for children. Activities include tattoos, face painting, games, bouncy pirate castle, treasure hunt, arts and crafts and boat rides. Rain or shine. (last Saturday in October)*

PORT COLUMBUS NATIONAL CIVIL WAR NAVAL MUSEUM - VICTORIAN HOLIDAY HOUSE

Columbus - *1002 Victory Drive, 31901. Phone: (706) 327-9798. www.portcolumbus.org. America's Civil War Era Santa makes an appearance each December at Port Columbus. Photos with Santa, Breakfast with Santa, holiday decorations, and FREE admission. (select days and times each December)*

COUNTRY INN & SUITES, COLUMBUS

Columbus - *1720 Fountain Court (I-185 exit 12) 31904. Phone: (706) 660-1880. As you head in on I-185 towards town, drop your bags at the Country Inn & Suites. They offer complimentary light & hearty breakfast, high speed internet and an outdoor pool. A nice place to base from for just over $100/night. www.countryinns.com/hotels/gacolumb. Free airport shuttle.*

COLUMBUS MUSEUM

Columbus - *1251 Wynnton Road (off 10th Avenue, outskirts of downtown) 31906. Phone: (706) 649-0713. www.columbusmuseum.com. Hours: Tuesday-Saturday 10:00am-5:00pm, Thursdays until 8:00pm, Sunday 1:00-5:00pm. Closed legal holidays. Admission: FREE. Educators: Resources - www.columbusmuseum.com/programs/school/teacher-resources/*

The second-largest art museum in Georgia and one of the largest in the Southeast, the Columbus Museum is particularly known for its concentration on American art and the history of the Chattahoochee River Valley. Even if you're not a big fan of modern art - what family can resist the tempting colors and forms of Chihuly's Boat Installation - spikes of colored glass in a 17-foot wood river dory. In addition to its 15 permanent collection and

traveling exhibition galleries of fine and decorative art, the Museum offers visitors the chance to investigate color and texture in Transformations, a hands-on discovery gallery. In this area, kids can create patterns on a magnet board, mix colors on a light table, explore basic shapes in a building block room, and step into works from their permanent collection. Visitors also can trace the development of the Chattahoochee Valley area in Chattahoochee Legacy, a regional history gallery displaying artifacts with its own award-winning film (shown several times daily). Visitors can see replicas of an archaeological dig, an urban slave cabin, a one-room school house, and a cotton loom, in addition to other full-scale replicas. Also on display in the gallery are Native American artifacts, Civil War-era weapons, and other cultural items from Columbus' history.

A dog effigy pipe

DINGLEWOOD PHARMACY LUNCH COUNTER

Columbus - *1939 Wynnton Road, 31906. Phone: (706) 322-0616. Hungry? Visit a pharmacy for lunch! This is a Columbus tradition and the place to get the original Scrambled Hot Dog! (no eggs, but everything imaginable on top of a hot dog) It's nothing fancy…just your typical pharmacy with a lunch counter, but you'll see everyone from construction workers to CEOs.*

COUNTRY'S BARBEQUE

Columbus - *1329 Broadway 31909. www.countrysbarbeque.com. Phone: (706) 596-8910. Located in an art deco-style bus station (1950s), there is even a bus from that era attached to the building and you can dine in it. Honk the bus's horn, make the bus station sounds or play with a viewmaster dessert menu. While you wait for your order, have some fun listening to a wide variety of FREE jukebox songs from the 50's to the 80's. The BBQ is good (love the Shoop sauce). Just follow your nose to the downtown location – hickory wood wafts in the air. Open daily 11:00am-10:00pm. Work of all that food walking or biking along the* ***CHATTAHOOCHEE RIVERWALK*** *– a 15 mile paved trail south along the river to Fort Benning.*

NATIONAL INFANTRY MUSEUM

Columbus - ***The museum is just off Fort Benning Road, about two miles south of Victory Drive. If you are using a GPS, enter 3800 South Lumpkin Rd., Columbus, GA 31903. www.nationalinfantrymuseum.org. Hours: Tuesday-Saturday 9am-5pm, Sunday 11am-5pm.***

The National Infantry Museum and Soldier Center sits on a 200-acre campus outside the gates of Fort Benning in Columbus, Georgia. Fort Benning Infantry school soldiers graduate on a parade field behind the museum every week, marching across ground that has been seeded with soil from major Infantry battlefields around the world. Graduations are open to the public.

World War II Company Street is a collection of seven buildings constructed in the 1940s when the Army signed up 16 million Americans to defend the nation. They include authentically recreated barracks, mess hall, chapel and the headquarters building and sleeping quarters General George S. Patton used while stationed at Fort Benning in 1941.

The Family Gallery, which recognizes the sacrifices made by those who love an Infantryman, includes a child-size area where kids can try on soldier uniforms and peer from inside of a pretend Bradley Fighting Vehicle at a humanitarian mission in Iraq. One of the Museum's galleries, the Fort Benning Gallery, demonstrates what it takes to turn a young farm boy from Ohio or a football star from Texas into an Infantryman. Heritage Walk links the museum with the parade field and is lined with U.S. state and territory flags and thousands of commemorative granite pavers purchased to honor an individual or unit and to support the museum. Inside the museum is the EST 2000, a rifle range simulator exactly like what soldiers train on at For Benning. The museum is the only public facility in the nation with this attraction.

Flovilla

INDIAN SPRINGS STATE PARK

Flovilla - ***678 Lake Clark Road (I-75 southbound, exit 205 to Jackson, south on GA 42 to the park) 30216. www.gastateparks.org/IndianSprings/. Phone: (770) 504-2277. Hours: Daily 7:00am-10:00pm Admission: $5.00 vehicle entrance fee. Fee for camping and cottages. Educators: Brief brochure on plants and animals from the area is online under: Indian Springs School Program Brochure.***

Indian Springs is thought to be the oldest state park in the United States. The area was once home to Creek Indians who used the springs for centuries to heal the sick and impart extra vigor to anyone. Then, the area became a bustling resort town. Today, visitors can still sample the spring water while enjoying the park's cottages, camping, swimming, boating and fishing. Many structures were built during the Great Depression by FDR's Civilian Conservation Corps. A museum highlights the original inhabitants, the Creeks, the resort era and the CCC building projects. There is also a 3/4 mile nature trail and a miniature golf course within the park.

Fort Valley

LANE SOUTHERN ORCHARDS

Fort Valley - *50 Lane Road (I-75 exit 142 west on Hwy 96. Look for the rows and rows of crop trees - you can't miss it) 31030. Phone: (478) 825-3592 or (800) 277-3224. www.lanesouthernorchards.com. Hours: Daily 9:00am-5:00pm. Admission: FREE. $5-$7.00 for orchard tours or field trips. Tours: Individuals can take the self-guided tour at anytime during the day. Viewing the entire process should take about 30 min. There is no charge for the tours. Due to the nature of the peach crop, they cannot guarantee the packing line will run every day. Guided tours are reserved. Note: Roadside Market includes the Café serving lunch and desserts daily and Gift Shop.*

The peaches march in like "little soldiers" here...

This fun and educational attraction grows and ships Georgia peaches and pecans. Lane Packing Company farms over 2,700 acres of peach trees and 2100 acres of pecans. Currently, they grow over 30 varieties of peaches. Begin your visit by watching the farm video in the market. How do they make new peach varieties? In the summer, take a self-guided tour of the packing operation from an elevated platform. Informational signs describe each step of the process. See the peaches line up like soldiers to get their baths! It's different and fun to watch.

ORCHARD TOUR - Summer or Fall. Riding tour through the peach and pecan orchards. Tour guides will explain the history of the peach industry in Georgia as well as how these crops are grown and harvested. Call in advance for group reservations. Small fee.

STRAWBERRY FIELD TRIP - Springtime. Young students will enjoy this package tour. Tour guides will explain how strawberries are grown. Each student picks one pound of berries and enjoys a cup of fresh strawberry ice cream. A strawberry coloring book is sent home with each child. Small fee.

LANE SOUTHERN ORCHARDS - CORN MAZE DAYS

Fort Valley - *50 Lane Road, 31030. www.lanesouthernorchards.com. Phone: (478) 825-3592 or (800) 277-3224. Visit Lane Southern Orchards giant, 6-acre corn maze and play Cornundrum. Find the corny signs hidden along secret paths for a chance to win prizes while you find your way out. Admission. (October)*

Gay

COTTON PICKIN' FAIR

Gay - *GA Hwy 85. Phone: (706) 538-6814. www.cpfair.org. Share remnants of farm life on a festival ground dotted with sheds, farm buildings and a cotton gin from the early 1900s. The Logan Turnpike grist mill will turn out cornmeal and flour; the blacksmith will forge functional art work and Uncle Lonnie shares farm stories. The Royal Scottish Country Dancers and Bagpipers lead visitors to music, dance, puppetry, and storytelling. Try baked, fried broiled, boiled, steamed and stewed tasty Southern foods. Admission. (first weekend of May and October)*

Hamilton

OSSAHATCHEE INDIAN FESTIVAL AND POW-WOW

Hamilton - *Harris County Soccer Field, GA 116E. www.ossahatchee.org. You will witness American Indian dances and stories that have been passed down through the ages. Taste authentic American Indian Foods. Vendors from all over the United States display and sell American Indian Arts and Crafts from artwork to pottery to intricately designed jewelry and leather goods. Primitive Skills from basket weaving to primitive weapons construction are demonstrated by some of the most highly skilled artisans in North America. Admission. (third weekend in October)*

Jackson

HIGH FALLS STATE PARK

Jackson - *76 High Falls Park Drive (nearly 2 miles east of I-75 exit 198) 30233.*

Phone: (478) 993-3053. www.gastateparks.org/HighFalls/. Hours: Daily 7:00am-10:00pm. Admission: $5.00 vehicle parking fee. Fee for camping.

This site was a prosperous industrial town with several stores, a cotton gin, a grist mill, blacksmith shop and hotel. Even a shoe factory was in town until a major railroad bypassed it and it became a ghost town in the 1880s. You can enjoy the scenic waterfall or hike to the remaining grist mill foundation. A campground, mini-golf, swimming pool and canoe rental are also available. Boating is allowed, 10 HP limit.

Juliette

JARRELL PLANTATION HISTORIC SITE

Juliette - ***711 Jarrell Plantation Rd., Route 2 (I75 exit 185 or 171, follow signs) 31046. Phone: (478) 986-5172. www.gastateparks.org/JarrellPlantation. Hours: Thursday-Saturday 9:00am-5:00pm. Admission: $4.00-$6.50 per person. Note: Watch the intro video to get an overview.***

This middle Georgia plantation consists of 20 buildings dating between 1847 and 1945. The cotton plantation was owned by a single family for more than 140 years. It survived General Sherman's "March to the Sea", typhoid fever, Emancipation, Reconstruction, the cotton boll weevil, the advent of steam power and a transition from farming to forestry. His success might be credited to the many trades produced here by several generations - especially "ginning" and "milling".

Among the buildings, machines and tools once used by the Jarrells are a three-story barn, smokehouses, wheat houses, a cane press, cotton gin, grist mill, saw mill, syrup mill, etc. Visitors can tour the 1847 plantation house, carpenter shop, blacksmith shop and other buildings. Inside the 1847 house, you'll see original furnishings, including a baby cradle and a cobbler's bench, many of which were built by family members. During seasonal programs, spinning, weaving, woodstove cooking, blacksmithing and other skills are demonstrated (best time to interactively visit). Kids like seeing crops growing and visiting with the mule.

JARRELL PLANTATION HISTORIC SITE - OLD FASHIONED JULY 4TH

Juliette - *711 Jarrell Plantation Rd. Route 2 31046. www.gastateparks.org. Phone: (478) 986-5172. This celebration features a noon reading of the Declaration of Independence followed by three-legged races, sack races, and bygone crafts and chores. Admission. (July 4th)*

SYRUP MAKIN' & STORYTELLIN'

Juliette - 711 Jarrell Plantation Rd. Route 2, 31046. www.gastateparks.org. Phone: (478) 986-5172. The traditional syrup cook-off was an important fall event on middle Georgia farms and featured family and community getting together for work and play. This program brings this event back to life with demonstrations of the sugar cane mill, syrup kettle, steam engine, woodstove cooking, and also storytelling. Admission. (second weekend in November)

JARRELL PLANTATION HISTORIC SITE - PLANTATION CHRISTMAS

Juliette - 711 Jarrell Plantation Rd., Route 2, 31046. www.gastateparks.org. Phone: (478) 986-5172. Tour this plantation by luminary and candlelight, then enjoy a campfire, carols, and Christmas stories from long ago. Admission. (first or second weekend in December)

WHISTLE STOP CAFÉ - FRIED GREEN TOMATOES

Juliette ***- 443 McCracken Street (I-75 exit 186 east 9 miles) 31046. Phone: (478) 992-8886. www.thewhistlestopcafe.com. Hours: Daily 11:00am-4:00pm.***

In the early 1900s, Juliette was a booming community along the railroad tracks and the Ocmulgee River. As time went on the economy left Juliette a ghost town. Then, in 1991, the town was re-discovered by the producers of the movie "Fried Green Tomatoes". The quaint buildings and the railroad provided just the right ingredients for the movie. Visitors from all over the country now come to taste those famous fried green tomatoes at the real-life café and enjoy walking down the streets of this very small town. After you dine on original tomatoes and southern food, take a walk and look for the burial site of "Buddy's arm" or the Juliette "Little Opry". Cute town...and the trains come through faithfully at noon.

LaGrange

EXPLORATIONS ANTIQUITY CENTER

LaGrange ***- 130 Gordon Commercial Drive (I-85 exit 13, head north, then west) 30241. Phone: (706) 885-0363. www.explorationsinantiquity.com. Hours: Tuesday-Saturday 10:00am-6:00pm. Admission: $10.00.***

An interfaith museum, the folks here produce full-scale archaeological reconstructions of discoveries from the ancient world and display them in authentic settings. People understand the Bible and ancient life better with almost real visuals of a grape press, aqueducts, a tomb, an Israelite altar and the nativity cave. Travel back in time some 2,000 years and pretend you're a shepherd, a farmer, or a villager. Dig for artifacts or sit on camel-hair rugs learning how to make bread by hand. The theme each December is "the Long Road to Bethlehem," following the shepherds walks.

AZALEA STORYTELLING FESTIVAL

LaGrange - *LaGrange College. www.lagrange.edu/azalea/index.html. Phone: (706) 880-8276. Nationally acclaimed storytellers will visit LaGrange to spin comedic, nostalgic and moving tales at the annual Azalea Storytelling Festival. Admission (students half price). (first full weekend in March)*

Macon

AROUND TOWN TOURS - MACON

Macon - *450 Martin Luther King, Jr. Blvd. (trolley leaves from Welcome Center, Terminal Station. I-16, exiting and turning onto M.L. King, Jr. Blvd.) 31201. Phone: (800) 768-3401. www.visitmacon.org. Hours: Monday-Saturday 9:00am-5:00pm. Admission: $18.00 adult, $8.50 youth (downtown tour). Note: Tickets are available at the Downtown Visitor Center located in the Terminal Station where you'll find free all day parking.*

Around Town Tours offer friendly, local trolley operators who kindly answer questions and give you quick tidbits and access to historical sites around town. Trolley offeredduring weekends and events but you can walk it too. It features free trolley transportation & admission into the following attractions:

The DOWNTOWN TOUR ticket includes free admission into the following attractions: Georgia Sports Hall of Fame and Tubman African American Museum. See separate listings for reviews of each attraction. (most recommended for families)

Tour INTOWN HISTORIC MACON. You'll feel like royalty at the HAY HOUSE (www.hayhouse.org), also known as "The Palace of the South." This 24-room, 18,000 sq. ft. Italian Renaissance Revival mansion is full of surprises including a secret room where legend has it that Confederate gold was hidden! Next, visit the CANNONBALL HOUSE and imagine seeing an enemy cannonball crashing through your house during a Union Army attack on Macon in 1864! See the cannonball along with the furnishings, lifestyles and clothes of that era. Don't miss the Civil War museum in the old kitchen & servants quarters out back. And, finally, the SIDNEY LANIER COTTAGE - see separate listing.

After dinner get outside and take a stroll through Lights on Macon...Historic Intown Illumination Tour. This safe, self-guided walking tour features over 30 antebellum and historic mansions throughout Macon's historic in-town neighborhood. These homes are dramatically lit up at dusk to showcase their unique architectural features.

AROUND TOWN TOURS - MACON - CHRISTMAS OPEN HOUSE

Macon - 450 Martin Luther King, Jr. Blvd. (trolley leaves from Welcome Center, Terminal Station. I-16, exiting and turning onto M.L. King, Jr. Blvd.) 31201. Phone: (800) 768-3401. www.visitmacon.org. Miscellaneous: Tickets are available at the Downtown Visitor Center located in the Terminal Station where you'll find free all day parking. The tradition of grand holiday decorating continues today. In addition to tours of the historic home decorated for the holiday season, special events are offered such as children's Victorian Christmas parties, catered lunches in the house museums including the House, the Cannonball House, and the Sidney Lanier Cottage. A special program book designed for the Christmas season is distributed to guests throughout the month. Admission. (December)

GEORGIA SPORTS HALL OF FAME

Macon - ***301 Cherry Street (I-75 to exit I-16 east to MLK, Jr. exit to Cherry St) 31201. Phone: (912) 752-1585. www.gshf.org. Hours: Tuesday-Saturday 9:00am-5:00pm. Admission: $8.00 adult, $6.00 senior (60+), Military, College Students; $3.50 child (6-16).***

Mom, Jenny & Daniel experience the "Thrill of Victory"...

Begin your sports experience in the museum's theater with a high energy, high emotion film about Georgia sports legends. Next, it's on to the actual exhibit hall, which takes you through sports from prep to professional, including collegiate, amateur, and Olympic achievements such as record home run hitter Henry "Hank"

Aaron and football legend turned sports announcer Fran Tarkenton.

Along the way, you'll have the chance to shoot hoops, kick field goals, throw passes, slam a jump ball, drive a NASCAR simulator and use specially themed computers to see how academics like geography, math and history are critical to athletes and many careers in sports from playing to sports casting to managing.

The 43,000 sq ft. GA Sports Hall of Fame is the largest STATE sports hall of fame in the country.

There's even an area to be a media announcer and make your own calls on famous ball plays! That was our favorite part - how excited can you sound? Be ready for action as this museum is the most interactive Hall of Fame you'll ever visit!

NU-WAY WEINERS

Macon - ***428 Cotton Avenue, downtown Macon (I-75 exit 164 follow signs to downtown, corner of Cherry & Cotton) 31201. www.nu-wayweiners.com. Phone: (478) 743-6593.***

Nu-Way has been serving up the best hot dogs in Macon for 87 years through three generations of the same family. Recently cited as being among the top

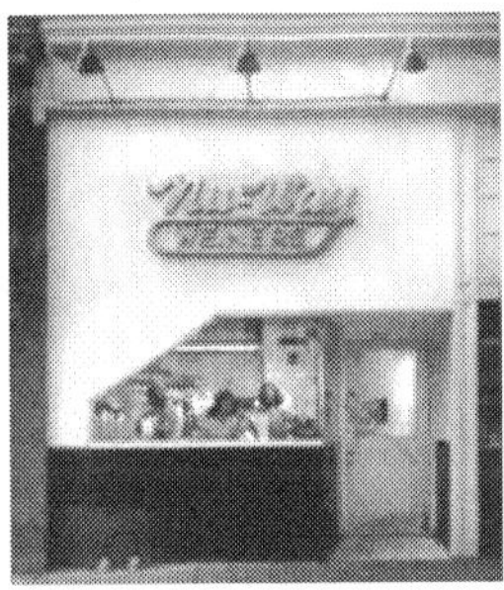

10 in the nation, these Central Georgia restaurants serve up secret-recipe chili sauce and homemade slaw. (10 other locations, include Zebulon Road at I-475; Northside Drive near I-75 and North Avenue at I-16). Hours: 6:00am-7:00pm. Breakfast, lunch and supper. Closed: Sunday. Price range: About $5.00 for a complete lunch. A delectable selection of hot dog toppings, hamburgers, sandwiches and old fashioned chocolate malts can be enjoyed while sitting at a nostalgic stainless lunch counter or booth in the original downtown eatery or at one of ten other locations throughout Macon and Middle Georgia. Kids meals are served in "Dog Houses" and include a treat and toy. For about $1.89, you can order their signature red-colored hot dogs "all the way" - the best way is Nu-Way. Yum!

 ____________________

SIDNEY LANIER COTTAGE

Macon - ***935 High Street (downtown, I-75 exit 164 into town) 31201. Phone: (478) 743-3851. www.historicmacon.org. Hours: Thursday-Saturday 10:00am-4:00pm. Admission: $3.00-$5.00 per person. Educators: Lanier bio online link.***

Step back in time with a guided tour of this 1840 cottage that is the birthplace of Sidney Lanier (1842 - 1881), famous poet and musician of the Old South, who penned "The Marshes of Glynn" and "Song of the Chattahoochee." He served in the Confederate Army until captured aboard a blockade runner and confined at Fort Lookout, Maryland. Kids' group tours explore 1800s toys and the influences of nature on Lanier's music and poetry. At an early age, Sidney learned to play the flute, violin and many other instruments that imitate sounds in nature (ex. Birds). The museum displays Lanier memorabilia and the gift shop sells books on the Civil War, items on Lanier, and other related articles. Kids with an interest in The Arts are best influenced by sites like this.

TUBMAN AFRICAN AMERICAN MUSEUM

Macon - ***340 Walnut Street (I-75 exit 165 to I-16 east to exit 2, MLK, Jr. Blvd. And turn right. Turn right on Walnut) 31201. www.tubmanmuseum.com. Phone: (478) 743-8544. Hours: Tuesday-Friday 9:00am-5:00pm. Saturday 11am-5:00pm. Admission: $8.00 adult, $4.00 child (age 3-17)***

Along the trolley tour, the Tubman is a wonderful experience to learn about African American art, history and culture. Your visit starts with a 63-foot long mural that documents history from ancient Africa to today's leaders and heroes. Hear the exciting stories of Harriet Tubman, Dr. Martin Luther King, Jr., Otis Redding, Ellen Craft and many more. A hands-on inventors gallery and musical instrument station are favorites for kids of all ages.

TUBMAN AFRICAN AMERICAN MUSEUM - PAN AFRICAN FESTIVAL

Macon - *340 Walnut Street 31201. www.tubmanmuseum.com. Phone: (478) 743-8544. Event includes concerts, soul food, Pan African Parade Family Day @ Central City Park, Health Fair, and Children's Village. (third week of April)*

☒

COURTYARD BY MARRIOTT, MACON

Macon - *3990 Sheraton Drive (I-75 exit 169). 31210. Phone: (478) 477-8899. Unwind and relax in one of the 108 spacious and comfortable guest rooms available at this hotel that features large sitting areas, spacious work desks, coffee makers, voice mail, and high speed Internet access in all of the rooms. Amenities on site include a restaurant, a seasonal outdoor pool, an indoor whirlpool, an exercise room, guest laundry facilities, and meeting rooms. A breakfast buffet is served daily for around $8.00/$4.00. Rooms from $99.oo. Just 2 exits north (I-75 exit 172) is Starcadia Entertainment Complex. www.starcadia.net. They have go-karts, mini-golf, bumper boats, batting cages, arcade, flying swings, junior go-karts, rock climbing, trampoline and even a couple of kiddie rides. Each activity averages around $5.00/person. www.marriott.com/hotels/travel/mcnga-courtyard-macon/.*

MACON LITTLE THEATRE

Macon - ***4220 Forsyth Road (I-75 exit 164) 31210. www.maconlittletheatre.org. Phone: (478) 477-3342.***

Take in a show. The nationally acclaimed Macon Little Theatre is Georgia's oldest and largest community theatre with a season of classic musical productions including the beloved Annie, The Sound of Music, and Scrooge. Tickets run $10.00-$18.00. All shows start at 8:00pm except for Sunday Matinees which start at 2:30pm.

MUSEUM OF ARTS AND SCIENCES

Macon - ***4182 Forsyth Road (I-75 exit 164) 31210. www.masmacon.org. Phone: (478) 477-3232. Hours: Tuesday-Saturday 10:00am-5:00pm, Sunday 1:00-5:00pm. Admission: $10.00 adult, $8.00 senior, military; $5.00 students (3-17). Educators: Time Traveler and Holiday themed celebrations change each month.***

At the Museum of Arts & Sciences, a whimsical, three-story Discovery House with interactive exhibits proves that learning about art, science and the humanities can be fun. Take a stroll through the enclosed Back Yard and look for live animals living around a man-made banyan tree and the gator in the mini swamp! The museum features changing and permanent exhibits like daily live animal shows, daily planetarium shows, an observatory, and nature trails. Examine the beauty of original works of art in an artist's garret, peek into a scientist's workshop and then journey into space. Maneuver a robot thru the Great Pyramid, sit in the cockpit of Amelia Earhart's plane, steer a canoe, track elephants, rover the surface of Mars and then search for Blackbeard's pirate ship. In the Inventor's Basement, become a mad scientist for the day or simply enjoy watching nature unfold from our window of winged wonders.

OCMULGEE NATIONAL MONUMENT INDIAN MOUNDS

Macon - *1207 Emery Highway (I-75 exit 165 onto I-16 east to exit 2 on US 80 east) 31217. Phone: (478) 752-8257. www.nps.gov/ocmu. Hours: Daily 9:00am-5:00pm. Closed Christmas and New Years only Admission: FREE. $3-$6 admission for events. Note: The Ocmulgee Heritage Trail is near here. The main access point to the Ocmulgee Heritage Trail, the Spring Street (Interstate 16, exit 1A) entrance provides ample parking and the only boat access to the river along the trail. Gateway Park is at the southern end of the trail, at the Martin Luther King Jr. Bridge (Interstate 16, exit 2) on the South side of the river. It features a spectacular overlook with steps down to the water, an interactive fountain, and a 7-foot bronze statue of late soul singer and Macon native, Otis Redding. FREEBIES: printable Word Find online under: For Kids/Park Fun.*

The long boardwalk to the mound ...

Between AD 900 and 1100 a skillful forming people lived on this site. They were known as Mississippians - a sedentary people who lived mainly by farming bottomlands for crops of corn, beans, squash, pumpkins, and tobacco. They built a compact town of thatched huts on the bluff overlooking the river. The visitor center houses a museum of items found on site and shows a short film "People of the Macon Plateau" (shown every 30 minutes). Among the artifacts found in the Funeral Mound were a pair of copper sun disks and a copper covered puma jaw, part of a head-dress. Survey the landscape from atop ancient Indian Mounds, listen to tales of the past inside a 1,000 year old ceremonial earth-lodge, hike along nature

We made it, now...what's inside?

trails and study archeological remains. Why did they build trenches? What is different about their arrowheads (vs. northern Woodlands)? Our favorite part? - the earthen lodge and oral program inside. What happens to the lodge twice a year (once on Michele's birthday)? Would you be comfortable in their "seats"? This is an excellent place to play archeologist or explorer for the day!

OCMULGEE NATIONAL MONUMENT INDIAN MOUNDS - OCMULGEE INDIAN CELEBRATION

Macon - *1207 Emery Highway, 31217. Phone: (478) 752-8257. www.nps.gov/ocmu. America's first music makers. Native Americans representing at least five different Nations (Creek, Choctaw, Chickasaw. Cherokee and Seminole), return to the place where man first sat down to celebrate their heritage. Ceremonial stomp dance performances, authentic arts & crafts, storytelling, music. and native cuisine. Picnics welcome. Admission ($5.00 age 13+). (third weekend in September)*

CHERRY BLOSSOM FESTIVAL

Macon - *Many events occur on the Great Lawn of Wesleyan College. Events range from live animal shows to hot-air balloon festivals, parades, arts and crafts and live theatre productions to amusement rides, fireworks, historic tours and dances. Complimentary horse-drawn carriage rides and refreshments are also provided, including Cherries 'n Cream, an ice cream made specifically for the festival. Concerts held daily. Ninety percent of events are FREE. www.cherryblossom.com. (ten days beginning mid-March)*

GEORGIA STATE FAIR

Macon - *Central City Park. Phone: (800) 768-3401. www.georgiastatefair.org. Games, carnival, fair food, Animal Magic Shows, Wildlife Educational Shows, Duck Races, Reptile Shows, Hillbilly Comedy Shows, contests, and livestock exhibits and competitions. Admission. (third week of September)*

FIRST NIGHT MACON

Macon - *Downtown Historic area. www.midsummermacon.org/firstnight.htm. First Night is a family-oriented non-alcoholic celebration of the arts held each year on New Year's Eve. First Night begins with a Children's Festival featuring magic shows, puppets. and crafts. Following the Children's Festival, families are invited to enjoy indoor performances of all kinds including; Country, Rock, Jazz, Irish Folk, Magic, and more. The grand finale begins at 11:30pm around the Main Stage on the downtown square. At midnight, thousands of people ring in the New Year with a large fireworks show. Admission buttons. (December 31st, New Years Eve)*

Omaha

FLORENCE MARINA STATE PARK

Omaha - ***(16 miles west of Lumpkin at the end of GA 39C) 31821. Phone: (229) 838-6870. http://gastateparks.org/info/flormarin/. Hours: 7:00am-10:00pm Admission: $5.00 daily vehicle parking fee.***

This park offers the perfect setting for those who love water sports. It is adjacent to a natural deep-water marina with an accessible deep-water fishing pier, boat slips and boat ramp. The park's Kirbo Interpretive Center teaches visitors about Native Americans, local history and nature, and it displays artifacts from the prehistoric Paleo-Indian period through the early 20th century. The park also offers camping, cottages, a swimming pool and 3/4 mile nature trail.

Perry-Warner Robins

MOSSY CREEK BARNYARD FESTIVAL

Perry-Warner Robins - *Deep Piney Woods (6 miles east of I-75, exit 138, Thompson Road). Phone: (478) 922-8265. www.mossycreekfestival.com. Step into an enchanted forest full of Appalachian mountain music, hammered dulcimer, folk songs, Fantasy Forest storytelling, and Ragtime piano. Watch wood-carving, weaving and hand-building fishing rods. There is also animal petting areas and hayrides. Admission. (mid-April weekend)*

MOSSY CREEK BARNYARD FESTIVAL

Perry-Warner Robins - *Deep Piney Woods (6 miles east of I-75, exit 138, Thompson Road). www.mossycreekfestival.com. Step into an enchanted forest full of Appalachian mountain music, hammered dulcimer, folk songs, Fantasy Forest storytelling, and Ragtime piano. Watch wood-carving, weaving and hand building fishing rods. There is also animal petting areas and hayrides. Admission. (mid-October weekend)*

Pine Mountain

BUTTS MILL FARM

Pine Mountain - ***2280 Butts Mill Road (Hwy 27 north to town. Left on Butts Mill Rd) 31822. Phone: (706) 663-7400. www.buttsmillfarm.com. Hours: Daily 10:00am-5:00pm except closed on Wednesdays. Admission: $15.95 adult, $13.95 child (3-9). Extra fees: Horseback riding $26.00; $8.00 go karts; $5.00-$50 paintball.***

Visit this fully operational farm with miniature golf, train rides, bungee bull rides, pony rides, cow milking, Wild West Playground, petting farm, Wild Animal exhibits (cougar, camel, lion, tiger and bears), and a seasonal swimming hole with waterslide and swings. Plan to get your money's worth by staying a half-day or so. Rides and events occur on a daily schedule. Barn dances and concerts on occasional weekends.

CALLAWAY GARDENS

Pine Mountain - ***(either I-85 or I-185, exit east on Hwy. 18 to The Gardens at Callaway) 31822. www.callawaygardens.com. Phone: (706) 663-5187 or (800) 225-5292. Hours: Daily 9:00am-5:00pm. Extended summer hours. Beach open seasonally Memorial Day weekend through mid-August plus Labor Day weekend. Butterfly Center open mid-March through October only. Admission: $18.00 adult, $15.00 senior (65+), $9.00 child (6-12). Daily admission to Callaway Gardens includes the Discovery Center, Day Butterfly Center, Horticultural Center, Mr. Cason's Vegetable Garden, Azalea Bowl, Overlook Garden, Discovery Bicycle Trail, Pioneer Log Cabin, Callaway Memorial Chapel, nature trails and daily programs. Note: Summer peaks at the Surf & Sand Spectacular July 4th event and packages.***

There are so many activities offered that you never could do them all in one day. The Gardens offer a rock wall garden, sculpture garden, fern grotto, floral conservatory, Vegetable Garden, Pioneer life Log Cabin, hiking and biking trails, Robin Lake Beach (world's largest man-made, white sand beach), and Aqua Island Floating Water Playground. Also within the property is:

BIRDS OF PREY: The mighty birds of prey featured in these outdoor, free-flighted shows, demonstrate their strength, speed and natural instincts at a lakeside amphitheater that allows the creatures to swoop directly over spectators' heads.

BUTTERFLY CENTER: The Butterfly Garden is so colorful and we promise you'll find a different species of butterfly every time you visit. The tropical atrium setting for the Butterfly Garden delights the senses and young and old were "tickled" by the "flybys" of a few creatures here and there.

Add a dash of high-flying adventure (circus camps and daily summer performance of an entertaining and surprising Flying High Circus).

Pass or Pay for Play options. If you decide NOT to purchase a Pass ($49/person), most activities are available for a fee. The fees start at $10.00/person and go up to $30.00/person. Seasonal Activities include: riding the miniature train, paddle boating, miniature golf, laser tag AND the

TREETOP ADVENTURE: Take your love of nature to new heights through a dizzying course of zip lines, swinging bridges, nets, logs and other aerial challenges that are woven into the natural forest behind the Discovery Center. Trusty guides instruct you, secure you in your harness and away you go on a birds-eye view adventure at your own pace. What's unique is that, once trained, you can move at your own pace through the course.

Don't forget the sandy beach and the famous ROBIN LAKE (super warm and clean – bring rafts, toys and coolers), the floating water park (parents of young ones under 10, best to go along to Aqua Island to help boost the little legs up the giant icebergs – separate admission wristband, $10.00 per person/per hour), water ski lessons, and a nationally acclaimed family golf program.

The family camps offer signups for hiking, biking, fishing, boating, tennis, golf, arts and crafts and more during the day. When night falls the fun continues with the circus, campfires, movies, games and more.

Make your own fun biking the 10 miles of trails (many folks brought their own bikes but you can rent them, too), hiking together, just beaching (apply that sunscreen - often), or sightseeing the Discovery Center, or Pioneer Cabin. Add the nation's oldest family summer camp and you'll have a host of memory makers.

CALLAWAY GARDENS - SKY HIGH HOT AIR BALLOON FESTIVAL

Pine Mountain - *(either I-85 or I-185, exit east on Hwy. 18 to The Gardens at Callaway) 31822. www.callawaygardens.com. Phone: (706) 663-5187. Hot air balloons fill the sky. Balloon Glow on Friday night. Family activities include tethered balloons, helicopter rides, line dancing, and live entertainment. Kite building, swimming, sandcastle building, mini golf and kids crafts too. Admission. (Labor Day weekend)*

CALLAWAY GARDENS - AUTUMNFEST

Pine Mountain - *(either I-85 or I-185, exit east on Hwy. 18 to The Gardens at Callaway) 31822. Phone: (706) 663-5187. www.callawaygardens.com. Mr. Cason's Vegetable Garden is a bushel of fun for everyone. Basket weavers, quilters, storytelling, apple bobbing, and making your own corn-shuck dolls are just some of the creative activities that fill this festival. Scarecrow Contest. (weekends in October)*

CALLAWAY GARDENS - FANTASY IN LIGHTS

Pine Mountain - *(either I-85 or I-185, exit east on Hwy. 18 to The Gardens at Callaway) 31822. Phone: (706) 663-5187. www.callawaygardens.com. Celebrate the shining glory of the holiday season with one of the world's largest light and sound shows featuring 8 million lights stretching more than six and a half miles long, creating more than a dozen larger-than-life holiday scenes. (they use green power - wind power credits offset conventional electricity). Visitors embark on the "Jolly Trolley" or drive through the lighted scenes in their vehicles to enjoy more than a dozen scenes including Snowflake Valley, a winter wonderland filled with enormous snowflakes and thousands of white lights. Two spectacular scenes are set apart from the drivable route and incorporate narration, music and choreographed lights to tell the story of 'Twas the Night Before Christmas and The Nativity on Robin Lake Beach. Advance tickets required. (Mid-November thru December)*

Rockin Robins Soda Shop was a great place to cool off...

CALLAWAY GARDENS RESORT

Pine Mountain - ***(either I-85 or I-185, exit east on Hwy. 18 to The Gardens at Callaway) 31822. Phone: (800) 225-5292. www.callawaygardens.com.***

CALLAWAY GARDENS reminds us of resort properties from the 50s – hundreds of cottages and a massive inn complete with daily activities for each family member. It is quaint yet modernized for extended families vacationing together. . . in any season. Their 50 years of experience and great family packages (such as the recommended annual Summer Family

Adventure Program) and activities satisfy and delight every generation. They offer accommodations in the Inn and Cottages (start around $129 per night). Summer Family Adventure: stay overnight for several days and sign up for bike hikes (up to 10 miles long), storytelling, campfires, theme dinner, arts & crafts, Discovery programs, tours, circus performances, adventure challenge on the ropes course, aerobics, water skiing, Callaway Olympics, movies, bingo, and trail hikes (easy .5 to 1.2 mile trails). We'd recommend staying at the cottages with plenty of space and privacy w/ screened decks and a grill and full kitchen.

Check out Rockin Robins soda shop themed diner w/ pizza and great shakes plus wonderful sandwich melts. Play pinball or bop to tunes on the jukebox.

F. D. ROOSEVELT STATE PARK

Pine Mountain - ***2970 Georgia Highway 190 (I-185 near Callaway, west of Warm Springs on GA 190, or south of Rine Mountain off US 27) 31822. Phone: (706) 663-4858 park or (877) 696-4613 stables. http://gastateparks.org/info/fdr/. Hours: Daily 7:00am-10:00pm. Admission: $5.00 daily vehicle parking fee.***

This park is deeply rooted in the historical era of four-time President Franklin D. Roosevelt. Seeking a place for treatment after he was stricken with polio in 1921, he traveled to the "curing" springs of the area and built a house. Several structures within the park, including the stone swimming pool, were built by the Civilian Conservation Corps during the Great Depression. Dowdell's Knob, Roosevelt's favorite picnic spot overlooking a magnificent view of the valley below is special. Hikers will enjoy the scenic trails (37 miles of) in the state's largest park. Camping, cottages, fishing, boating and horseback riding (stables, horse rentals, and 20 miles of trails) are here, too. Wolfden Loop (6.5 mile loop) travels past beaver dams, over Hogback Mountain and along Mountain Creek Nature Trail.

WILD ANIMAL SAFARI

Up close and personal for sure here...

Pine Mountain - ***1300 Oak Grove Road (I-185 North to Exit 42. Head east. Go approximately 6.7 miles) 31822. www.animalsafari.com. Phone: (706) 663-8744 or (800) 367-2751. Hours: Daily 10:00am-5:30pm. Extended evening hours late spring thru summer. Closed Christmas day. Admission: $16.95-$19.95 (age 3+). Extra fees for Zebra Van Rentals (if***

desired). Note: Just remember, domestic pets are not allowed on the property. Safari Cafe. To stave boredom on the road trip there, print off some animal word games from their website under Kid Zone.

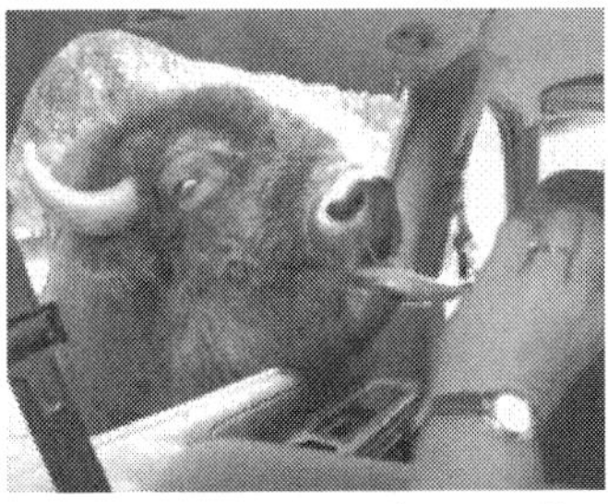

Some were cute, others, well "not so cute?"

See, feed and touch hundreds of exotic animals in this 250-acre park. Take a complimentary guided Zebra Bus or motor your own vehicle past giraffes or through the "Rhino Riviera".

Upon entering the drive-through section, you immediately begin to see animals that come right to the vehicle and see others in the distance that give you the feeling of being on a safari in the Serengeti. It's recommended (and we agree) to go on a safari bus/van tour vs. riding your own vehicle. It will be covered with slobber.

This is one of those "you have to be there" experiences. The acres of valley safari land provide dozens of opportunities to see, touch and feed (giant pellet cookies) hundreds of animals. Choose to feed timid deer or aggressive ostrich. Our favorites: the elk, cattle (wait till you see their tongues!) and the pot bellied pigs. (if you're timid about hand feeding animals, just toss the food pellets out on to the ground)

After your tour of the Park, visit their Winding Path and the Walk-About which is similar to a "zoo environment". The animals are penned and viewed from a walk through setting. Hand feed a Four-Horned Sheep, an Alpaca, Zedonk, or even a Wallaby

Thomaston

SPREWELL BLUFF STATE PARK

Thomaston - ***740 Sprewell Bluff Road (10 miles west of town. From GA 74 turn on Old Alabama Road and go south) 30286. http://gastateparks.org/SprewellBluff/. Phone: (706) 646-6026. Hours: Daily 7:00am- Sunset. Admission: $5.00 daily vehicle parking fee.***

Visitors can cool off in the gently flowing river, skip rocks across the water, picnic on the river's edge or toss horseshoes in a grassy field. A three-mile trail winds along a bank and up rocky bluffs, offering excellent views from high above the river. A boat ramp is available for canoeists, kayakers, rafters and fishermen. Canoes may be rented from several nearby outfitters, and camping is available 25 miles away at F. D. Roosevelt State Park in Pine Mountain.

ROCK RANCH

Thomaston - ***5020 Barnesville Hwy (I-75 south to exit 201. Take Hwy 36 west through town about 8 miles) 30385. www.therockranch.com. Phone: (706) 647-6374. Hours: Saturdays 10:00am-10:00pm throughout the Fall Family Fun Days. Also open for other special events throughout the year. Tours: $8.00 each for students and non-teaching adults. Teachers are FREE. Field Trips are available Mondays thru Fridays 10:00am or 11:30am (Spring, Summer or Fall). Each tour includes a hayride of the ranch and seasonal zipline opps. Educators: An excellent PDF of 21 page Georgia history booklet is available online under Field Trips/Just for Teachers/Miscellaneous. Note: Don't forget to wear your farm attire - wear old shoes, dress comfortably and for the weather. Bring a sack lunch to enjoy at the pavilion before returning home. Home cooked concessions and beverages are available for sale. There is no Chick-fil-A restaurant on the premises.***

The Rock Ranch is a 750-acre working cattle farm, owned by S. Truett Cathy, founder of Chick-fil-A. They offer many seasonal events and other "agritainment" or field trips. Some of the group tours available are: What's in a Farm? Learn about different animals in FarmLand...which of them have rectangular pupils, which ones can see in color? Let the goats entertain you on The Great Goat Walk.

Pond Adventure! A pond is a really fun place to be in the spring. Learn about the delicate web of life and what we can do to preserve it, and the importance of conserving our wetlands. You'll dip your net into the water and examine dragonfly nymphs and other aquatic creatures under microscopes.

Nature Hike - Observe animals and plants in their natural habitats. Watch the master builders and woodcutters at work, and search for the shy critters who like to hide! Pilgrim to Pioneer Days - Meet Pilgrims, dressed in period attire, and discover how they lived, and what they ate. Learn the relationship Native Americans had with these early settlers, and how those relationships shaped our country's early history. Students will meet and feed Farmland animals and learn how to care for them.

ROCK RANCH - FALL FAMILY FUN DAYS CORN MAZE

Thomaston - *5020 Barnesville Hwy (I-75 south to exit 201. Take Hwy 36 west through town about 8 miles) 30385. Phone: (706) 647-6374. www.therockranch.com. Hours: Saturdays 10:00am-10:00pm throughout the Fall Family Fun Days. Each year the Rock contracts a pro maze company to help you get lost in a corn maze. Don't worry about the maze being too difficult, they have trained employees stationed in observation towers to help. Fall Family fun Days coincides with this providing Saturday entertainment with wranglers, comedians, music, hot air balloons and Pumpkin Destruction Day. Admission. (early September thru early November)*

Warm Springs

BEST WESTERN WHITE HOUSE INN

Warm Springs - *White House Pkwy. (Hwy 85W) 31830. Phone: (706) 655-2750. If you just want to sightsee, try the Best Western White House Inn. They have spacious rooms with a free warm breakfast and outside patio pool. Many families we met were basing from this property for days, visiting sites within a 60 mile radius (see MW chapter). http://book.bestwestern.com/bestwestern/productInfo.do?propertyCode=11158*

BULLOCH HOUSE

Warm Springs - *47 Bulloch Street (Hwy 41 south of Broad Street/Hwy 27A) 31830. Phone: (706) 655-9068. www.bullochhouse.com. Plan to do lunch at a classic Southern favorite: BULLOCH HOUSE. Their home-cooked meals have the charm of the South with classic surroundings. The 1892 House buffet features fried green tomatoes, fried apples, real potatoes, pork and even pulley bones (yummy fried chicken). We loved the stewed pureed tomatoes for dipping our veggies and fruit. Lunch served daily, dinner Friday and Saturday, brunch Sunday. Prices $8.95-$11.95 for buffets.*

ROOSEVELT'S LITTLE WHITE HOUSE HISTORIC SITE

Warm Springs - ***401 Little White House Road (1/4 mile south of Warm Springs on GA 85 Alt - Hwy 27 Alt) 31830. http://gastateparks.org/info/littlewhite/. Phone: (706) 655-5870. Hours: Daily 9:00am-4:45pm. Last full tour at 4:00pm. Admission: $6.00-$10.00.***

Franklin Delano Roosevelt first came to Warm Springs in 1924 hoping to find a cure for the infantile paralysis (polio) that had struck him in 1921. Swimming in the warm, buoyant spring waters brought him no miracle cure, but it did bring improvement. He built the Little White House in 1932 while governor of New York, prior to being inaugurated as president in 1933. During FDR's presidency and the Great Depression, he developed many New Deal Programs based upon his experiences in this small town.

His actual Ford convertible complete with hand controls for driving...

Begin with the orientation video and preview the time line. Now, enter the museum and learn from the museum exhibits. How was Eleanor a 6th cousin to her own children? What is polio? Feel the temperature difference of warm vs. cold springs. How do you drive a vehicle without use of your legs? Why did President Franklin Roosevelt always have breakfast in bed? Look for FDR's 1938 Ford convertible with hand controls. Fireside Chats play over a 1930s radio and there is also a theatre. Visitors can tour FDR's home (looks like he just left it), and the servants and guest quarters. Nestled a mile down the road (in town, Hwy 27 Alt. west) is the Roosevelt Institute for Rehab and the FDR Pools Museum where you can feel the real waters of Warm Springs (get directions from the Historic Site). He was so charming and loveable, your heart will sink when you see the unfinished portrait partially complete at the time of his death at Warm Springs. So much to learn about times of Depression and War and the American spirit lead by a compassionate man.

The unfinished portrait...

ROOSEVELT'S LITTLE WHITE HOUSE HISTORIC SITE - FALA DAY TRIBUTE

Warm Springs - *401 Little White House Rd. 31830. Phone: (706) 655-5870. Join the Greater Atlanta Scottish Terrier Association for an opening parade, costume parade, grooming exhibits and bagpipe music. All Scotty dogs welcome on a six-foot leash. Free admission to the program held in the picnic area. Admission. (first Saturday in November)*

Warner Robins

MUSEUM OF AVIATION

Warner Robins - ***GA Hwy 247 S and Russell Pkwy. (I-75 exit 146. Take US 247C to Robins Air Force Base) 31099. www.museumofaviation.org. Phone: (478) 926-6870 or (888) 807-3359. Hours: Daily 9:00am-5:00pm except Thanksgiving Day, Christmas Day and New Year's Day. Admission: FREE. Tours: pre-arranged guided tours are scheduled on Tuesday-Saturday $3.00. Note: Victory Café. Freedom Park playground and picnic pavilion area. "Transporter." Visitors are transported to virtual reality locations like man's first walk on the moon, Christopher Columbus' ships, a ride through a volcano, a Grand Prix Race and a fighter jet strike mission during Operation Desert Storm. A total of twelve different 6-minute ride experiences are available in the enclosed capsule with seven seats (fee per ride). FREEBIES: 2 Scavenger Hunts are available to download/print from the tours page: www.moaeducation.com/tours.php***

This huge, ever-updated museum includes historical displays of military aircraft and the aviation pioneers who "kept them flying" for freedom around the world. Different buildings or hangars house exhibits on artifacts, aircraft, missiles and engines. Many especially like the Vistascope Theater, "We the People" Theatre and the Presidential and combat helicopters or wartime planes. The older kids can't wait to have the controls in their hands in the air traffic or fighter plane simulators. With names like "Destroyer" and "StratoFortress", this place appeals to a sense of freedom and strength. Try to catch a presentation, demonstration (posted daily at the reception area) or "dress-up" flight area.

West Point

BATTLE OF WEST POINT REENACTMENT

West Point - *Fort Tyler (I-85, west on US 29). www.forttyler.com/reenactments.htm. The Battle of West Point was fought on April 16, 1865 in West Point, Georgia, during the American Civil War. This battle was fought at Fort Tyler seven days after Confederate General Robert E. Lee surrendered to Union General Ulysses S. Grant, making it one of the last battles of the Civil War east of the Mississippi and Fort Tyler the last Confederate fort captured by the Union. The annual commemoration of the April 16, 1865, Battle of West Point is held at the reconstructed Fort Tyler off Sixth Avenue. Living history demonstrations ending with a candlelight memorial service. FREE. (mid-April weekend)*

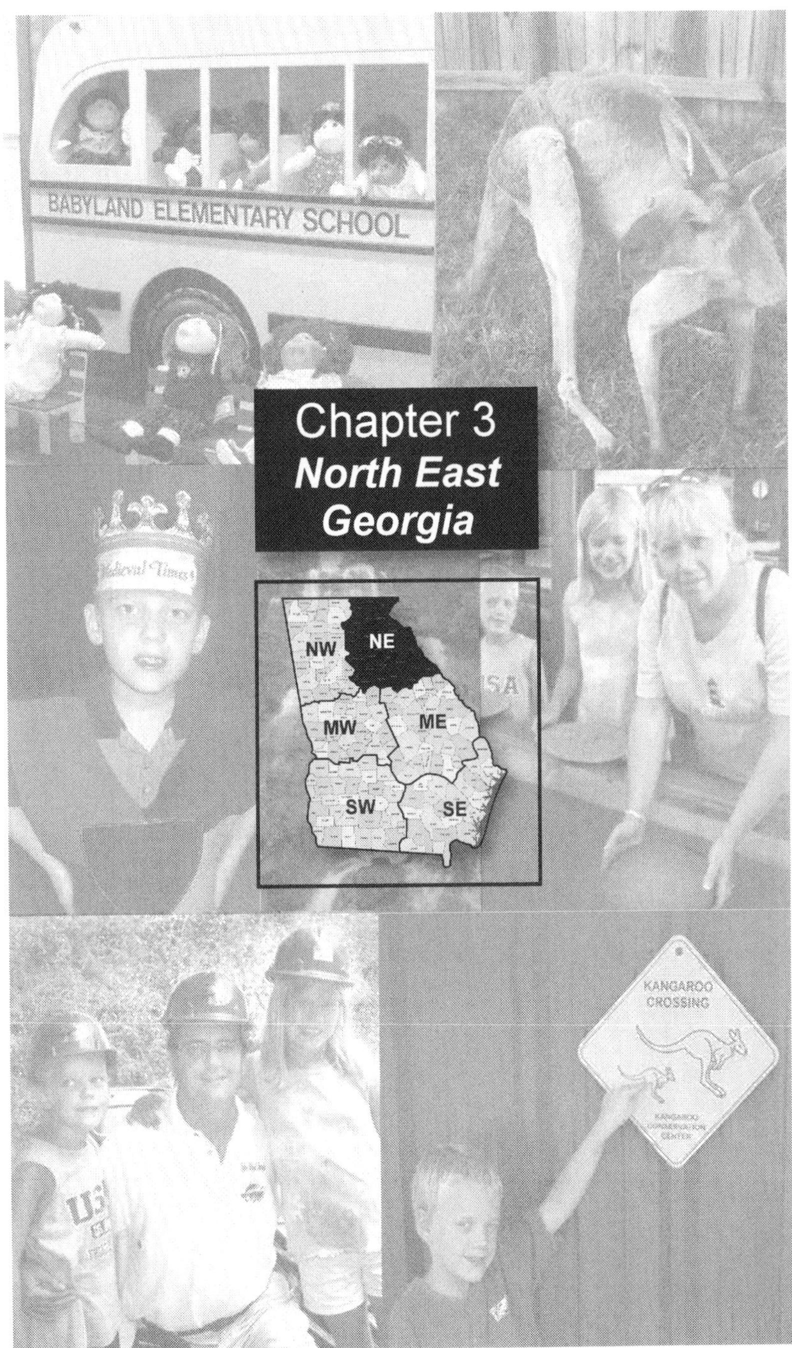
BABYLAND ELEMENTARY SCHOOL
Chapter 3
North East
Georgia
NW
NE
MW
ME
SW
SE
KANGAROO
CROSSING

Athens
- University Of Georgia
- Bear Hollow Wildlife Trail
- Sandy Creek Nature Center

Blairsville
- Brasstown Bald
- Misty Mountain Model Railroad
- Trackrock Archaeological Area
- Vogel State Park
- Vogel State Park - July 4th Celebration
- Scottish Festival & Highland Games
- Pumpkins, Pumpkins, Pumpkins
- Sorghum Festival

Blue Ridge
- Blue Ridge Scenic Railway
- Blue Ridge Scenic Railway - Santa Express

Braselton
- Mayfield Dairy Farms

Clarkesville
- Moccasin Creek State Park

Cleveland
- Babyland General Hospital

Comer
- Watson Mill Bridge State Park

Conyers
- Cherry Blossom Festival

Crawfordville
- A. H. Stephens Historic Park

Dahlonega
- Chestatee Wildlife Preserve
- Consolidated Gold Mine Tour
- Crisson Gold Mine
- Dahlonega Gold Museum Historic Site

Dawsonville
- Amicalola Falls State Park And Lodge
- Amicalola Falls State Park And Lodge - All American Happy Daze
- Amicalola Falls State Park And Lodge - Christmas Open House
- Georgia Racing Hall Of Fame

Dawsonville *(cont.)*
- Fall At Burt's Farm
- Uncle Shuck's Corn Maze And Pumpkin Patch

Duluth
- Southwestern Railway Museum

Elberton
- Bobby Brown State Park
- Nancy Hart Cabin
- Richard B. Russell State Park

Flowery Branch
- Atlanta Falcons Training Camp

Gainesville
- Ink Interactive Neighborhood
- Northeast Georgia History Center
- Elachee Nature Science Center
- Elachee Nature Science Center - Winter In The Woods Holiday Celebration

Greensboro
- Scull Shoals Festival

Hartwell
- Hart State Park

Helen
- Black Forest Bear Park
- Charlemagne's Kingdom Model RR
- Buggy Rides
- Remember When Theatre
- Smithgall Woods Conservation Area
- Unicoi State Park And Lodge
- Unicoi State Park And Lodge - Deck The Halls
- Helen To The Atlantic Hot Air Balloon Race

Hiawassee
- Crystal River Ranch Llama Treks
- High Shoals Falls & Scenic Area
- Georgia Mountain Fair
- Georgia Mountain Fall Festival

Jefferson
- Crawford W. Long Museum
- Mule Day

Lake Lanier Islands
- Lake Lanier Islands

- Lake Lanier Islands - Magical Nights Of Lights
- Lake Lanier Resort

Lakemont

- Hillside Orchard Farms

Lavonia

- Tugaloo State Park

Lawrenceville

- Medieval Times

Lilburn

- Yellow River Game Ranch
- Yellow River Game Ranch - Groundhog Day Celebration

Lincolnton

- Elijah Clark State Park

Mansfield

- Charlie Elliott Wildlife Center

Mountain City

- Black Rock Mountain State Park
- Foxfire Museum

Royston

- Ty Cobb Museum
- Victoria Bryant State Park

Rutledge

- Hard Labor Creek State Park

Sautee Nacoochee

- Sautee Nacoochee Center

Stockbridge

- Panola Mountain State Park

Suches

- Chattahoochee Forest National Fish Hatchery

Tallulah Falls

- Tallulah Gorge State Park

Toccoa

- Traveler's Rest Historic Site
- Traveler's Rest Historic Site - Christmas For Travelers

Toccoa Falls

- Toccoa Falls

Washington

- Callaway Plantatlon
- Robert Toombs House Historic Site

Winder

- Fort Yargo State Park
  Fort Yargo State Park - A Fort Yargo Christmas

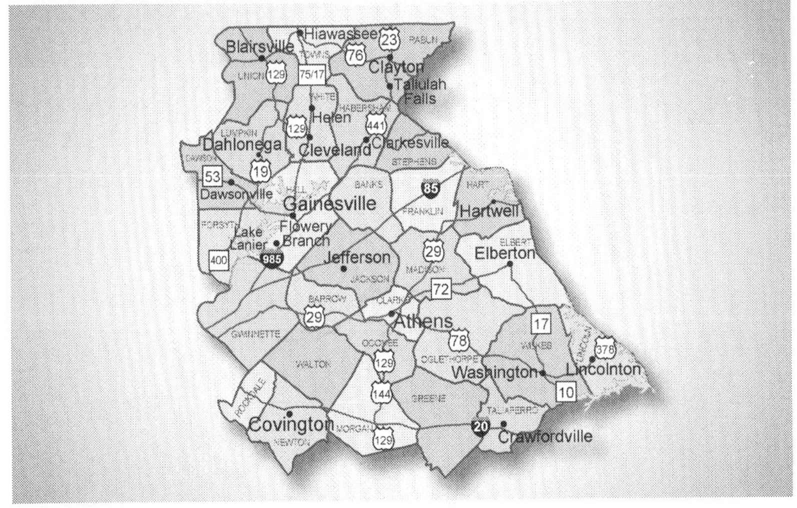

A Quick Tour of our Hand-Picked Favorites Around...

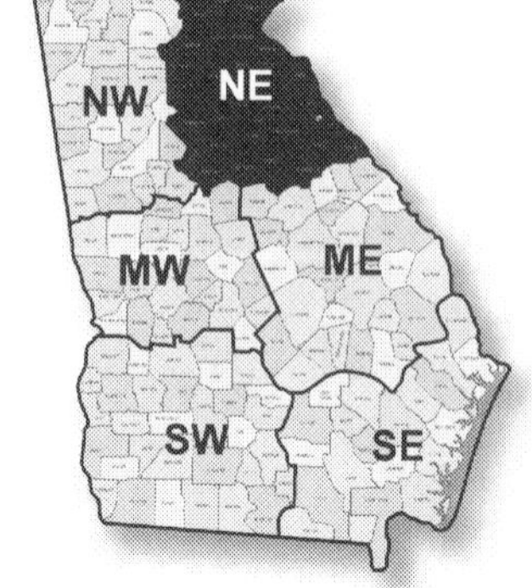

North East Georgia

Head to the mountains of northeast Georgia, and with the mountains come waterfalls – tall **Waterfalls**. Amicalola, a Cherokee Indian word meaning "tumbling waters," is an appropriate name for these 729-foot falls - the tallest cascading waterfall east of the Mississippi River. Other notable waterfalls are found on numerous State Park hiking trails – many only short walking journeys to the overlooks. . . a great reward after some uphill exercise.

Thar's gold in them thar hills! **Consolidated Gold Mine** in Dahlonega was the site of America's first gold rush. After the underground tour you will do some gold panning and gem grubbing…with a real miner at your side. Amazingly, you can still find gold in these hills!

Want to hold some more cute creatures? Head over to Cleveland, Georgia – the home of **Babyland General Hospital**, birthplace of the Cabbage Patch Kids dolls. Walk into the magical Cabbage Patch town starting in the nursery, then to the school house and playgrounds. When you hear a nurse call "Delivery Room STAT!" you need to hurry to the Patch. Here, you'll witness the birth of another one-of-a-kind, soft Cabbage Patch Kid.

Lake Lanier Islands invites your family to discover an abundance of activities from playing at the Beach & WaterPark to boating, equestrian and much more. Be sure to plan your trip around one of the special events that take place each summer for an extra added surprise!

Sites and attractions are listed in order by City, Zip Code, and Name. Symbols indicated represent:

☒ Festivals  Restaurants  Lodging

NORTHEAST GEORGIA WATERFALLS

http://georgiamountains.org/page/waterfalls. Phone: (706) 782-3320 (Clayton) or (706) 754-6221 (Helen).

Only a few waterfalls are visible from the road or parking lots. But most waterfalls can be easily reached, requiring varying lengths of walks or hikes.

BLAIRSVILLE / CLARKSVILLE:

- **DESOTO FALLS** (Chestatee Ranger District) - There are five beautiful waterfalls located in the 650-acre recreation area. Three of these falls are maintained for the hiker's viewing convenience and are designated as the lower, middle, and upper DeSoto Falls. DeSoto Falls got its name from a legend that tells of a piece of armor found near the falls. It was decided that the armor belonged to Hernando DeSoto or one of his fellow explorers. Directions: From Cleveland, take US 129 north 15 miles to DeSoto Falls Recreation Area.
- **PANTHER CREEK FALLS** (Chattooga Ranger District) - Panther Creek Falls Trail (5.5 miles in length) follows Panther Creek through stands of hemlock and white pine along steep, rocky bluffs of the creek. The trail passes a series of cascades, as well as, the falls. Directions: From Clarkesville, take U.S. 23/441 north for 10 miles to the Panther Creek Recreation Area. (706) 754-6221. Admission: $5.00 per vehicle.

CLAYTON - Start close to downtown Clayton at **BECKY BRANCH FALLS** (Warwoman Road), a 20-foot cascade easily accessible with a walk up a trail to a bridge at the base of the falls. **DICK'S CREEK FALLS** (off Sandy ford Road) is 60 feet high and makes a sheer drop over a granite mound into the Chattooga River. At the top, there's a viewing area. Finally, the Holcomb Creek Trail passes **HOLCOMB CREEK FALLS** (Hale Ridge Road), which drops and flows over the shoals for approximately 150 feet, and Ammons Creek Falls, where there is an observation deck.

HELEN - In Helen, there's **HORSE TROUGH FALLS** (GA 75 & Forest Service Rd 44) - follow the Falls Trail (.04 mile in length) leading to the beautiful falls. Also, the **RAVEN CLIFF FALLS** (off Russell-Brasstown Scenic Byway) - perhaps one of the most unusual in the area because the water flows through a split in the face of a solid rock outcropping and plummets to the ground 100 feet below.

Athens

UNIVERSITY OF GEORGIA

Athens - ***Visitors Center - Four Towers Building, College Stadium Road (I-85 to Georgia Highway 316 (Exit 106). Proceed east on GA 316 for approximately 40 miles until you see signs for Athens Perimeter (GA Loop 10). 30602. Phone: (706) 542-0842. www.uga.edu/profile/visit.html. Hours: Visitors Center Info: Monday-Friday 8:00am-5:00pm, Saturday 9:00am-5:00pm, Sunday 1:00-5:00pm. Closed on UGA holidays and breaks. Admission: FREE. Tours: Self-guided, or call for guided tours.***

Located in a former dairy barn on East Campus, the Visitor Center occupies the southern wing of the Four Towers Building (the four towers representing the building's four silos). The center assists visitors and maintains up-to-date information about campus, local accommodations, special events and campus maps.

- **BUTTS-MEHRE HERITAGE HALL & SPORTS MUSEUM** - One Selig Circle, (706) 542-9036 or www.georgiadogs.com. Here, in the rotunda under the domed roof, are many exhibits and memorabilia tracing the long and proud heritage of all Georgia's athletic programs. In addition, recently upgraded touch-screen displays containing video highlights of Georgia's football history offer the chance to relive great Bulldog moments. (Call for hours)
- **ITA COLLEGIATE TENNIS HALL OF FAME** - UGA South Campus, (706) 542-8064 or www.uga.edu/uga/bottom-va.html. Famous inductees include Arthur Ashe, Jimmy Connors, and Stan Smith. (Monday-Friday 9:00am-Noon, 2:00-5:00pm)
- **GEORGIA MUSEUM OF ART** - 90 Carlton Street. www.uga.edu/gamuseum. (706) 542-4662. Their permanent collection focuses on 19th-and early-20th century American paintings. Just My Imagination Workshops provide adults and their children a chance to create art together. The workshops are led by artists from Georgia and are free to participants. (Tuesday-Saturday 10:00am-5:00pm, Wednesday until 9:00pm, Sunday 1:00-5:00pm)
- **STATE BOTANICAL GARDEN OF GEORGIA** - 2450 South Milledge Avenue, (706) 542-1244 or www.uga.edu/botgarden. The three-story tropical conservatory dominates this 313-acre preserve. (Daily 8:00am to dusk)

- <u>HORTICULTURE TRIAL GARDEN</u> - 1111 Plant Science Building, Dept. of Horticulture, (706) 542-2471. Ornamental plants are performance-tested in seasonally rotating gardens. (Daily 8:00am-dusk)
- <u>OCONEE FOREST PARK</u> - UGA Recreational Sports Complex, College Station & E. Campus Roads, www.forestry.uga.edu/warnell/ofp/. (706) 542-1571. Home to the Tree Trail, a network of trails with more than 100 native Georgia trees and shrubs identified by tags. The forest park also has lakeshore hiking, mountain bike trails, and a picnic area. (Daily 8:00am to dusk)

BEAR HOLLOW WILDLIFE TRAIL

Athens - ***293 Gran Ellen Drive, Memorial Park (one street north of the East Campus Drive traffic light. Memorial Park is about two blocks down) 30606. Phone: (706) 613-3580 or (706) 613-3616 zoo. www.athensclarkecounty.com/~bearhollow/. Hours: Daily 9:00am-5:00pm. Trails open until dark. Admission: FREE, donations accepted. Tours: Every Saturday (and many Sundays) they offer either guided feeding tours or a classroom project. They also have Wee walks through the park on school year Thursdays.***

Wear your tennis shoes to experience 80 acres of rolling hills, a lake, walking trails, picnic spots, a playground area, and a small zoo. Resident animals include black bears, owls, otters, deer and bobcats. Keep your eyes and ears open and you may see the resident pair of red-shouldered hawks flying in the tree tops overhead.

SANDY CREEK NATURE CENTER

Athens - ***205 Old Commerce Road (exit the 10 loop at 441 N) 30607. Phone: (706) 613-3615. www.sandycreeknaturecenter.com. Hours: Tuesday-Saturday 8:30am-5:30pm. Admission: FREE.***

Explore over 225 acres of woodland, marshland, and fields that support a variety of wildlife along five miles of trails. Check out beavers at the clay pit pond. See ruins of a turn-of-the-century brick factory and an 1800's log house. Visit the Oconee River and Sandy Creek. Walk the Greenway or Cook's Trail.

The ENSAT (Environment, Natural Science and Appropriate Technology) Center features live animal exhibits and wheelchair accessible trails. Meet a live sea turtle. Delve into an interactive wetlands exhibit complete with microscopes and a beaver lodge. View live venomous snakes from our region and other non-venomous species. Use the resource library to learn about natural science and ecology. Create nature crafts in the children's classroom or enjoy a story in the reading loft.

Blairsville

BRASSTOWN BALD

***Blairsville** - 4811 Teague Road (take US 19/129 south of town 8 miles. East onto SR 180 another 12 miles) 30512. www.aboutnorthgeorgia.com/ang/Brasstown_ Bald Phone: (706) 896-2556. Hours: Daily (Memorial Day - October). Weekends only (March-May). Admission: $2.00 per car into Anna Ruby Falls parking lot.*

Georgia's highest mountain, visitors can enjoy spectacular 360 degree views at an elevation point of 4,784 feet above sea level (Georgia's highest). To reach the bald's summit, families can either hike a half-mile trail or take a shuttle from the parking lot. The surrounding area is home to a wide variety of plants and animals. The Visitor Information Center, located on the summit of the Bald, offers exhibits, video presentations and interpretive programs. For those seeking a great outdoor experience, there are four hiking trails ranging from 1/2 to 6 miles in length. Seasonal activities include kite-making, wood-carving and mountain music festivals. It includes picnicking as well as an observation deck. On a clear day, you can see Atlanta.

MISTY MOUNTAIN MODEL RAILROAD

***Blairsville** - 4381 Misty Mountain Lane on Town Creek Road 30512. Phone: (706) 745-9819. www.mistymountaininn.com/train.htm. Admission: $5.00 donation requested (age 17+). Tours: One hour tour begins promptly at 2:00pm every Monday, Wednesday, Friday and Saturday. No Friday tours (January-April).*

America's largest o-gauge train display, the 3,400 square foot layout features 14 O-gauge Lionel trains traveling on a mile of track over 12 bridges and four trestles and through 15 tunnels. Many displays represent North Georgia and Atlanta. Trains run at floor level so that the children can get a good look. There is lots to see at every turn including Blairsville, Gainesville, Dahlonega, Blue Ridge, Gainesville, historic Atlanta, Stone Mountain, and even Tara from "Gone with the Wind."

TRACKROCK ARCHAEOLOGICAL AREA

Blairsville - ***Trackrock Gap Road (US Hwy 76/GA Hwy 515 E for 5.8 miles; turn R (S) on Trackrock Gap Rd.) 30512. Phone: (706) 745-5493. www.fs.usda.gov/goto/conf/trackrock.***

Once covered by the waters of a great ocean, Track Rock Gap is now dry land. Georgia's Cherokee Indians simply called it "printed place." This 52 acre area contains preserved petroglyphs of ancient Indian origin with carvings resembling animal and bird tracks, crosses, circles, and human footprints. Look for the historical marker. This park is open daylight hours and is FREE.

VOGEL STATE PARK

Blairsville - ***7485 Vogel State Park Road (11 miles south of Blairsville via US 19-129) 30512. Phone: (706) 745-2628. http://gastateparks.org/info/vogel/. Hours: Daily 7:00am-10:00pm. Admission: $5.00 daily vehicle parking fee.***

Vogel is located at the base of BLOOD MOUNTAIN in the Chattahoochee National Forest. Most popular in the fall, when the Blue Ridge Mountains transform into a rolling blanket of red, yellow and gold leaves. Cottages, campsites and primitive backpacking sites provide overnight accommodations. HELTON CREEK FALLS Trail (.3 mile in length) follows Helton Creek to two waterfalls. The trail accesses the lower falls at both the bottom and top of the falls and ends at the bottom of the upper falls. The total vertical drop is more than 100 feet. The rocks are deceptively slippery around these falls. Exercise caution! Go 2.2 miles to a small pullout parking area. Trailhead will be on the right. Outdoor activities include 17 miles of hiking to the falls (Appalachian Trail also nearby), fishing, swimming, pedal boat rental and miniature golf.

VOGEL STATE PARK - JULY 4TH CELEBRATION

Blairsville - *7485 Vogel State Park Road 30512. Phone: (706) 745-2628. Admission: $5.00 daily vehicle parking fee. Celebrate with a flag-raising ceremony, bicycle parade, paddle boat races. sandcastle building and watermelon eating contests, sack races, egg tosses and greased pole climb. (July 4th)*

SCOTTISH FESTIVAL & HIGHLAND GAMES

Blairsville - *Meeks Park. Phone: (706) 745-5789. www.blairsvillescottishfestival.org. Catch the excitement of clan gatherings, Scottish vendors, pipe and drum bands, parade of Tartans, athletics, border collie demonstrations, children's games, Scottish dancing and music in the village. Admission. (second weekend in June)*

PUMPKINS, PUMPKINS, PUMPKINS

Blairsville - *Southern Tree Plantation (4.7 miles south of town). Phone: (706) 745-0601. www.southerntreeplantation.com. Hayrides, kids train ride, petting farm, maze, marshmallow roasting, pony rides and inflatable slides. Admission. (weekends – Friday thru Sunday in October)*

SORGHUM FESTIVAL

Blairsville - *Downtown. http://sorghum.blairsville.com. Celebrating the lost art of sorghum syrup-making, the festival will have live demonstrations showing how the cane is crushed and cooked as well as jars of the sweet syrup for sale. Participate in contests such as Bisket Eatin', Pole Climbin", Syrup Soppin', Rock Throwin", Horseshoe Throwin", and Log Sawin". There's also live country music, singing, square dancing, and a Sorghum Parade and Car Show. FREE. (two full weekends in October)*

Blue Ridge

BLUE RIDGE SCENIC RAILWAY

Blue Ridge - ***241 Depot Street (I-575 north to town. Turn right at second light. Follow signs to railroad tracks) 30513. Phone: (706) 632-9833 or (800) 934-1898. www.brscenic.com. Admission: $32.00-$66.00 adult, $25.00-$39.00 senior (65+), $17.00-$25.00 child (2-12). Advanced Reservations Recommended. 48 hours notice required to cancel. Tours: Seasonal schedule with departures at 9:45am, 11:00am, 1:30pm or 2:45pm. Daily summers, mostly weekends spring and fall. (March through mid-November) Note: Commissary car with snacks and souvenirs. Restrooms on board.***

Nestled in the mountains of Georgia in the Chattahoochee National Forest, historic Blue Ridge awaits you and your family. Rent a cabin, climb a mountain, hike a trail and ride the Blue Ridge Scenic Railway. The train route consists of a 26-mile round trip through historic Murphy Junction along the beautiful Toccoa River. This railroad was built over 100 years ago. Choose from vintage, climate controlled coaches or open air rail cars. Each trip includes a stop in McCaysville which permits passengers to stretch their legs while exploring the downtown shops of McCaysville, Georgia and Copperhill, Tennessee. The sister towns divided by the TN-GA state line have fresh mountain air and little eateries or ice cream shops for a treat or light lunch or snack. Each round trip takes approximately 3 1/2 hours.

BLUE RIDGE SCENIC RAILWAY - SANTA EXPRESS

Blue Ridge - *241 Depot Street. 30513. Phone: (706) 632-9833 or (800) 934-1898. www.brscenic.com. Miscellaneous: Commissary car with snacks and souvenirs. Restrooms on board. Treat your family to an old-fashioned Christmas singing carols, listening to the story of the Polar Express, and visiting with Santa and his elves at Santa's Village stop in McCaysville. Admission (slightly higher than normal fare). Trips are 2.25 hours long. (weekends beginning thanksgiving weekend in November thru third weekend in December, some December Christmas break weekday trains, too)*

Braselton

MAYFIELD DAIRY FARMS

Braselton ***- 1160 Broadway Avenue (I-285 East to I-85 North. Turn right at Exit 126) 30517. Phone: (706) 654-9180 or (888) 298-0396. www.mayfielddairy.com. Hours: Monday-Friday 9:00am-5:00pm, Saturday 9:00am-2:00pm. Admission: FREE. Tours: Weekday tours (except Wednesdays) begin every 30 minutes. Saturday tours begin every hour. Last tour begins 1 hour before closing. Reservations recommended for groups. Educators: Online Lesson Plans & Activities are under the icon Fun & Learning/For Teachers.***

Get the "scoop" on the history of this dairy through a film presentation followed by a plant tour that includes how milk is bottled. Begin by watching all the swirling and twirling and spinning and turning and churning of jugs. The fun tour includes a great look at how they make plastic milk jugs from a handful of tiny pellets...melted and molded. See the Aro-Vac that removes unwanted flavors from milk or how they homogenize, pasteurize, and add vitamins to milk. After the guided visual tour - taste some of their ice cream creations for sale (cheap!). Try Snow Cream.

Why does Mayfield Milk come in a yellow jug?

(Answer - for freshness and it seals in the vitamins)

Clarkesville

MOCCASIN CREEK STATE PARK

Clarkesville - *3655 Georgia Highway 197 (20 miles north of town on GA 197 or 15 miles west of Clayton via GA 76 & GA 197) 30523. http://gastateparks.org/info/moccasin/. Phone: (706) 947-3194. Hours: Daily 7:00am-10:00pm. Closed December thru mid-March. Admission: $5.00 daily vehicle parking fee.*

Moccasin Creek is nestled in the Blue Ridge Mountains on the shores of Lake Burton. Despite its mountain location, the park is relatively flat, offering easy navigation for biking. A fully accessible fishing pier sits above a trout-filled creek open only to physically challenged visitors, senior citizens and children. Tour the adjacent trout rearing station or hike on several nearby mountain trails (2 mile Hemlock Falls Hiking Trail). The park also offers seasonal canoe and jon boat rentals.

Cleveland

BABYLAND GENERAL HOSPITAL

Cleveland - *300 NOK Drive (US 129, downtown - look for the signs) 30528. Phone: (706) 865-2171. www.cabbagepatchkids.com. Hours: Monday-Saturday 9:00am-5:00pm, Sunday 10:00am-5:00pm. Admission: FREE.*

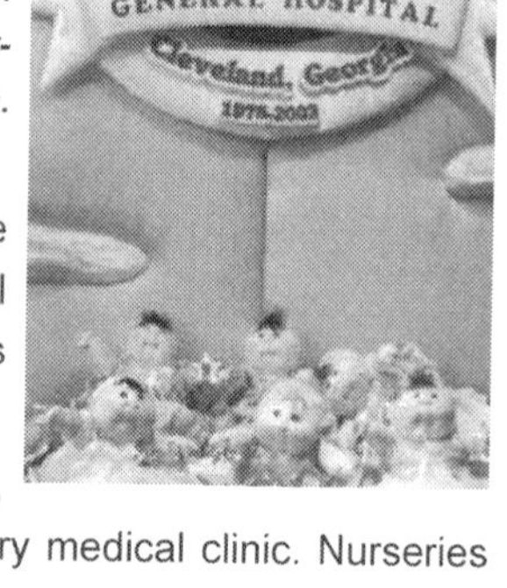

Enter the Babyland General Hospital, birthplace of the Cabbage Patch Kids and home to original artist Xavier Roberts' creations from the early 80s to now.

Polished floors lead up to simple double doors, recreating a sense of a former turn of the century medical clinic. Nurseries are lined with cribs filled with hand-sculpted Preemies and Lullabye Babies. Displays include a spectacular Cabbage Patch under the Magic Crystal Tree, the Fantasy Forest and Clubhouse tree house. Licensed Patch Nurses and Doctors are on call to assist Mother Cabbages in labor and provide advice for on-site adoptive parents. When you hear a nurse call "Delivery Room STAT!" you need to hurry to the Patch. Here, you'll witness the birth of a one-of-a-kind, soft Cabbage Patch Kid. Wander through the rest of the "Hospital" gift shop and maybe fall in love with a baby and adopt it to take home. Fun is born here!

Comer

WATSON MILL BRIDGE STATE PARK

Comer - ***650 Watson Mill Road (3 miles south of Comer off GA 22) 30629. Phone: (706) 783-5349. http://gastateparks.org/info/watson/. Hours: Daily 7:00am-10:00pm. Admission: $5.00 daily vehicle parking fee.***

Watson Mill Bridge contains the longest original-site covered bridge in the state, spanning 229 feet across the South Fork River. Built in 1885, the bridge is supported by a town lattice truss system held firmly together with wooden pins. Hiking (7 miles), biking (5 miles) and horseback riding (12 miles) trails allow visitors to enjoy the thick forest along the river or travel into the park's backcountry. During summer, kids often play in the cool river shoals just below the bridge.

Conyers

CHERRY BLOSSOM FESTIVAL

Conyers - *Georgia International Horse Park, Centennial Olympic Parkway (I-20 east exit 82, GA 138 north 4 miles). www.conyerscherryblossomfest.com. In an attractive setting with woods and rolling meadows, this park was the scene of several Olympic events. For two days the City of Conyers will come alive as the pink blossoms begin to bloom on the cherry trees. The contemporary art festival includes 300 artist and crafter booths, a variety of food booths, an interactive children's area, and entertainment from diverse cultures on multiple stages. They have a nature preserve with miles of trails on the property, too. FREE admission with a $5.00 parking fee. (last weekend in March)*

Crawfordville

A. H. STEPHENS HISTORIC PARK

Crawfordville - ***(north of I-20 exit 148 and go north on GA 22 for 2 miles. Then, go east on US 278) 30631. http://georgiastateparks.org/AHStephens/. Phone: (706) 456-2221. Hours: Park: 7:00am-10:00pm. Historic Site: Wednesday-Sunday 9:00am-5:00pm. Closed Monday except holidays. Admission: $1.50 - $3.00 fee. Note: Victorian Christmas decorations and refreshments each December.***

This site combines recreation with education. The park features a Confederate museum with one of the finest collections of Civil War artifacts in the state, including uniforms and documents. Stephen's home, Liberty Hall, is renovated to its 1875 style, fully furnished and open for tours. There are cottages, campgrounds and large overnight group camps. The park area offers fishing, boating and boat rentals, horseback riding trails, pedal boat rentals, and 3 miles of walking trails.

Dahlonega

CHESTATEE WILDLIFE PRESERVE

Dahlonega - ***469 Old Dahlonega Hwy (Hwy 400N to end, go straight and then right onto Hwy 115) 30533. www.chestateewildlife.com. Hours: Daily 9:00am-4:00pm. Admission: $10.00 adult, $5.00 child (11 years and under). All money goes to the feeding and care of the animals.***

The kids loved seeing the animals so close and the adults were very impressed how clean the cages are kept and well-cared for animals too. There is such a wide variety from one pen housing two gray wolves with a black bear, grizzly, and cinnamon bear. Another with deer and young zebras. The white and Bengal tigers are magnificent, and Mufasah the big male lion. Currently two baby leopard cubs are here along with over a hundred other species.

CONSOLIDATED GOLD MINE TOUR

Dahlonega - ***185 Consolidated Gold Mine Road (main crossroad of town where US 19, GA 60, GA 9 & GA 52 run together - the mine is under the Wal-Mart) 30533. www.consolidatedgoldmine.com. Phone: (706) 864-8473. Hours: Daily 10:00am-4:00pm (winter) or 5:00pm (summer). Admission: $15.00 adult, $9.00 child (4-14). Tour not recommended for 3 & Under. (Admission includes 40 - 45 minute underground tour and FREE Sampler gold panning) Tours: Tours are guided and run daily year-round. The mines remain at a comfortable 60 degrees year round.***

Did You Know...
Gold was first discovered in the Dahlonega area in 1828, twenty years before the Gold Rush to California.

Thar's gold in them thar hills! When Gold was discovered, it was completely by accident – a deer hunter, Benjamin Parks, tripped over a rock 2½ miles south of what is now Dahlonega. Upon inspecting the rock, he discovered that it was full of gold! Within one year's time, some 15,000 miners heard about that and rushed to find some gold for themselves. This authentic mine site offers underground tours of a hard rock gold mine and gold panning.

Panning for real gold...

Once in the massive underground network of tunnels (complete with the original track system), you'll learn about techniques used by early miners. Hear a loud air hammer drill bit demonstrated! The tour introduces guests to the geology of the gold belt including the quartz and pyrite formation which early miners were working at the turn of the century. Amazingly, you can still find gold in these hills! Look for it underground. Once you're done with the geology tour, try your hand at gold panning using techniques you just learned about.

"Gold miners"...sure has a good sound to it...

CRISSON GOLD MINE

Dahlonega - ***2736 Morrison Moore Parkway East (2 1/2 miles north of town on US 19 Connector) 30533. Phone: (706) 864-6363. www.crissongoldmine.com. Hours: Daily (except Christmas) 10:00am-6:00pm. Admission: varies with choice of bucket size and methods of "hounding" for gold.***

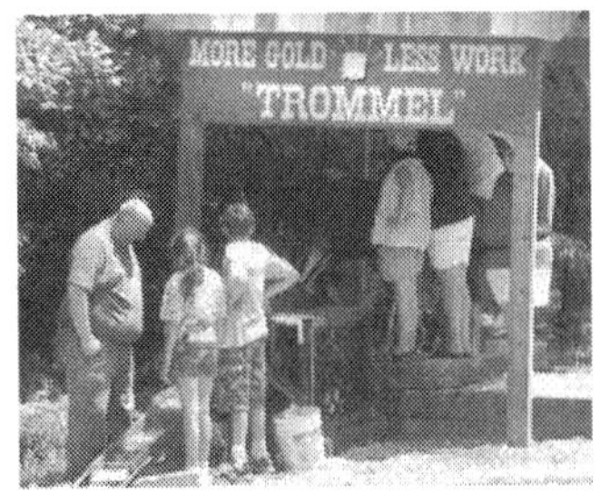

The Crisson Gold Mine, dating back to 1847, is open for tours and gold panning. Crisson Gold Mine is an actual open pit gold mine, not underground in "mines." Antique gold mining machines along with an open pit mine can be seen on the tour. The operating 10-stamp mill is demonstrated as part of the Crisson Gold Mine Tour. Pan for gold or try you luck at gem grubbin', where you can find rubies, emeralds, garnets, and more. They sell ore by the 5-gallon bucket and even offer tools, "trommels", and larger buckets for serious rock hounds.

DAHLONEGA GOLD MUSEUM HISTORIC SITE

Dahlonega - ***1 Public Square (Public Square in town, 5 miles west of GA 400) 30533. Phone: (706) 864-2257. http://gastateparks.org/info/dahlonega/. Hours: Monday-Saturday 9:00am-5:00pm, Sunday 10:00am-5:00pm. Closed major winter holidays. Admission: $3.50-$6.00 per person. Note: Gold Rush packages include discounted tickets and a gold panning dish. The friendly Welcome Center offers directions and tickets (located in the town square).***

Many years before the Gold Rush out west, thousands of gold seekers flocked into the Cherokee Nation in North Georgia. In the mid-1800s, more than $6 million in gold was coined by the US Mint. Located in the old county

DAHLONEGA GOLD MUSEUM HISTORIC SITE *(cont.)*

Did you know they've found trace amounts of gold in bricks made around town?

courthouse, this museum tells the story of the mining history of Georgia and displays many large gold nuggets and coins. A 17-minute film, "America's First Gold Rush," describes the mining techniques and lifestyles of the prospectors through interviews with mining families. Look at and discover what a stamp machine is. Or, what is a water cannon and why was it so helpful to miners? Gold now can be processed so thin, it looks like paper. Very interesting and educational.

Dawsonville

AMICALOLA FALLS STATE PARK AND LODGE

Dawsonville - *240 Amicalola Falls State Park Road (Hwy 53 west to Hwy 183 north to Hwy 52 east. 15 miles NW of town) 30534. Phone: (706) 265-4703 or 265-8888 (lodge). www.gastateparks.org/info/amicalola. Hours: Daily 7:00am-10:00pm. Admission: $5.00 daily vehicle parking fee.*

Amicalola is a Cherokee Indian word meaning "tumbling waters" - an appropriate name for the 729-foot falls - the tallest east of the Mississippi River. Numerous trails are available for short journeys. The lodge is popular with guests who prefer hotel-like comforts (private porches with breathtaking glass-walled views) but they also offer cottages and camping. Find activities that combine both adventure and accommodations: spend the night at the Len Foote Hike Inn, with a warm bed and tasty dinner, accessible only by foot over a 5 mile hiking trail originating at the top of Amicalola Falls. Accommodations run $60.00-$160.00 per night and the lodge has a restaurant. The park office has nature displays, live creature exhibits and a gift shop.

Hiking the APPALACHIAN TRAIL is on the 'to do' list of many adults. Some try to hike it in one trip while others take it in small chunks. The southern terminus of this 2176-mile footpath is in Georgia at Springer Mountain. The 76 mile Georgia section of the trail may be the most rugged and difficult and yet is as beautiful as any section along the trail. On your trek, stop at Mountain Crossings at Neel's Gap and visit the Boot Museum, seeing the many hikers' boots left behind as a reminder of their journey. An 8.5 mile approach trail leads from the state park to Springer Mountain.

AMICALOLA FALLS STATE PARK AND LODGE - ALL AMERICAN HAPPY DAZE

Dawsonville - *240 Amicalola Falls State Park Road 30534. Phone: (706) 265-4703 or 265-8888 (lodge). www.gastateparks.org/info/amicalola. This weekend is filled with old-fashioned games, patriotic crafts, watermelon seed spitting contest, pie-eating contest, greased pole climb, Hula Hoop contests, hayrides and more. Each day ends with a nostalgic visit back to the '50s as the park's restaurant transforms into the Amicalola Diner. $2.00 parking. (three days around July 4th)*

☒

AMICALOLA FALLS STATE PARK AND LODGE - CHRISTMAS OPEN HOUSE

Dawsonville - *240 Amicalola Falls State Park Road 30534. Phone: (706) 265-4703 or 265-8888 (lodge). www.gastateparks.org/info/amicalola. Visit with Santa and enjoy choir performances, hayrides, artwork by local children and gingerbread displays. A holiday buffet will be served in the park's restaurant. Some fees. (first or second weekend in December)*

☒

GEORGIA RACING HALL OF FAME

Dawsonville - ***415 Hwy 53 east (GA 400 exit Hwy 53 west) 30534. Phone: (706) 216-RACE. www.georgiaracinghof.com. Hours: Weekdays 10:00am-4:00pm. Weekends 10:00am-2:00pm. Closed Christmas only. Holiday hours vary. Admission: Museum FREE, donations accepted. Note: Champions Café is on the fast track to great southern cooking and icy cold Sweet Tea...served up fast in the retro-style diner.***

This museum's theme is realistic old streets, garages and race cars. Sit in old cars and on tailgates to view custom films on racing at the "Drive-in". Follow Elliott family and famous racing legends in the Hall of Fame - see many cars which won Daytona. Exhibits change monthly.

FALL AT BURT'S FARM

Dawsonville - *Burt's Farm (4801 Highway 52). www.burtsfarm.com. Phone: (800) 600-BURT. Come out to the fall foliage in a sea of orange created by thousands of Burt's pumpkins. They offer hayrides and field trips pulled by John Deere tractors that take you through a winding trail filled with nature and beauty. Stop at the Pumpkin House to hear Autumn and Gourdy...the talking pumpkins. The hayride ends hilltop with a view of Amicalola. Admission. (weekends early-September to mid November)*

UNCLE SHUCK'S CORN MAZE AND PUMPKIN PATCH

Dawsonville - *4525 Hwy 53E (I-295 exit GA 400 north to GA 53). Phone: (888) OSHUCKS. www.uncleshucks.com. Explore the Corn Maze, Pick a Pumpkin, Shoot the Corn Cannon, try some fall foods, bonfires and hayrides. Admission. (Labor Day weekend thru long weekends in November. Extended to weekdays in October only)*

Duluth

SOUTHWESTERN RAILWAY MUSEUM

Duluth - ***3595 Peachtree Road (I-85 north of Atlanta, turn west past Gwinnett Place Mall and follow the signs) 30096. Phone: (770) 476-2013. www.srmduluth.org. Hours: Thursday, Friday, Saturday 10:00am-5:00pm (April-December). Saturdays only (January-March). Admission: $9.00 adult, $7.00 senior (65+) & child (2-12). Entry to exhibit hall and train rides included with admission. Note: this facility is not a glamorous site, but, instead a way to see restoration in progress. Educators: Online lesson plans for elementary aged kids on Field Trips/tours link.***

See over 80 pieces of rolling stock, including vintage steam locomotives, historic wooden cars and Pullmans up close. Count how many beds are in the Sleeper/Lounge cars. Then, take as many short train rides aboard restored cabooses, as you like. We suggest standing out on the back platform.

Elberton

BOBBY BROWN STATE PARK

Elberton - ***2509 Bobby Brown State Park (21 miles southeast of Elberton off GA 72) 30635. Phone: (706) 213-2046. http://gastateparks.org/info/bobbybrown/. Hours: Daily 7:00am-10:00pm. Admission: $3.00 daily vehicle parking fee.***

The park is named in memory of Lt. Robert T. Brown, US Navy, who gave his life in World War II. When water levels are low, visitors can see some foundations of the old town that was once there and imagine large plantations flourishing. The park's strategic location on the largest man-made lake east of the Mississippi River provides excellent boating, skiing and fishing. New yurts (like tents but make of canvas and wood) offer a new way to camp. The park offers almost 2 miles of hiking trails, a seasonal swimming pool, and canoe, pedal or fishing boat rentals.

On GA 72 east of town, look for "Old Dan Tucker's" Gravesite. Tucker is a minister whose empathy for slaves inspired the American folk song by his name.

NANCY HART CABIN

Elberton - ***River Road (off Highway 17, south of Elberton-near Bobby Brown St. Pk.) 30635. Phone: (706) 283-5651. Hours: Monday-Saturday 9:00am-5:00pm, just to look around and read markers. Admission: FREE.***

During the American Revolution, a party of British Tories came to Mrs. Hart's home. Single-handedly she killed one and wounded another. The remainder of the party surrendered and were later hanged by her and a few of her neighbors. A replica of her cabin, complete with gun holes is open to visitors. Call ahead and arrange a tour so you can hear the fabulous stories of how her size and character gained her notoriety as a colonial spy during the American Revolution.

RICHARD B. RUSSELL STATE PARK

Elberton - ***2650 Russell State Park Road (8 miles northeast of town off GA 77 on Ruckersville Road) 30635. http://gastateparks.org/info/richbruss/. Phone: (706) 213-2045. Hours: Daily 7:00am-10:00pm. Admission: $3.00 daily vehicle parking fee.***

This state park offers some of the state's finest fishing and boating. A nature trail follows the shoreline to one of the oldest steel pin bridges in the area, loops through the adjoining woods and returns to the beach. The park's campground and fully equipped cottages are located on or near the water's edge for relaxation. There are canoe and pedal boat rental and six miles of hiking and biking trails. Several Indian sites were excavated near the park in 1980 before the lake was filled, indicating that Paleo-Indians lived in the area more than 10,000 years ago. All Park facilities are designed for wheelchair accessibility, including the swimming beach.

Flowery Branch

ATLANTA FALCONS TRAINING CAMP

Flowery Branch - *4400 Falcon Parkway (I-985 northeast, exit 12) 30542. Phone: (770) 965-3115. www.atlantafalcons.com/schedules/schedule.html.*

Fans can watch most practices during Falcons Training Camp, which is held at the team's headquarters in Flowery Branch. In addition, the team usually has Rookie Mini Camp during the week following the NFL Draft. Each year at training camp (July and August), the team's practices are open and free to the public. Occasionally after practice, some fans will receive autographs from the players as they exit the field.

Gainesville

INK - INTERACTIVE NEIGHBORHOOD FOR KIDS

Gainesville - *999 Chestnut Street, Featherbone Center (I-985 exit 22 toward Gainesville on US 129) 30501. Phone: (770) 536-1900. www.inkfun.org. Hours: Monday-Saturday 10:00am-5:00pm. Sunday 1:00-5:00pm. Admission: $8.00 per person. Sunday afternoon admission is $6.00. Note: Café, library corner and performing arts stage. "You're Fired" Pottery Studio. Create your own take home masterpiece at "You're Fired" Pottery Studio at INK. Kids and adults can choose from a variety of pieces from $3.00 and up.*

INK strives, through the exhibits, to create a unique environment in which children of all ages, abilities, and experience can feel free to imagine, create, and explore beyond their dreams. Children can role play and learn through practical experiences about being a banker, grocery store clerk, doctor, dentist and much more. Check out the vehicles area, too. Their newest space includes towers and rope to climb and crawl through and a special Airplane space that explores flying, travel time and professions like pretending to be a pilot, air traffic controller, flight attendant or passenger.

NORTHEAST GEORGIA HISTORY CENTER

Gainesville - *322 Academy Street (Brenau University) 30501. Phone: (770) 536-0889. www.negahistorycenter.org. Hours: Tuesday-Saturday 10:00am-4:00pm or by appointment. Admission: $5.00 adult, $4.00 senior (65+), $3.00 students (18 and under). Free for kids under six years of age. Educators: lesson plans- www.negahc.org/pages/44/lesson-plans*

This regional history museum includes a replica country store, artifacts from the 1996 Olympics, a "whirlwind" diorama of items that might have been tossed around in the 1936 Gainesville tornado, and a doctor's office from the 1940s. See what home life was like for both the Cherokee Indians (just prior to the removal) and early white settlers in the Chief White Path's Cabin. The Northeast Georgia Sports Hall of Fame is here, too (look for artifacts from Tommy Aaron, golf; Ty Cobb, baseball; Bill Elliott, racing). Another exhibit space highlights the drawings by local Ed Dodd, creator of the Mark Trail comic strip.

Chief White Path's cabin

ELACHEE NATURE SCIENCE CENTER

Gainesville - ***2125 Elachee Drive (I-985 exit 16 onto Mundy Mill Road, SR53. Follow signs to Elachee and SR 13 to Chicopee Woods area) 30504. Phone: (770) 535-1976. www.elachee.org. Hours: Trails open 8:00am-dusk. Nature Center open daily (except Sunday) 10:00am-5:00pm. Reduced hours each spring. Admission: Trails are FREE. Center charges $3.00-$5.00 per person (age 2+).***

Elachee's sprawling campus consists of a woodland refuge and an interactive museum that will excite and educate visitors of all ages. In the Museum Center visitors can tour three discovery areas that explore local archaeological history, astronomy and the solar system, and native wildlife. Visit animal exhibits and feel free to use their "touch tables" to examine a selection of unique nature objects.

Surrounding the Center is the 1,400 acre Chicopee Woods Nature Preserve laced with over 12 miles of nature trails. Their "Budding Naturalists" program introduces nature to 3, 4 and 5 year olds and also increases parents' comfort level and knowledge in the out-of-doors. Songs, creative movement, crafts, storytelling, mini-hikes, visits with live animals, and learning about different nature topics each day are all part of the fun and adventure.

ELACHEE NATURE SCIENCE CENTER - WINTER IN THE WOODS HOLIDAY CELEBRATION

Gainesville - *2125 Elachee Drive 30504. Phone: (770) 535-1976. www.elachee.org. Take a break from your hectic holiday schedule to enjoy the natural beauty and spirit of the season. Create some natural decorations, explore the winter woods, decorate a cookie, and enjoy a cup of cocoa while listening to the sounds of the season provided by the Chicopee Woods Elementary Chorus. Inside search for candy canes in the museum and check out the Duck Stamps Student Art Tour. Youngsters can create their own holiday crafts and go on an outdoor scavenger hunt. Admission. (second Saturday long morning in December)*

Greensboro

SCULL SHOALS FESTIVAL

Greensboro - *Scull Shoals. Chattahoochee-Oconee National Forest. Macedonia Church Road. Phone: (800) 886-5253. www.scullshoals.org/. Scull Shoals is an extinct town on the Oconee River, site of a 19th century mill village which included Georgia's first paper mill. The 2,200 acre experimental forest area, containing the mill town, a prehistoric mound complex dating from 1250-1500 AD, and beaver ponds and streams along the Oconee River. Archeological digs and old-fashioned food and games. (first Saturday in May)*

Hartwell

HART STATE PARK

Hartwell - ***330 Hart State Park Road (drive north of town on US 29, turn left on Ridge Road and proceed 2 miles to the park) 30643. http://gastateparks.org/info/hart/. Phone: (706) 376-8756. Hours: Daily 7:00am-10:00pm. Admission: $3.00 daily vehicle parking fee.***

The park's boat ramps and docks offer easy access to all water sports. Swimming, boating, water skiing and fishing at Lake Hartwell are the prime reasons folks visit this park. A swimming beach and picnic tables along with cottages and most campsites are located on the scenic lake shore. There are canoe, jon boat and pontoon boat rentals and a short hiking and biking trail.

Helen

Did you know?
Black bears do not hibernate during the winter, instead they remain dormant.
(Dormant animals can awaken if there is danger, hibernating do not)

BLACK FOREST BEAR PARK

Helen - ***8160 South Main Street 30545. www.blackforestbearpark.com. Phone: (706) 878-7043. Hours: Monday-Friday 10:00am-7:00pm, Saturday 10:00am-8:00pm, Sunday 11:00am-6:00pm. The park closes mid-December thru February. Weekends only in March. Admission:***

$5.00 per person. Note: The reptile exhibit has numerous types of large snakes for observation including all the poisonous snakes found in this country.

This park educates people about many different species of bears commonly found in the state of Georgia. Some of the species you will observe are the American Black Bear, Grizzly Bear, Cinnamon Bear, Syrian Brown Bear, and others. At each exhibit, there is a map showing where they live and some detailed information about each species.

Not only do you get to see these animals up close, but you get to feed them as well. Visitors may buy food trays that consist of sliced apples, lettuce and bread to feed the bears. The owners of the park have over 10 years of experience in breeding and keeping animals alive. Many of these bears would be destroyed because of no more use in circuses or they are troubled bears that raided campgrounds. How many parks actually WANT you to feed the bears?

CHARLEMAGNE'S KINGDOM MODEL RAILROAD

Helen - ***8808 North Main Street 30545. www.georgiamodelrailroad.com. Phone: (706) 878-2200. Hours: Daily 10:00am-6:00pm. Admission: $2.50-$5.00 per person.***

Charlemagne's Kingdom is an Alpine Model railroad layout, in HO scale miniature. All of the buildings are replicas of buildings existing in Germany, with over five thousand hand painted figures, 400' of railroad track, computerized trains, and hot air balloons, three ring circus, mountains 22' tall, and much more. The crowning piece of the multi-featured land-scape is the 22 ft. high "Matterhorn", built up over a framework with more than 300 gallons of plaster sculpted into its "icey" slopes. While you are here, watch the Glockenspiel dancer in the Gingerbread House (dances occur at Noon, 3:00pm & 6:00pm).

ALPINE CARRIAGE BUGGY RIDES

Helen - ***(corner of River and Main Street in downtown) 30545. Phone: (706) 878-3658. www.alpinecarriage.com. Admission: $7.00 adult, $5.00 child.***

Buggy rides through the streets of Helen, an old Bavarian town. Pictures with the horse are welcome.

REMEMBER WHEN THEATRE

Helen - *115 Escowee Drive (one block from SR 75, near Main Street) 30545. Phone: (706) 878-SHOW. www.rememberwhentheatre.com. Hours: Shows start at 8:00pm every Saturday. Doors open at 7:00pm. Concessions at 6:30pm. Season runs early May - late September w/ occasional fall themed events each Autumn. Admission: $16.00 adult, $8.00 child (under 12).*

The Remember When Theatre was specifically built in 2001 for a "Reflections of Elvis" show. "Elvis" is known to spoil the kids by throwing out teddy bears and the moms by giving scarves to all the ladies. An exciting Entertainer, the Elvis tribute performer captivates the heart and soul of Elvis Presley on stage. He brings back wonderful memories of America's most loved and missed entertainer.

SMITHGALL WOODS CONSERVATION AREA

Helen - *61 Tsalaki Trail (on GA 75A, 3 miles west of town, just south of GA 348) 30545. Phone: (706) 878-3087. http://gastateparks.org/info/smithgall/. Hours: Daily 7:00am-6:00pm. Admission: $5.00 parking fee.*

A premier trout stream, Dukes Creek runs through the mountain property and is a favorite for catch-and-release fishing. Four miles of trails and 18 miles of roads allow hikers and bicyclists to explore the woods, wildlife and streams. Van tours are offered daily at 12:30pm and guided hikes with crafts or activities are scheduled several times per month. The Lodge at Smithgall Woods is an elegant mountain retreat perfect for getaways. Five cottages provide 14 bedrooms with private baths (rates include accommodations, meals and activities). Reservations are required for trout fishing.

UNICOI STATE PARK AND LODGE

Helen - *(2 miles northeast of Helen via GA 356) 30545. Phone: (706) 878-2201 (lodge) or (706) 878-0983 (programs). http://gastateparks.org/info/unicoi/. Hours: Daily 7:00am-10:00pm. Admission: $5.00 daily vehicle parking fee.*

Guests will find a variety of activities including swimming, fishing hiking, biking, wildlife viewing or relaxing in the Lodge's retreat-like atmosphere or in one of the numerous cottages or campsites. Outdoor enthusiasts will enjoy hiking and biking on scenic mountain trails, especially those leading to Helen and ANNA RUBY FALLS. The falls form a twin cascade into Smith Creek. The visitor center has a viewing deck where visitors can feed the trout. The Lodge provides a restaurant and the marina docks have canoe and pedal boat rentals.

UNICOI STATE PARK AND LODGE - DECK THE HALLS

Helen - *(2 miles northeast of Helen via GA 356) 30545. Phone: (706) 878-2201 (lodge) or (706) 878-0983 (programs). http://gastateparks.org/info/unicoi/. This holiday celebration includes making holiday crafts, hayrides and an evening of music. Festival of trees - Saturday after thanksgiving. $3.00 parking. (first Saturday of December)*

HELEN TO THE ATLANTIC HOT AIR BALLOON RACE

Helen - *downtown. www.helenballoon.com. This race, the only long distance hot air balloon race in the world, begins in Helen, Georgia. The finish line is I-95 - anywhere between Maine & Miami. While the competition continues, other balloonists compete in local events beginning Thursday, continuing Friday & Saturday with approx flight times of 7:00am and 6:00pm. Many experiences are available to the public; assisting with inflations, being part of a chase crew or taking tethered rides. (first weekend in June)*

Hiawassee

CRYSTAL RIVER RANCH LLAMA TREKS

Hiawassee - ***7316 US Hwy 76E 30546. www.crystalriver-ranch.com. Phone: (706) 896-5005. Hours: Most Saturdays from 11:00am-4:00pm. Tours: Treks depart from the ranch at 10:00am and usually last from 3 to 4 hours.***

On Saturdays, you can hand feed the llamas, take them for a hike, and learn about all of their uses. Or, plan Guided Day Hikes in the beautiful North Georgia mountains without carrying all of the necessities. Llamas will be your trail companions while you enjoy the scenery, exercise, and fresh mountain air.

HIGH SHOALS FALLS & SCENIC AREA

Hiawassee - ***Forest Service Road (off GA 75 north to Indian Grave Gap Road, Service Road 283) 30546. Phone: (706) 745-6928. www.fs.usda.gov/conf. Admission: FREE.***

Follow the creek hiking path to the viewing platform at two waterfalls. Open daily, be sure of weather conditions for hiking and driving to the trailheads. In winter with snow, often four-wheel drive vehicles are required.

GEORGIA MOUNTAIN FAIR

Hiawassee - *Georgia Mountains Fairgrounds. www.georgiamountainfairgrounds.com. Phone: (706) 896-4191. The Exhibit Hall is open daily with exhibits, antique machinery and area information from the Forest Service, 4-H, etc. Country music and gospel concerts. Admission. (last eleven days of July)*

GEORGIA MOUNTAIN FALL FESTIVAL

Hiawassee - *Georgia Mountains Fairgrounds. www.georgiamountainfairgrounds.com. Includes arts and crafts, kiddie rides, demos by craftsmen (board splitting, blacksmithing, quilting, corn milling, shake making, cider squeezing, soap making). Visitors can tour the Pioneer Village, a replica of an old mountain town with a mercantile store, one room schoolhouse, log home, smokehouse, barn, and corncrib. Watch country and gospel singing, clogging or attend the Georgia State Fiddlers convention. Admission. (second full week of October)*

Jefferson

CRAWFORD W. LONG MUSEUM

Jefferson - ***28 College Street (off US 129, in the heart of downtown) 30549. Phone: (706) 367-5307. www.crawfordlong.org. Hours: Tuesday-Saturday 10:00am-5:00pm. Admission: $3.00-$5.00 (age 6+).***

This is the site of the first painless surgery.

Dr. Crawford W. Long was the physician who, on March 30, 1842, first used ether for surgical anesthesia. While yet a young doctor, he observed the frolicking actions of youth around him using ether to kill the pain of their recreation. Soon after, a patient requested he remove a cyst from the neck. Using ether, the operation was successful and the patient felt no pain.

Personal artifacts of Dr. Long, as well as early anesthesia equipment are displayed in the Medical Museum. The antebellum Pendergrass Store Building houses a recreated 1840s doctor's office and apothecary shop. Exhibits on making medicine focus on the obstacles the early country doctor was forced to overcome. The building also includes a replica of a 19th century General Store and serves as the performance area for Museum programs such as storytelling, live music, craft and historical demonstrations. Take a stroll outside in the Knot Garden to learn the culinary and medicinal uses of the herbs and plants growing there.

MULE DAY

Jefferson - *Shields Ethridge Heritage Farm. www.shieldsethridgefarm.com. Phone: (706) 367-2949. Events are open to the public including demonstrations of traditional farm equipment and animals. The farm has a commissary, blacksmith shop. cotton gin, grist mill, wheat house, and many other historic farm buildings. (May)*

Lake Lanier Islands

LAKE LANIER ISLANDS

Lake Lanier Islands - ***7000 Holiday Road (I-985 north, exit 8, then GA 347 west or GA 400 north exit 14. Then, left on GA 20 for 10 miles, left on Peachtree and left again on Friendship Road) 30518. www.lakelanierislands.com. Phone: (770) 932-7200 or (800) 840-5253. Hours: Waterpark: Daily 10:00am-6:00pm (mid- May thru Labor Day). Admission: Waterpark: $28-$30.00 general, $16-$18.00 senior and child (under 42" tall). Mid afternoon rate approximately half price. Save with online tickets.***

About a half-hour drive north from Atlanta, The Lake Lanier Islands Resort is a year-round vacation spot located on the pristine southernmost shore of Lake Lanier. Accommodations include deluxe waterfront lake house rentals, hotel and a lakeside campground. A beach and water park, golf course, heated swimming pool, and boat rentals are available.

WATER PARK - incredibleFunDunker, with more than 100 ways to get wet! Hang Ten on the Surf Wave®; ride Wild Waves, Georgia's largest wave pool; and real thrill seekers go to extremes on the Intimidator, the Twister, SplashDown, and Triple Threat. Plus, the little ones will love Kiddie Lagoon and Wiggle Waves. Looking for a little R&R? Troubles melt away on their mile-long, sandy white beach. (Must be more than 42" tall to ride most slides. Must be 48" tall to ride the Surf Wave and FunDunker drop). Boating - from houseboats to pleasure cruising, they have gorgeous, large boats to rent on this beautiful lake. See separate listing for Lake Lanier Resort Lodging.

LAKE LANIER ISLANDS - MAGICAL NIGHTS OF LIGHTS

Lake Lanier Islands - *7000 Holiday Road, 30518. Phone: (770) 932-7200 or (800) 840-5253. www.lakelanierislands.com. Visit the world's largest animated light extravaganza. Bring the whole family a drive through tour of over six miles of twinkling, holiday light displays and a live nativity scene complete with live actors and animals! But that's not all! The Holiday Village awaits you with carnival rides, pony rides and holiday treats. Warm up with a sweet marshmallow roast or step inside the Santa Shop for some holiday shopping. Share your wish list with Santa and snap a picture too. Hotel package rates include breakfast with Santa. Admission ~$25.00 per carload. (nightly week before Thanksgiving thru December)*

LAKE LANIER RESORT

Lake Lanier Islands - ***7000 Holiday Road (GA 400 north exit 14, follow signs) 30518. Phone: (770) 945-8787. www.lakelanierislands.com.***

The New England-style LakeHouses On Lanier are nestled among towering Georgia pines on a private, gated peninsula. Just steps away from the waters of Lake Sidney Lanier, these quaint, waterfront villas offer much more than a "traditional" lake house. Equipped with all the conveniences of home but complemented with "creature comforts," including two spacious bedrooms and baths, a great room with a fieldstone fireplace, and a modern kitchen. Each cottage has a deck and full kitchen (except oven). Settle into overstuffed chairs with a good book, relax in the spa (on the deck), throw a steak on the grill or take a walk. Cozy rooms inspire memorable family time! Activity Package Rates begin around $379.00 per night for lake houses, near $179.00 per night for hotel rooms. Accommodations only Weekday, AAA and Family Fun discounted rates, too.

The cottage was a great place to unwind...

Lakemont

HILLSIDE ORCHARD FARMS

Lakemont - *18 Sorghum Mill Drive (Located on Historic 441 south of Clayton and north of Tallulah Falls) 30552. Phone: (706) 782-2776. www.hillsideorchard.com. Note: The Old Fashion Fall Farm Day is the last Saturday in October. Easter Egg Hunt, Spring Farm Day, etc. Farm tours now available for groups.*

Activities include a corn maze (opens in September and ends late October), sorghum and apple cooking, and music. Take a hay ride to Grandpa's Barnyard to visit and feed the goats, donkeys, pigs and rabbits. In the spring, see plowing, farm demos, and take a wagon ride. Pan for gold at the Little Mitcham Gem Mine (indoors) open from April to November. The Country Store has lots of jams and jellies as well as lots of other farm fresh items.

Lavonia

TUGALOO STATE PARK

Lavonia - *1763 Tugaloo State Park Road (I-85 exit 173 north on GA 17, follow park signs) 30533. Phone: (706) 356-4352. http://gastateparks.org/info/tugaloo/. Hours: Daily 7:00am-10:00pm. Admission: $3.00 daily vehicle parking fee.*

The name "Tugaloo" comes from an Indian name for the river which once flowed freely prior to the construction of Hartwell Dam. Tugaloo's cottages and camping offer spectacular views of Lake Hartwell. Some cottages even have private boat docks for overnight guests. Ten campers can choose modern or primitive campsites. Fishing is excellent and during the summer, the lake is a popular destination for swimming, water skiing, sailing and boating. Both the Crow Tree and Muscadine nature trails wind through oak, walnut, mulberry and cherry trees.

Lawrenceville

MEDIEVAL TIMES

Lawrenceville - *5900 Sugarloaf Pkwy, Discover Mills (I-85 north exit 107) 30043. Phone: (888) WE-JOUST. www.medievaltimes.com. Showtimes: vary by season. Generally matinee and evening performances most weekends. Admission: $51.95adult, $35.95 child (12 and under). Add-on Royalty packages add $10.00-$20.00 to ticket price per person.*

The Castle is 87,000 square feet and comfortably holds 1,100 Noble Guests per performance. In addition to the 200 employees staffing the Castle, there are 22 Andalusian stallions in residence. The Castle, an anchor attraction at Discover Mills, includes a stone façade, Dungeon, Bar and Gift Shop. Guests enjoy the Castle's medieval theme throughout the interior. When the lances splinter, swords clash and sparks fly during the medieval jousting tournament, the 1,100 revelers inside the arena join the action by cheering for their favorite Knight. Serfs and wenches dressed in period costumes serve guests a feast of fresh vegetable soup, roasted chicken, spare rib, herb basted potato, a pastry and beverages. In order to honor medieval tradition, guests eat their meals without silverware (your kids will love having to eat with their hands!). Andalusian horses and remarkable displays of choreographed sword and jousting ability make this show so engaging!

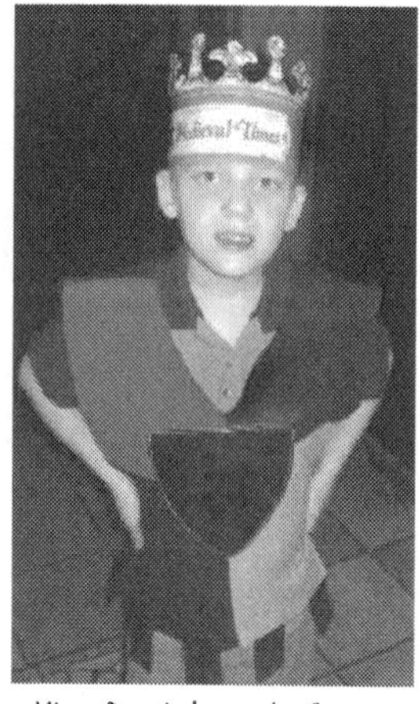

King Daniel ready for a "knight" of excitement...

Lilburn

YELLOW RIVER GAME RANCH

Lilburn - ***4525 Highway 78 (I-285 exit 39B) 30047. www.yellowrivergameranch.com. Phone: (770) 972-6643. Hours: Daily 9:30am-6:00pm. Admission: $8.00 adult, $7.00 child (2-11).***

Visit with more than 600 friendly animals that enjoy food and petting. There are deer, mountain lion, bobcat, bear, farm animals, ducks and squirrels living along the naturally wooded path by the river. There's the "Billy Goat Gruff Memorial Bridge" and the super popular "Bunny Burrows." They even have one of the largest herd of buffalo east of the Mississippi, roaming in the back meadow. Don't forget to stop by and say "hello" to General Beauregard Lee, Georgia's official groundhog weather predictor!

YELLOW RIVER GAME RANCH - GROUNDHOG DAY CELEBRATION

Lilburn - *Yellow River Game Ranch (east of Stone Mountain on Hwy 78) 30047. www.yellowrivergameranch.com. At Sunrise, each Groundhog Day, General Beau Lee, Georgia's Official Weather Prognosticator, peeks out to share or hide his shadow. Georgia's Secretary of State, proclaims the news in usually nippy weather. What food do they use to lure the animal out? Beau has a 93% rate of accuracy. The other one does not. (February 2)*

Lincolnton

ELIJAH CLARK STATE PARK

Lincolnton - *2959 McCormick Highway (7 miles northeast of Lincolnton on US 378) 30817. Phone: (800) 864-7275. http://georgiastateparks.org/ElijahClark/. Hours: Daily 7:00am-10:00pm. Admission: $5.00 daily vehicle parking fee.*

This park is named for a frontiersman and state war hero who led pioneers during the Revolutionary War. A renovated and furnished log cabin museum displays furniture, utensils and tools and is open for weekend only tours (April-November). Look for the graves of Clark and his wife, Hannah. The park is located on a large lake - cottages are located on the lake's edge, and the spacious campground is nestled into the forest. The park also offers hiking trails (3.75 miles), swimming, shuffleboard, and miniature golf.

Lula

NORTH GEORGIA CANOPY TOURS

Lincolnton - *5290 Harris Road (I-85/I-985 corridor), 30554. www.northgeorgiacanopytours.com. Fees: $69-$89 (kids/military/group discounts also). Bring picnic to watch others on the Observation Deck.*

Experience a heightened perspective on life at North Georgia Canopy Tours! Both Eco-Tour Adventures begin “low and slow,” but you'll soon find yourself zipping at greater heights and speeds through the lush canopy. Soar through the air attached to a steel cable—which will soon disappear from your consciousness. While you are zipping along, enjoy a birds-eye view of the North Oconee River, ravines, ponds, pastures and wildlife. The guides say the best time to see wildlife is in the early morning or late evening. Two certified eco-trained guides lead up to eight participants on both Tours, which include ziplines, sky bridges, moderate hikes through a naturally beautiful area, and a dual zip over a pond in front of the Tour Observation Deck. In the summer, folks on the ground can bring their super soakers and try to hit the zip liners.

Mansfield

CHARLIE ELLIOTT WILDLIFE CENTER

Mansfield - *543 Elliott Trail (I-20 east to Exit 98, south on Georgia Highway 11, Monroe-Monticello) 30055. http://georgiawildlife.com/PFA/CharlieElliott. Phone: (770) 784-3059. Hours: Tuesday-Saturday 9:00am-4:30pm. Sunday 1:00-4:30pm (April-October only) Admission: FREE.*

The property has dozens of ponds with a large rock outcropping. Activities include hiking, fishing, birdwatching, archery, and primitive camping. Visitors Center and Museum.

Mountain City

BLACK ROCK MOUNTAIN STATE PARK

Mountain City - ***(3 miles north of Clayton off US 441, follow signs) 30562. Phone: (706) 746-2141. http://gastateparks.org/info/blackrock/. Hours: Daily 7:00am-10:00pm. Admission: $5.00 daily vehicle parking fee.***

Named for its sheer cliffs of dark-colored biotitic gneiss, this park encompasses some of the most outstanding country in Georgia's Blue Ridge Mountains. At an altitude of 3,640 feet, Black Rock Mountain is the highest state park in Georgia. Numerous scenic overlooks provide spectacular 80-mile vistas of the Southern Appalachians. Several hiking trails (10 miles worth) lead past wildflowers, streams, small waterfalls and full forests. There are also camping and cottage facilities plus the summit visitor center.

FOXFIRE MUSEUM

Mountain City - ***2839 US Hwy 441S (near US 441 & US 76 intersection, far northeast corner of GA) 30562. www.foxfire.org/museum.html. Phone: (706) 746-5828. Hours: Monday-Friday 8:30am-4:30pm. Closed holidays. Admission: $6.00 general (age 11+). Educators: Download a 16-page pdf booklet explanation of historical aspects of life at Foxfire (find the sidebar note link on the main page). Note: The Museum also includes a scenic nature trail and cabins that are available for vacation rentals. A gift shop filled with folk art, handcrafted items, and books, including The Foxfire Book series, is located in the Gate House, the first log cabin you'll see on Foxfire Lane.***

The Foxfire Museum focuses on Appalachian life and is rooted in the work that hundreds of regional high school students (in The Foxfire Magazine classes) have put into documenting their local history. Visitors see a glimpse of what life was like for the mountaineers who settled this area over 150 years ago as they tour over 20 historic log cabins. Buildings include a chapel, blacksmith shop, mule barn, wagon shed, single-room home, gristmill, and smokehouse. Included on the property is a wagon used in the Trail of Tears - the forced Cherokee migration from these mountains to Oklahoma.

Many of the cabins contain artifacts and crafts of early Appalachian life, including toys, wagons, cabin-building tools, blacksmithing instruments, woodworking tools, handmade items, household items, logging tools, shoemaking equipment, animal trapping and hunting equipment, and farm and agricultural equipment. As with any historical village, this is best to tour as a pre-arranged group. Docents' insights and stories really help bring the cabins to life.

Royston

TY COBB MUSEUM

Royston - *461 Cook Street, Joe A. Adams Professional Bldg. Of Cobb Healthcare System (15 miles from I-85) 30662. www.tycobbmuseum.org. Phone: (706) 245-1825. Hours: Monday-Friday 9:00am-4:00pm, Saturday 10:00am-4:00pm. Closed all major holidays. Admission: $3.00-$5.00 (age 5+). Active Military are FREE.*

Relive baseball history by viewing artifacts, original works of art and visual accounts of the brilliant player known as "The Georgia Peach." Cobb Theater features stadium-style seating surrounded by a beautiful mural collage. A moving video tribute, narrated by Georgia broadcasting legend Larry Munson, features rare action footage and interviews with Cobb. Cobb's controversial personality earned him the reputation as baseball's fiercest competitor. That zeal carried over to his life outside of baseball, making him a multimillionaire with significant generosity to the community.

VICTORIA BRYANT STATE PARK

Royston - *1105 Bryant Park Road (I-85 exit 160, 2 miles north of Franklin Springs on GA 327) 30662. Phone: (706) 245-6270. http://gastateparks.org/info/vicbryant/. Hours: Daily 7:00am - dark. Admission: $3.00 daily vehicle parking fee.*

Nestled in the rolling hills of Georgia's upper piedmont, a beautiful stream flows through the park. Hikers can follow either the short nature trail or the longer perimeter trail that winds through hardwoods and crosses creeks. There is also 8 miles of biking trails, fishing - ponds open to campers and disabled visitors only, and swimming.

Rutledge

HARD LABOR CREEK STATE PARK

Rutledge - ***(I-20 exit 105 into town, then 3 miles on Fairplay Road) 30663. Phone: (706) 557-3001. http://gastateparks.org/info/hardlabor/. Hours: Daily 7:00am-10:00pm. Admission: $5.00 daily vehicle parking fee.***

This creek is thought to have been named by slaves who tilled the fields or by Native Americans who found it difficult to work. The park offers a wide range of recreational opportunities in a beautiful wooded setting. Over 24 miles of trails are available for hikers and horseback riders, and a lakeside beach is open for swimming during warmer months. Camping and cottages are available and there are 30 horse stalls, a riding ring and 12 Equestrian Campsites.

Sautee Nacoochee

SAUTEE NACOOCHEE CENTER

Sautee Nacoochee - ***283 Ga Hwy 255 N 30571. www.snca.org. Phone: (706) 878-3300. Hours: Monday-Saturday 10:00am-5:00pm, Sunday 1:00-5:00pm and during evening performances. Admission: Museums are FREE admission. Classes and productions fees vary. Note: Tellabration, Yuletide Festival, music concerts and children's theatre productions are some of their biggest events. Headwaters: Stories from a Goodly Portion of Beautiful Northeast Georgia play performances run each year in July, Thursdays thru Sundays.***

Nestled in the Appalachian foothills of Northeast Georgia, the Center is a thriving cultural and community center housed in a restored rural schoolhouse, offering a Folk Pottery Museum, Theatre, Art Studio, Dance Studio, History Museum, Heritage Site, and Nature Preserve.

<u>HISTORY MUSEUM</u>: A walk through history begins with the earliest inhabitants of the valleys, the Cherokee Indians. Names of the 62 white families who came across the Southern Appalachians from North Carolina to settle the valleys are listed. With them came slaves, descendants of whom still live nearby, continuing their influence though many generations. Next came the gold rush of Georgia and asbestos mining, railroading and the lumber industry.

<u>NATURE CENTER</u>: Can you help count the number and different species of birds that flutter through?

Stockbridge

PANOLA MOUNTAIN STATE PARK

Stockbridge - ***2600 Highway 155 SW (18 miles southeast of Atlanta on GA 155 via I-20 exit 68) 30281. http://gastateparks.org/info/panolamt/. Phone: (770) 389-7801. Hours: Daily 7:00am- dark. Admission: $5.00 daily vehicle parking fee. Tours: Guided 3.5 mile hikes to the mountain are offered Tuesday-Saturday (call for reservations).***

This unusual park was created to protect a 100-acre granite monadnock (mountain) often compared to Stone Mountain. Panola Mountain shelters rare plants of the Piedmont region. Hikers may explore the park's watershed and granite outcrop on their own or go on a guided hike onto the restricted-access mountain. The interpretive center has live exhibits, including bees, bats, snakes and turtles. Color-lovers can also take the Fall Color Half-Day Hike at Panola Mountain State Park. Because of delicate ecological features of the park, pets and bicycles are not allowed on trails.

Suches

CHATTAHOOCHEE FOREST NATIONAL FISH HATCHERY

Suches - ***4730 Rock Creek Road (400 North to Dahlonega. Hwy. 60 North to Suches. Continue another 11 miles on Hwy. 60 North. Turn left on Rock Creek Rd) 30572. Phone: (706) 838-4723. www.fws.gov/chattahoocheeforest. Hours: Monday-Friday 8:00am-3:00pm. Admission: FREE. Educators: BiT - Biologist in Training fact sheet is online under the icon: For Kids, Parents and Educators. Note: U.S. Forest Service campgrounds are located both above and below the hatchery. Family Fish Festival and Kids Day are held annually to promote recreational fishing.***

The beautiful surroundings and natural environment draw a lot of visitors to the hatchery. A visitor center, an education center, a visitor kiosk and an opportunity to view the fish in various stages of production draws a crowd. Visitors tour the hatchery annually (call ahead for group tours). Rock Creek, which runs through hatchery property, offers a great trout fishing opportunity. The hatchery annually distributes 324,000 catchable-size rainbow trout to statewide waters allowing thousands of anglers to land a trout.

Tallulah Falls

TALLULAH GORGE STATE PARK

Tallulah Falls - ***(US 441) 30525. http://gastateparks.org/info/tallulah/. Phone: (706) 754-7970. Hours: Daily 8:00am-dark (park). Center hours 8:00am-5:00pm (plus $4.00 parking). Admission: $5.00 daily vehicle parking fee. Note: Nantahala Outdoor Center (Chattooga Ridge Road, 864-638-5980 or 800-232-7238 or www.noc.com) offers white-water rafting and kayaking trips from Clayton.***

Tallulah Gorge is two miles long and nearly 1,000 feet deep. Visitors can hike rim trails to several overlooks. Exhibits in the Interpretive Center highlight the history of the old Victorian resort town, as well as the geography and fragile ecosystem of the area. Additionally, the park has produced a film that takes viewers on the dramatic journey through the gorge. Some like to whitewater paddle (first two April weekends and first three November weekends). There are more than 20 miles of hiking and mountain biking trails and a separate 1.7 mile paved "Rails to Trails" path. A suspension bridge sways 80 feet above the rocky bottom, providing spectacular views of the river and waterfalls. Swimming and camping are available, too.

Tiger

GOATS ON THE ROOF

Tiger - ***3026 Hwy 441 South. 30576. Phone: (706) 782-2784. www.goats-on-the-roof.com. Hours: Daily 10:00am-6:00pm (plus $4.00 parking).***

A retail store and gift shop, and entertainment center, Goats on the Roof is a unique, out of the ordinary experience. Children can feed goats, roast marshmallows over an open pit fire, mine for gemstones, or grab an ice cream cone. You may even see Conway Twitty, the proud and colorful rooster strutting his stuff around the yard. Keep an eye out for some of our free roaming bunnies as they graze on the fresh green grass. But, the highlight is the goats on the roof! We suggest you humor the goats with kind words, Goat Chow, and perhaps a carrot at Christmas. Find out why they climb the rooftops and cling to the shingles.

Toccoa

TRAVELER'S REST HISTORIC SITE

Toccoa - ***8162 Riverdale Road (six miles east of Toccoa via US 123) 30577. Phone: (706) 886-2256. http://gastateparks.org/info/travelers/. Hours: Saturday 9:00am-5:00pm. Admission: $3.00-$5.00 per person.***

Traveler's Rest was a stagecoach inn and 1815 plantation home of the "richest man in the Tugaloo Valley". To accommodate the growing number of travelers to northeast Georgia, he added on to the structure to house overnight travelers. Today, visitors receive a guided tour of the plantation home with its 90-foot long porch and original antiques, some made by local craftsman, Caleb Shaw.

TRAVELER'S REST HISTORIC SITE - CHRISTMAS FOR TRAVELERS

Toccoa - *(six miles east of Toccoa via US 123) 30577. Phone: (706) 886-2256. http://gastateparks.org/info/travelers/. Enjoy music, treats, crafts and dancing in an 1800s decorative holiday setting. Free, but donations appreciated. (second Sunday in December)*

Toccoa Falls

TOCCOA FALLS

Toccoa Falls - ***GA Hwy Alt. 17, Toccoa Falls College campus (from town, take GA Alt 17 one mile) 30598. Phone: (706) 886-6831 or (800) 868-3257. Admission: Small admission per person.***

On the campus of Toccoa Falls College sits 186-foot high Toccoa Falls, 26 feet higher than Niagara Falls. The Cherokee word "toccoa" means beautiful. From the gift shop and parking area, it is just a short walk along the stream to the base of the falls. A monument reminds visitors of the tragic loss of lives when the earthen dam broke back in the 1970s. The Gate Cottage Restaurant, above the gift shop, has a wonderful buffet on Sundays.

Washington

CALLAWAY PLANTATION

Washington - ***US Hwy 78 (US Hwy 78, west of town, across from the Washington-Wilkes Airport) 30673. www.historyofwilkes.org/sites-callaway.html. Phone: (706) 678-7060. Hours: Tuesday-Saturday 10:00am-5:00pm. Closed on Thanksgiving, Christmas and New Years. Admission: $1.00-$4.00 per person.***

Step back in time at Callaway Plantation, a living history museum. The Plantation consists of three restored homes as well as the fields of the farm. The main house (1869) with Greek Revival columns, was the center piece of a 3,000 acre plantation. Virtually unaltered since that time, the home is furnished by period pieces. The oldest building is a hewn log cabin and is believed to have been the home of an early settler. It is a single room cabin with a fireplace for cooking and heating. There is also a 2 story home typical of the 1890 period and an one-room schoolhouse. The entire family will enjoy picking cotton, touring the plantation houses, and seeing primitive crafts.

ROBERT TOOMBS HOUSE HISTORIC SITE

Washington - ***216 E. Robert Toombs Avenue 30673. Phone: (706) 678-2226. http://georgiastateparks.org/RobertToombsHouse/. Hours: Wednesday-Saturday 10:00am-4:00pm. Closed Monday (except holidays). Admission: $1.00-$5.00 per person.***

Robert Toombs was a successful planter and lawyer who lead a whirlwind career as a state legislator, US Congressman and Senator. "Defend yourselves, the enemy is at your door…!" thundered Toombs from the Senate floor in January, 1860. The following year, Georgia seceded from the Union and Toombs personified the South by evolving from conservative Unionist to fire-breathing secessionist. Ten years later, as the Reconstruction Era drew to a close in Georgia, Toombs felt that Georgia should live under their own constitution. It was not amended until 65 years later. Visitors can tour the house and grounds, view exhibits and watch a dramatic film portraying an elderly Toombs relating his story to a young reporter.

Winder

FORT YARGO STATE PARK

Winder - ***(1 miles south of Winder on GA 81) 30680. Phone: (770) 867-3489. http://gastateparks.org/info/ftyargo/. Hours: Daily 7:00am-10:00pm. Admission: $5.00 daily vehicle parking fee.***

This historical park features a log fort built in 1792 by settlers for protection against Creek and Cherokee Indians. Fort Yargo offers great camping, hiking and biking (5 miles of trails) and fishing for families. There is also a 260-acre lake with a swimming beach, fishing areas and boat ramps. Many campsites are near the water's edge, and hiking/biking trails follow the lake shore. The park also has pedal boat rentals and miniature golf.

FORT YARGO STATE PARK - A FORT YARGO CHRISTMAS

Winder - *(1 miles south of Winder on GA 81) 30680. http://gastateparks.org/info/ftyargo/. Phone: (770) 867-3489. Hours: Daily 7:00am-10:00pm. Admission: $3.00 daily vehicle parking fee. Join them for Christmas carols, refreshments, hay rides and a visit from Santa. $3.00 parking. (second Saturday in December)*

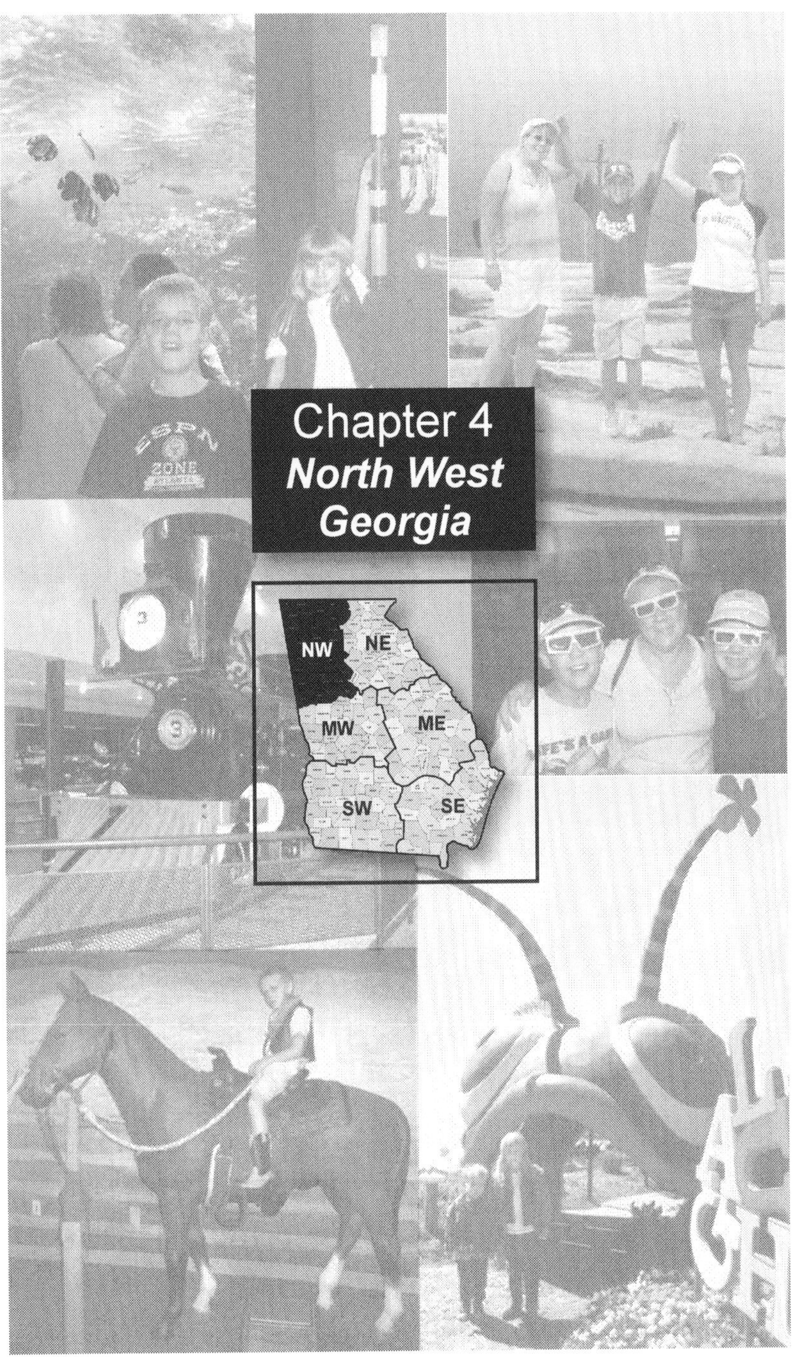
Chapter 4
North West
Georgia
NW
NE
MW
ME
SW
SE

Acworth

- Cauble Park

Adairsville

- Great Locomotive Chase Festival

Atlanta

- Apex Museum
- Atlanta Hawks Basketball
- CNN Studio Tour
- Philips Experience
- Atlanta History Center
- Fernbank Museum Of Natural History
- Fernbank Science Center
- Jimmy Carter Library And Museum
- The Varsity
- Atlanta Botanical Garden
- Atlanta Botanical Garden - Scarecrows
- Atlanta Botanical Garden - Holiday Garden
- Atlanta Symphony Orchestra
- Center For Puppetry Arts
- Federal Reserve Bank Of Atlanta Visitors Center & Monetary Museum
- High Museum Of Art
- Margaret Mitchell House & Museum
- Martin Luther King Jr. Nat'l Historic Site
- Atlanta Falcons
- Centennial Olympic Park
- Centennial Olympic Park - 4th Of July
- Centennial Olympic Park - Holiday Lights
- Georgia Aquarium
- Georgia Dome Tours
- Imagine It! Children's Museum of Atlanta
- World Of Coca-Cola
- Atlanta Braves
- Atlanta Braves Museum / Turner Field
- Atlanta Cyclorama
- Zoo Atlanta
- National Museum Of Patriotism
- Paper Museum At Ipst
- Georgia State Capitol & Museum
- Dogwood Festival
- Easter Eggstravaganza
- Atlanta Greek Festival
- Peach Drop

Atlanta (Austell)

- Six Flags Over Georgia

Atlanta (Dunwoody)

- Dunwoody Nature Center
- Dunwoody Nature Center - Cocoa And Candles / Light Up Dunwoody

Atlanta (Lithia Springs)

- Sweetwater Creek State Park

Atlanta (Morrow)

- Reynolds Memorial Nature Preserve

Atlanta (Sandy Springs)

- Chattahoochee River Nat'l Rec. Area

Atlanta (Stone Mountain)

- Stone Mountain Park
- Stone Mountain Park - Easter Service
- Stone Mountain Park - Highland Games
- Stone Mountain Park - Pumpkin Fest.
- Stone Mountain Park - Pow Wow & Indian Festival
- Stone Mountain Park - Christmas

Calhoun

- New Echota Historic Site
- New Echota Historic Site - Christmas Tour

Canton

- Cagle's Farm
- Cagle's Farm - Maize

Carrollton

- John Tanner State Park

Cartersville

- Bartow History Center
- Booth Western Art Museum
- Etowah Indian Mounds Historic Site
- Red Top Mountain State Park
- Red Top Mountain SP - Christmas Cabin
- Tellus NW Georgia Science Museum
- Battle Of Allatoona Pass Encampment
- Etowah Valley Indian Festival
- Pumpkin Fest
- Pettit Creek Christmas Holiday Lights

Cave Spring

- Cave Spring And Rolater Park

Chatsworth

- Chief Vann House Historic Site
- Chief Vann House Historic Site - Christmas Candlelight Home Tour
- Fort Mountain State Park

Dallas

- Pickett's Battlefield Historic Park

Dalton

- Hampton Inn Dalton
- Dalton Carpet Mill Tours
- Dalton Depot Restaurant
- Battle Of Resaca Civil War Reenactment
- Battle Of Tunnel Hill Reenactment
- Prater's Mill Country Fair

Ellijay

- Apple Pickin' Jubilee, Hillcrest Orchards
- Georgia Apple Festival

Fairburn

- Georgia Renaissance Festival

Fort Oglethorpe

- Chickamauga National Military Park
- Chickamauga National Military Park - War Between The States Day

Hampton

- Atlanta Motor Speedway Tours

Jonesboro

- Battle Of Jonesboro Reenactment

Kennesaw

- Southern Museum Of Civil War And Locomotive History
- Kennesaw Mountain Nat'l Battlefield

Marietta

- Georgia Ballet
- The Big Chicken
- Whitewater Park, Six Flags
- North Georgia State Fair

McDonough

- Southern Belle Farm
- Southern Belle Farm - Maize

Rising Fawn

- Cloudland Canyon State Park

Rome

- Chieftains Museum
- Chieftains Museum - Christmas

Roswell

- Bulloch Hall
- Bulloch Hall - Christmas For Kids
- Chattahoochee Nature Center
- Smith Plantation Home
- Andretti Indoor Karting

Summerville

- James H. "Sloppy" Floyd State Park

Waleska

- Funk Heritage Center

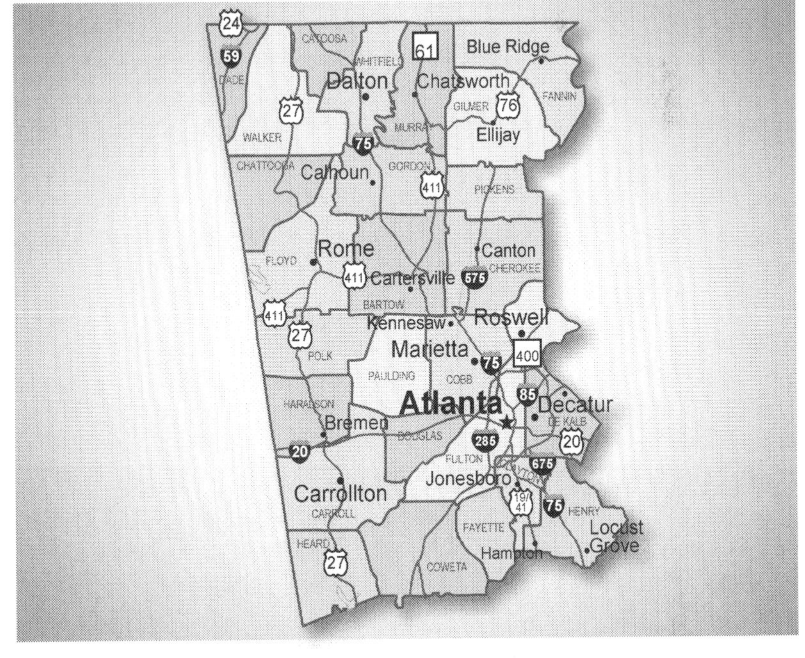

A Quick Tour of our Hand-Picked Favorites Around...

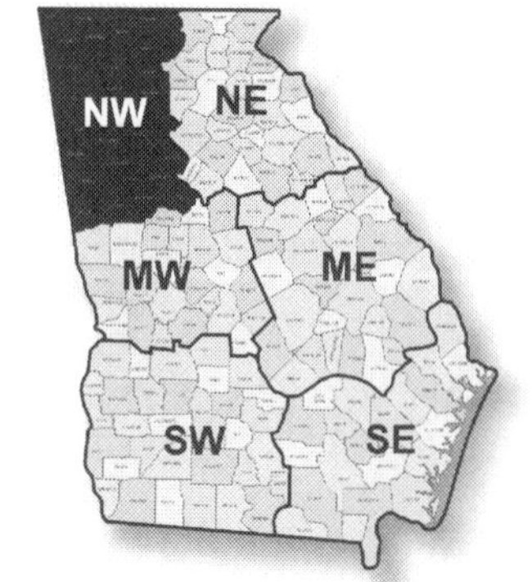

North West Georgia

Believe it or not, this is the land of Cowboys and Indians. Travel the scenic route of the Chieftains Trail through the Appalachian foothills to explore northwest Georgia's Native American heritage.

Follow a path from mysterious rock formations high atop a wind-swept summit and ceremonial Indian mounds on the river bank below (**Etowah Mounds**), to the "showplace of the Cherokee Nation," **New Echota**. And the cowboys – well, they are proudly displayed in art form at **Booth Western Art Museum**. Grab your saddlebag and go on an interactive art journey scavenger hunt upstairs, then play pretend cowboy or cowgirl in the clever discovery room downstairs.

Two things Atlanta is most known for: Coca-Cola and fish? Yes, the **World Of Coca-Cola** and the **Georgia Aquarium** are both in downtown Atlanta and worth a definite stop. After a brief orientation, guests are let loose exploring the land of cola at Bottle Works production line, meeting a soda jerk and ending your tour at Taste It – sampling galore! Beluga whales, whale sharks, 8 million gallons of water – oh my! The world's largest aquarium is separated into different "worlds" so every child can change his attention to the overwhelming new waters and sea critters in each world without burning out too fast. Expend whatever energy is left in the playspace area full of climbing and touching interactives that let kids act like fish swimming upstream...

From the battlefields of the Civil War to the center of the Civil Rights Movement, Georgia has been making history. In the 1860's, history took a turn for the worse with the advent of the Civil War. To get a feel for the state's pitied soul, plan a visit to **Margaret Mitchell's** (the author of Gone with the Wind) House in downtown Atlanta. She was quite a character. Another charismatic Georgian came forward 100 years after the Civil War. The transition from the Civil War era to the era of Civil Rights was successfully carried out by people like Atlanta native **Dr. Martin Luther King Jr**., a Nobel Peace Prize winner, who preached for justice and social change. His boyhood home is a National Park.

Two more tours that are unique to Atlanta: CNN Studio Tours and Turner Field Tours. For children four and older, the **CNN Studio Tour** is an exciting way to discover how a newsroom operates. Listen to behind-the-scenes action of the actual newsroom, see what it takes to put a news broadcast together and even learn how the weather map works. Another behind the scenes tour is open at the Atlanta Braves home field: **Turner Field Tours**. Go through the museum and then explore the ball park from the tippy top to the deep locker rooms.

Stone Mountain Park, east of Atlanta, is home to the world's largest relief sculpture, a carving that's larger than Mount Rushmore, and a spectacular, patriotic laser light show. With so many adventures to choose from (ex. Skylift, Skyride or hiking the mountainside), we recommend staying the night in the park's camping, hotel and resort options. For an outdoor display of nature on a smaller scale, check out **Atlanta Botanical Gardens** where plants help us laugh, live and learn.

Visit the **Center for Puppetry Arts** if you are looking for an outrageous or mildly eccentric show. Parents love the concept of the Puppetry center as it seeks to take the child through a process of creativity – some hands on. First, view famous puppets, then watch a flawless puppet show, and finally create your own puppet to take home.

Sites and attractions are listed in order by City, Zip Code, and Name. Symbols indicated represent:

 Restaurants 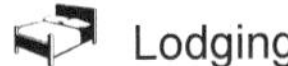 Lodging

Acworth

CAUBLE PARK

Acworth - ***(located on Beach Street on the North side of Lake Acworth, I-75 exit 278) 30101. Phone: (770) 917-1234. www.acworth.org/aprd/Parks.html.***

The 25-acre park contains fishing points, public restrooms, a boating ramp (for electric motor driven boats only), a boardwalk, a beach, volleyball net, rental facilities, two playgrounds, and an open play area. Cauble Park opens at 7:00am and closes at 11:00pm. Acworth Beach opens on Memorial Day weekend and closes Labor Day weekend. During the summer Coach's Café is open to meet all of your beverage and food needs. There is no lifeguard on duty and the beach opens at sun up and closes at sun down. There is a $10.00 parking fee on the weekends - only the weekends between Memorial Day thru Labor Day.

Adairsville

GREAT LOCOMOTIVE CHASE FESTIVAL

Adairsville - *Downtown Square (I-75 exit 306). www.visitcartersvillega.org/eventcal/293. Phone: (800) 733-2280. Arts and crafts festival in the town that witnesses Andrews' Raiders Civil War escapade. Today the entire town is on the National Register of Historic Places. Enjoy crafts, artwork, entertainment, food and parade with fireworks in the evening. Street dancing on Friday & Saturday evenings; Gospel singing Sunday. Admission. (first weekend in October)*

Atlanta

APEX MUSEUM

Atlanta - ***135 Auburn Avenue NE (I-75/85 North, take Exit # 248B or heading South, take exit 249A) 30303. Phone: (404) 521-2739. www.apexmuseum.org. Hours: Tuesday-Saturday 10:00am-5:00PM. Admission: $5.00-$6.00 (age 4+).***

The African American Panoramic Experience offers a variety of permanent and temporary exhibits ranging from art to politics. Visit the Yates and Milton Drug Store, one of Atlanta's first Black owned businesses. Hear the stories of early African American pioneers in Atlanta. Learn about the powerful Black Families that helped to make Atlanta great.

All Aboard! The Trolley Theater provides the right atmosphere for video presentations on African American experiences. Videos shown are: "Sweet Auburn: Street of Pride", "The Journey", and a number of children's shows (The Croations presentation of inventor Lewis Latimer & African Tales of courage, honesty and respect). Where Every Month is Black History Month®.

ATLANTA HAWKS BASKETBALL

Atlanta - ***Phillips Arena (home games), 30303. www.hawks.com.***

The Atlanta Hawks are back in action each winter and spring playing NBA games. Playoff games at Phillips Arena boast some of the largest crowds ever, packed with over 20,000 cheering fans. Kids, look for Harry the Hawk mascot and be sure to tell your folks about Chick-fil-A Family Nights.

CNN STUDIO TOUR

Atlanta - ***One CNN Center (I-75/85 exit International Blvd. exit 248, left on Olympic Park) 30303. www.cnn.com/tour/atlanta/. Phone: (404) 827-2300 or (877) 4CNN-TOUR. Admission: $15.00 adult, $14.00 senior (65+) & youth (13-18), $12.00 child (4-12). Parking $10.00. Tours: Daily from 9:00am - 5:00pm. Tours depart every 10***

minutes from Atrium. Tours last 55 minutes. Advance reservations suggested. The tour is closed on Easter Sunday, Thanksgiving day and Christmas Day. Insider's Tip: Don't spend vacation time waiting for an appointment. Make reservations in advance for the 45-minute tour.

This attraction showcases the CNN Studios. On tour, get a look INSIDE the CNN production studios and newsrooms. Begin by looking at 30+ monitors simulating the CNN control Room. A one-of-a-kind re-creation of CNN's main control room where guests will see and hear the truly behind-the-scenes elements of 24-hour news, live. Look for the monitor with the pre-shot - maybe catch an anchor powdering their nose! An interactive exhibit area follows. This is where guests can view video clips of the top 100 news stories that CNN has covered during the past 20 years, log on to CNN.com, and test their knowledge with the journalism ethics display. Next, see a sample studio - be sure to volunteer to do a short broadcast. Why can't weather people wear blue? Check out the robotic cameras. The Tour Finale features a special presentation showcasing the networks that make up the rest of the Turner Broadcasting family such as TBS, TNT, and the Cartoon Network. Great tour to see the glamour and electronic glitz it takes to pull off a 24-hour broadcast.

PHILIPS EXPERIENCE

Atlanta - ***1 Philips Drive (I-75/85 south exit 249C, heading north take exit 248C) 30303. Phone: (404) 878-3000 or (800) 326-4000. www.philipsarena.com. Hours: During arena games or events. Admission: included with event ticket price.***

Within this state of the art multi-purpose sports and entertainment complex (home to the NBA Hawks) there is tons of Philips technology. The Philips Experience is the first interactive space of its kind offering hands-on activities where visitors see, touch, move and control much of the action. Activities include Interactive Alley and Ready, Set, Shoot. While visitors dribble and shoot, specially placed cameras capture their moves from 360 degrees and project it onto screens surrounding the exhibit. This station lets the athlete in everyone shine through for all to see. Shot on Goal; Screen Test; and Digital Dream Set feature an interactive entertainment system designed to replicate the fun of shooting in true game situations. Or, take a photo celebrity shot and email it to friends. Fans can also keep tabs on the games by watching one of the over 600 Philips TVs throughout the arena.

ATLANTA HISTORY CENTER

Atlanta - *130 West Paces Ferry Road, NW (I-75 to exit #255, follow signs 2.5 m) 30305. Phone: (404) 814-4004. www.atlantahistorycenter.com. Hours: Monday-Saturday 10:00am-5:30pm, Sunday Noon-5:30pm. Closed most holidays. Admission: $16.00 adult, $13.00 senior (65+) and student (13+), $11.00 youth (4-12). Includes the Atlanta History Museum, Centennial Olympic Games Museum, historic gardens and tours of two Historic Houses, Swan House and Smith Farm. Plus, Margaret Mitchell House admission is included if visited in 9 days. Note: Lots of little theatre rooms with videos here. Ask for the Family Fun brochure. Take a walk outside to visit the Swan House 1928 Mansion or the Tullie Smith Farm. The farmhouse and other related buildings are from the 1840s and are best visited during special event programs. Gift shop and Coca-Cola Café.*

Jenny holding an actual Olympic Torch...

Educators: About a dozen excellent Lesson Plans are online under: Teachers/Educator Resources/Online Interactives (ex. Farms, Native Americans, Civil War); and History Live! Seasonal themed monthly events. FREEBIES: The Kids Corner onsite has a room full of activity sheet puzzles and coloring that you can do there or take with you.

Revisit the Civil War, discover southern folk arts and meet famous Atlantans. Kids will gravitate to these areas:

- CENTENNIAL OLYMPIC GAMES: The 1996 Centennial Olympic Games changed Atlanta forever - and accelerated its transformation from southern capital to international city. For seventeen days, Atlanta was the focus of the entire world. The favorite spot - the interactive Sports Lab.
- METROPOLITAN FRONTIERS (1835-present): Journey through four stages of Atlanta history, from early pioneer settlements to today's bustling city of international fame. See an entire 1894 shotgun house (why called that? Hint: long, narrow shape) moved from southwest Atlanta; an 1898 horse-drawn fire engine with a steam-driven pump used by the Atlanta fire department in the city's tragic 1917 fire; a 1920 Hanson car built in Atlanta and one of only two known in existence; a scale model of the "Spaghetti Junction".
- TURNING POINT: THE AMERICAN CIVIL WAR - Explore the stories of both Confederate and Federal soldiers, along with the heartache and hope of loved ones at home. Videos interpret what happened and why. Touch-screen computer learning stations can answer your questions and deepen your understanding. Did you know only 6% of slaves from Africa went to the States? Others went to the

Caribbean and South America.

- SHAPING TRADITIONS: FOLK ARTS IN A CHANGING SOUTH - Touch, see, and hear the folk arts that have defined the South for generations. It begins with sections asking "What's folk about folk arts?" and "What's southern about southern folk arts?"

Other Exhibits explore: Barbeque, Rednecks, Bobby Jones, and Native American history.

FERNBANK MUSEUM OF NATURAL HISTORY

Atlanta - ***767 Clifton Road NE (I-75/I-85 to downtown exit 248C (GA 10 east). Go 1.7 miles to Ponce de Leon Ave., turn right. Go 1/7 mile to left on Clifton Rd. Follow signs) 30307. Phone: (404) 929-6300. www.fernbankmuseum.org. Hours: Monday-Saturday 10:00am-5:00pm, Sunday Noon-5:00pm. Only closed Thanksgiving and Christmas. Admission: $18.00 adult, $17.00 senior (62+) and student, $16.00 child (3-12). IMAX extra $11.00-$13.00. Museum and IMAX combo pricing. Note: IMAX Theatre shows each day. View schedule and features online. Fernbank Café open for lunch. Educators: You can also stimulate your senses with lasers, mirrors, water, acoustics and more in Sensing Nature or walk through a World of Shells. Three different Scavenger Hunts (detailed, write in answers) and pdf Exhibition guides are online under: Education/Just for Educators/Online Resources.***

History comes alive at Fernbank Museum of Natural History. Giants of the Mesozoic features the world's largest dinosaurs. This area recreates a snapshot of what life was like years ago during the Cretaceous Period. The exhibit showcases the world's largest meat eater, the 47-foot-long Giganotosaurus as it prepares to make a meal out of the largest dinosaur ever discovered, the 123-foot-long plant-eating Argentinosaurus. Also featured in the exhibition are two species of flying reptiles. Twenty-four in all, the pterosaurs are shown reacting to the scene below. The terrain-like rockwork includes fossils of other animals and plants such as a prehistoric frog, crocodile and Auracaria tree, along with dinosaur tracks. A Walk Through Time in Georgia tells the two-fold story of Georgia's natural history and the development of our planet. Gobs of exhibits and realistic

dioramas take you on a journey that begins in the Piedmont, the region in Georgia with the oldest rocks. Then walk in the sand through a marsh or in the muddy swamp. Fish in the Okefenokee Swamp, dock up at the Jekyll Island Pier, encounter native wildlife at Turkey Mountain and more. Other highlights include the Cosmos Theatre, a six-foot sloth that lived during the Ice Age, and the Dinosaur Gallery.

FERNBANK SCIENCE CENTER

Atlanta - ***156 Heaton Park Drive NE (I-285 to exit 39A Decatur/Highway 78) 30307. Phone: (678) 874-7102. http://fsc.fernbank.edu. Hours: Museum: Monday-Friday Noon-5:00pm, Saturday 10:00am-5:00pm. Open until 10:00pm Thursday and Friday. Planetarium: General Times for Family Shows. Saturday & Sunday 1:30pm. Additional family shows during the summer and some holidays Tuesday-Friday at 11:00am and 1:30pm. Admission: Museum is FREE. $5.00-$7.00 for planetarium shows. Educators: Science Newsletter pdf's are found on the online Teachers section.***

This learning center has a 500-seat planetarium, an observatory, two electron microscopes, a distance learning studio, a NASA Aeronautics Education lab, and a 65-acre forest. The new animals exhibit at Fernbank Science Center has poison dart frogs, snakes, turtles, spiders, and more. Plan a group or school visit to get the benefit of guided programs - inside and outside.

JIMMY CARTER LIBRARY AND MUSEUM

Atlanta - ***441 Freedom Parkway (I-75/85 exit 248C, Freedom Pkwy) 30307. Phone: (404) 865-7100. www.jimmycarterlibrary.gov. Hours: Monday-Saturday 9:00am-4:45pm, Sunday Noon-4:45pm. Admission: $8.00 adult, $6.00 senior (60+), military and students, Free youth (16 and under). Note: restaurant serving lunch daily except Sunday. Educators: a biography of Jimmy Carter is online under: Information about Jimmy & Rosalynn Carter. Also curriculum under Education.***

The only Presidential Library in the southeast United States features an exact replica of the Oval Office, and the Nobel Peace Prize awarded to President Jimmy Carter. Exhibits change every six months.

THE VARSITY
ATLANTA

THE VARSITY

The Varsity is the world's largest drive-in offering fast-food dining.

e, N.W. (I-75/85 exit 249D, the Varsity is over bridge. Pull into first driveway) m. Phone: (404) 881-1706.

An Atlanta institution for over 80 years. You need to know everyone from businessmen to college students frequent here and it's always crowded (they serve over 10,000 customers each day) and noisy - but, it's a must see. You can sit in your car and get car-hop service or go inside. Whether it's a chili cheese dog, the rings, a Frosted Orange or maybe a fried pie, everyone has their favorites that keep them coming back. Everything is made fresh and all fried items are cooked in Canola Oil with No Cholesterol - no trans fat, low saturated fat; and they make their chicken salad and egg salad with Kraft Lite Mayonnaise. If you're just wanting to order for the experience, whatever you order, be sure to add one order of onion rings and a fried pie to split. If you're planning a trip to The Varsity, you should brush up on your Varsity Lingo to make sure you have your "order in your mind". "Walk a Dog" (hot dog to go); Sideways (onions on the side); or P.C. (Plain Chocolate milk always served with ice) are examples of shortcut chants the servers use to call out your order. One of those "you had to be there" diners.

A little "role-playing" after we got home from The Varsity...

ATLANTA BOTANICAL GARDEN

Atlanta - ***1345 Piedmont Avenue (I75/85 exit 250-14th St., left on Piedmont Ave. at The Prado, Midtown) 30309. www.atlantabotanicalgarden.org. Phone: (404) 876-5859. Hours: Tuesday - Sunday 9:00am-5:00pm, open till 7:00pm during Daylight Savings Time. Admission: $18.95 adult, $13.95 child (3 -12). Note: Tropical, desert and endangered plants from around the world are found at Fuqua Conservatory (on the other side of the park). FREEBIES: click on Kids & Schools for fun activity sheets like Critter Crawl or Scavenger Hunt.***

The Atlanta Botanical Garden features one of the world's largest permanent displays of tropical orchids, 15 acres of outdoor display gardens and the Fuqua Conservatory, home to rare and endangered tropical and desert plants. The Children's Garden, alone, is worth the visit here! Greeted by the "Green Man Fountain and "Plants Keep Us Well" atrium, you'll walk into a garden wonderland where plants help us LAUGH, LIVE AND LEARN. Special enclaves include the Laugh Garden, providing a space for little ones to wind through a cocoon tunnel and emerge as a butterfly as they swish around a maze beginning at a colorful caterpillar's mouth and ending at the Butterfly Pavilion. Dig for fossils at the Dinosaur Garden, learn about carnivorous plants in the Soggy Bog, and experience the singing stone at Rocky Pointe. Slide through a leaf, sit around storytime readings of Peter Rabbit, then walk through the story's scenery. Sit in an Indian hut, go to Grandma's House for a visit, play the bee game, and climb in a giant tree house. This is, by far, the best children's garden we've interacted with in the South!

ATLANTA BOTANICAL GARDEN - SCARECROWS IN THE GARDEN

The Children's Garden is sure worth the visit!

Atlanta - 1345 Piedmont Avenue 30309. Phone: (404) 876-5859. Imaginative scarecrows on display in the Children's garden. Special activities are scheduled every weekend in October from 1:00-4:00pm. Children of all ages are welcome to come and enjoy a fun-filled day of activities that include the following: Face Painting, Make a scarecrow puppet, Make a spider magnet, Craft corn activity, and Make A Scarecrow bookmark. Admission. (month-long in October)

ATLANTA BOTANICAL GARDEN - HOLIDAY IN THE GARDEN

Atlanta - 1345 Piedmont Avenue 30309. Phone: (404) 876-5859. Activities and crafts for children and their families, along with live holiday performances and entertainment, will enliven the afternoon. And to celebrate the holidays, admission is free for all children 12 and under. Parking available at Colony Square with free shuttle service to the Garden. Held rain or shine. (first Sunday in December)

ATLANTA SYMPHONY ORCHESTRA

Atlanta - ***1280 Peachtree Street N.E. (Atlanta Symphony Hall, Woodruff Arts Center. Take I-75 South to Exit 250 (10th Street/14th Street), turn left to Peachtree) 30309. Phone: (404) 733-5000, (404) 733-4900. www.atlantasymphony.org.***

Family Concerts-Crazy for Classical: Introduce your youngest family members to the fun world of symphonic music as dancers, puppeteers and your favorite storybook characters join the orchestra. Pre-concert cookies and juice are provided. Concerts are usually Sundays at 1:30 & 3:30pm. Each year the Youth Orchestra performs at least three subscription concerts.

CENTER FOR PUPPETRY ARTS

Atlanta - *1404 Spring Street, NW (I75 Exit #250 (10th/14th/GA Tech). Turn left on 14th Street, crossing over I-75. At 3rd traffic light, turn left on W. Peachtree Street) 30309. Phone: (404) 873-3391. www.puppet.org. Hours: Tuesday-Friday 9:00am-3:00pm, Saturday 10am-5pm, Sunday Noon-5:00pm. Admission: $16.00 per person per performance. Workshop and Museum admission included in single show ticket. Miscellaneous: Museum and performances change throughout the year. Excellent Education programs and study guides. Reservations suggested for activities. Take a special Behind-The-Scenes Tour at the Center for Puppetry Arts and get a peek at how puppet magic is made (weekends at 2:00pm for groups). Educators: click on Education, then Educator Resources for lesson and activity guides for current productions.*

Many famous puppets have spent the night here (how about Kermit the Frog). Can you imagine the stories this place could tell? So, let's start in the Museum. First of all, it's a little spooky and interactive (even the storage room is animated). The best part - the variety. Asians spend their lifetimes perfecting Shadow puppets and Bunraku puppetry requires three puppeteers to work one figure. Other puppets are much simpler. Kid's imaginations soar seeing household objects like scarves, cloth, and plastic tubing puppets. Now, attend a performance. Their shows are really several notches above any puppet shows elsewhere. Many are based on classic folk tales - some with a "twist". You are encouraged to laugh, giggle, sneer, clap or stomp approval or disapproval at the happenings on stage. The puppeteers greet the audience afterwards to enlighten the crowd and share their "tricks". Next, do a workshop. Learn about different types of puppets - hand, rod, string, marionette, shadow or body. Make your own hand puppet that resembles a character in the performance. Have a short time to perform with your puppet in the mini-stage. What a wonderful way to engage the kids into the art and entertainment of puppetry. This place is a wonderful surprise every visit and worth spending a good part of your morning / afternoon!

Learning how to make simple puppets...

FEDERAL RESERVE BANK OF ATLANTA VISITORS CENTER & MONETARY MUSEUM

Atlanta - *1000 Peachtree Street NE (I- 75/85 North, take Exit 250 (10th Street/14th Street/17th Street), turn right onto 10th Street, and left onto Peachtree Street) 30309. www.frbatlanta.org/about/tours/museum.org. Phone: (404) 498-8764. Hours: Monday-Friday 9:00am-4:00pm. Admission: FREE. Tours: Open for scheduled, guided tours only weekdays at 9:30am, 11:00am or 1:00pm. Recommended for pre-teens on up.*

The story of money—from bartering to modern times. In the museum, you'll see examples of rare coins and currency plus displays highlighting noted events in monetary history. After touring the museum, experience the rest of the Visitors Center, where interactive and multimedia exhibits provide in-depth lessons on the role of the Federal Reserve in the U.S. economy. Then, you can take a look inside their cash-processing operations, where millions of dollars are counted, sorted, or shredded daily. You'll also get a glimpse into the bank's automated vault and see the robotic transports that do the heavy lifting.

HIGH MUSEUM OF ART

Atlanta - *1280 Peachtree Street (I-75/85 exit 249 east) 30309. Phone: (404) 733-4400. www.high.org. Hours: Tuesday-Saturday 10:00am-5:00pm, Sunday Noon-5:00pm. Admission: $19.50 adult, $16.50 senior (65+), $12.00 child (6-17). Your ticket includes admission to the permanent collection, all current special exhibitions and family workshops. Walk-up admission is free for Fulton County residents on the first Saturday of each month. Tours: Guided tours Sunday and Wednesday at 1:00pm.*

This museum mostly displays European and American paintings and special exhibits including African, decorative, folk and modern art. The Learning to Look / Looking to Learn interactives are the best way to explore a classic art museum with kids. Learning Gallery: Before or after visiting the galleries, families can play together in five fun activity areas: Building Buildings, Making a Mark, Telling Stories, Sculpting Spaces, and Transforming Treasure. Designed for children ages 5-10 when accompanied by an adult.

MARGARET MITCHELL HOUSE & MUSEUM

Atlanta - *990 Peachtree Street (I-75, 10th Street exit 250 and Peachtree) 30309. Phone: (404) 249-7015. www.gwtw.org. Hours: Open daily 10am-5:30pm, except Sunday Noon-5:30pm. Admission: $13.00 adult, $10.00 senior (65+) and students over 12, $8.50 youth (4-12). Miscellaneous: Because Margaret was quite a character, ask for the family-friendly version of the apartment tour.*

In the "Gone With the Wind" movie museum, your girls will love to admire the doll collection and everyone will want to "walk thru" the actual doorway to "Tara"! Now, prepare, girls and boys, to be inspired! Tour the historic house and apartment where Margaret Mitchell wrote one of the classic beloved novels "Gone With the Wind". As you learn about the life (and death) of this fascinating woman you'll learn that she wrote short stories as a little girl - she even put on plays with neighboring children. The girls were always the heroine! Her Dad was a history buff and many characters are based on family and friends throughout Margaret's life history. Touch her lucky stair post or see her battered typewriter where she wrote most of her work. When friends came over, she'd hide her manuscript all over the house. She once forgot the first chapter was hidden in the refrigerator! Amusing stories abound while on tour. We promise, you'll be told a secret or two!

See the famous typewriter where the tale was told...

Although constantly hounded by publishers, Mitchell refused to write a sequel to her novel. She never published another book.

MARTIN LUTHER KING JR. NATIONAL HISTORIC SITE

Atlanta - *450 Auburn Avenue, N.E. (I-75 exit 248D, Sweet Auburn district) 30312. Phone: (404) 331-6922. www.nps.gov/malu. Hours: Daily 9:00am-5:00pm. Closed Thanksgiving Day, Christmas and New Years. Summers open until 6:00pm. The Home and Church may have shorter hours, please inquire at the Park Service desk for tour times. Admission: FREE. Tours: No special arrangements are needed since most of the park is self-guided. However, you will need to register to tour the Birth Home of Dr. King. Educators: click on For Teachers/LessonPlans &TeacherGuides.htm for some excellent exhibit-based activities and problem-solving projects.*

Open the door to see a future leader...

Now a National Historic Site, visit Dr. Martin Luther King Jr.'s Birthplace, Home and Church. Begin in the Visitor Center for orientation. The "Civil Rights Struggle" present emotional exhibits through movie and video clips. Most exhibits encourage children to carry on the dream of freedom, justice and world peace using interactive displays. The exhibits are extremely emotional and capture your attention and your heart. However, it may contain material that is best viewed by children who have studied segregation and Civil Rights beforehand. Otherwise, your children may be terrified how cruel people can be to one another. The Home is located in the residential section of "Sweet Auburn", the center of black Atlanta. Two blocks west of the home is Ebenezer Baptist Church, the pastorate of Martin's grandfather and father. The tour guide at the church "preaches" the church's history from near the pulpit! Here, "M.L." learned about family and Christian love, segregation in the days of "Jim Crow" laws, diligence and tolerance.

ATLANTA FALCONS

Atlanta - ***One Georgia Dome Drive 30313. Phone: (404) 249-6400 or (800) 326-4000. www.atlantafalcons.com.***

NFL Atlanta Falcons play each autumn and winter football season with an average of 10 games at home. Meet the mascot Freddie Falcon at most games. Falcons Landing is open to the public 3 hours prior to kick-off for all Falcon home games. At each home game, Falcons Landing features a different band, live on the Coca-Cola stage. Children and adults alike enjoy participating in a variety of free activities. Practice kicking field goals, fielding punts, or testing your quarterbacking skills on the gridiron. Check out Falcons central where you can have your face painted while listening to local radio stations broadcasting their pre-game shows live from the landing.

CENTENNIAL OLYMPIC PARK

Atlanta - ***285 International Blvd. (I-75/85 north to exit 248C or south to exit 249C) 30313. Phone: (404) 223-4412. www.centennialpark.com. Hours: Daily 7:00am-11:00pm. Admission: FREE.***

Look for the Fountain of Rings - the world's largest fountain utilizing the five interconnecting rings of the Olympic symbol with 25 water jets - and you've found the park. The water jets display four 20-minute musical water shows daily beginning at lunchtime, then every three hours. Today, the park features a wide variety of events including Fourth Saturday Family Fun Days, a free event with hands-on activities, April through September. There are also playgrounds, water gardens, a visitors center with Fountainside Cafe, and people-watchers plaza.

CENTENNIAL OLYMPIC PARK - 4TH OF JULY CELEBRATION

Atlanta - *285 International Blvd. 30313. www.centennialpark.com. Phone: (404) 223-4412. Celebrations of our nation's Birthday featuring live music, exhibits, concessions and fireworks. Arrive at the Park early to secure a good seat and enjoy fun for the whole family! Children's activities are in the south end of the Park around the Fountain of Rings from noon to 5:00pm. Entertainment includes arts and crafts, face painting, performances, inflatables, stilt walkers and more! Or families can relax on the Great Lawn and splash in the world famous Fountain of Rings. The free musical entertainment begins at 5:00pm. with a headline performance before the finale of the evening, Atlanta's best fireworks display synchronized to a special selection of patriotic music. Salute 2 American Parade is on Peachtree Street earlier that afternoon. (July 4th)*

CENTENNIAL OLYMPIC PARK - HOLIDAY IN LIGHTS

Atlanta - *285 International Blvd. 30313. www.centennialpark.com. Phone: (404) 223-4412. Hours: Daily 7:00am-11:00pm. Admission: FREE. In November, the Park transforms into a winter wonderland with thousands of lights that make up the dazzling display. Different and unique every year, the park also opens an outdoor skating rink during this time. Atlanta Christmas Parade has holiday bands and floats for a little holiday magic downtown (parade is first Saturday). The Park is open daily to view the lights from 7:00am -11:00pm, including Christmas Day, and there is no charge for admission. (mid-November thru early January)*

GEORGIA AQUARIUM

Atlanta - ***225 Baker Street (I-75 Williams Street exit 249C, follow signs) 30313. Phone: (404) 581-4000. www.georgiaaquarium.org. Hours: Sunday-Friday 10:00am-5:00pm, Saturday 9:00am-6:00pm. Extended hours during peak weekends or school breaks. Admission: $35.95 adult, $31.95 senior, $29.95 child (3-12). Includes 4D & Dolphin Tales show. Parking Garage $10.00. Café Aquaria Food Court on premises. Miscellaneous: Guarantee admission to the Aquarium by making advance reservations. We recommend that parents bring a pair of socks for children while playing in the Georgia Explorer gallery's children's play area. Educators: click on Education/ teachers online for fact sheets, lesson plans and Ask an Educator Q & A***

opportunities.

Beluga whales, whale sharks, 8 million gallons of water - oh my! The world's largest aquarium with more than 100,000 animals is dedicated to the waters of the world, and there's a children's play area with touch tanks for kids to get up close and personal with all kinds of sea critters. Kids love the "pretty colors" in Tropical Diver and the Touch Wall and bubbles and tunnels in Ocean Voyager. Learn about the Whale sharks' journey to Georgia and much more in the Ocean exhibit that cleverly takes you around the same tank of water, just from wall, bubble and tunnel views. No one can resist hanging around the giant two-story wall of live fish (it's like you're watching an IMAX film – only it's live)! The Belugas gracefully dance ballet to the music and the Penguins love getting close to humans behind "ice" in Coldwater Quest. Be sure to watch the Octopus action video and make time to be amused by all the Sea Otter and Sea Lion antics in Quest. River Scout and Georgia Explorer have displays of things you might find closer to home – don't be frightened by the Red Piranha or afraid to touch rays or shrimp at the various Touch Tanks in these areas. One of our favorite aquariums! We especially liked the way many paths led you around different sides of the same tank of fish. Especially amusing to kids as sometimes the fish were above you, below you or right up in your face!

Getting close with our penguin friends...

GEORGIA DOME TOURS

Atlanta - ***One Georgia Dome NW (I-75 exit 252. tours depart between Gates B & C) 30313. Phone: (404) 223-8600. www.gadome.com. Admission: $6.00 adult, $4.00 senior and child (5-12). Individual Tours: Tuesday-Saturday 10:00am-3:00pm during football season (except on days when events occur in the Dome). Tours leave every hour. Call ahead to be sure there's room.***

The world's largest cable-supported dome offers tours. Want to see behind-the-scenes, from the Falcons locker room, to the new turf everyone is talking about (wanna touch it)? Want to see the VIP views from the press box or Dome suites? Get a Falcons eye view of the stadium and then see the TV studio where broadcasted games originate from. Come see the site of the 1994 & 2000 Super Bowls. Visit the venue that hosted gymnastics & basketball for the 1996 Summer Olympics. Every year the Georgia Dome hosts the highest attended and highest rated non-BCS bowl game, the Chick-Fil-A Bowl, which often draws more than 75,000 spectators.

IMAGINE IT! THE CHILDREN'S MUSEUM OF ATLANTA

Atlanta - ***275 Centennial Olympic Park Drive NW (north exit 248C. south I-75/85 exit 249C-Williams Street. Turn right onto Baker Street) 30313. Phone: (404) 659-5437. www.childrensmuseumatlanta.org. Hours: Monday-Friday 10:00am-4:00pm, Saturday & Sunday 10:00am-5:00pm. Closed Wednesdays & major holidays. Admission: $12.75 per person age 1 and above. Note: Vending area. The Museum is also walking distance from The CNN Center, World of Coca-Cola, and other downtown restaurants.***

This is a museum where children can experience the power of imagination and the delight of learning. Primarily designed for ages two to eight, Imagine It! features hands-on, colorful exhibits and activities in which children look, listen, touch and explore. Kids and their adults can learn together where food comes from (and how the body uses it), work construction equipment, explore a barnyard, and make a craft to take home. Make music with bongos and such. The kids especially love the big ball popper that shoots out giant balls on command. You can even walk through a make-believe town and go shopping.

WORLD OF COCA-COLA

Atlanta - ***121 Baker Street (adjacent to Georgia Aquarium at Centennial Olympic Park Drive, I-75 exit 249C) 30313. www.worldofcoca-cola.com. Phone: (800) 676-COKE. Hours: Daily 10:00am-5:00pm. Longer open/close hours during peak season and most weekends. Closed Easter, Thanksgiving, Christmas. Admission: $16.00 adult, $14.00 senior (55+), $12.00 child (3-12). Online discounts. Timed entry***

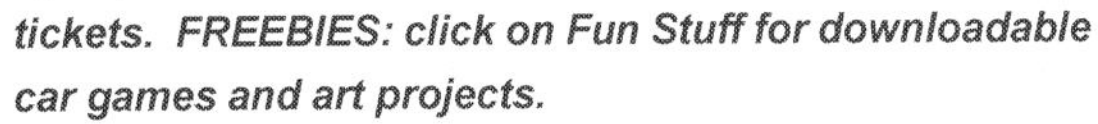

tickets. FREEBIES: click on Fun Stuff for downloadable car games and art projects.

Atlanta is the birthplace of Coca-Cola. The story is told through a bright collection of memorabilia, classic radio and television ads, a fantasy representation of the bottling process and a futuristic soda fountain. It started with a syrup created by a pharmacist. Accidentally, a soda jerk added carbonated water and the customers loved it - Coke was born! Guests are greeted by a enthusiastic guides who direct you to start by viewing the 4-minute audio visual history of the product (later you'll get a chance to watch the Secret Formula 3D movie with moving seats!). After that, you are turned loose to explore the many sections of the museum. At Bottle Works you'll view a slow-motion production line so you can see robots in action filling bottles. Really interesting history is found at Milestones of Refreshment. On display- a can that flew on the space shuttle and the original prototype bottle. The highlight of your visit is the last station - taste testing! Try flavors, old and new, plus many found in foreign countries. Some are quite unusual, some very sweet. If you try them all, like we did, you're bound to have a belly-ache - so, be wise, and choose carefully. Don't forget your free Coke as you leave.

> **Top Secret...**
> Did you know the secret formula is still a secret? Where is it kept?

ATLANTA BRAVES

***Atlanta** - 755 Hank Aaron Drive (Turner Field, just southeast of downtown) 30315. Phone: (404) 249-6400 or (800) 326-4000. http://atlanta.braves.mlb.com. Note: Grab a bite to eat at the Chop House, situated right over the Braves bullpen, or bring your own picnic. Tables are located right inside the ballpark's entrance.*

Major League Baseball team plays regular season March through September. Tickets range $1.00 (Skyline seats) to $45 (dugout). Turner Field combines the nostalgia and the atmosphere of old-time baseball with a state-of-the-art early at Turner Field and take advantage of activities such as pre-game pep rallies and posing for pictures with Scooby-Doo at Tooner Field. To keep the kids busy during the game try: Getting your face airbrushed at the Braves free Fun Zone; testing your baseball skills in Scouts Alley; or, bang the over-sized Braves drum. Kids 14 and under are invited to join the Atlanta Braves Kids Club. Your one-year membership is FREE and includes great gifts and discounts. Plus, learn about opportunities to meet and greet with the team mascot, Homer the baseball. Kids, run the bases after the game on Sundays.

Take me out with the crowd...

ATLANTA BRAVES MUSEUM / TURNER FIELD TOURS

Take me out to the ballgame...

Atlanta - *755 Hank Aaron Drive (I-75/85 exit 246, Fulton Street East) 30315. Phone: (404) 614-2310. http://atlanta.braves.mlb.com. Hours: The museum opens two and a half hours before each game and closes in the middle of the seventh inning. Admission: Museum Only: $2.00-$5.00. Tour/Museum: $12.00 adult, $7.00 child. FREE parking in the Green Lot. Tours: On non-game days, tours are offered Monday - Saturday from 9:00am-3:00pm, and Sundays from 1:00-3:00pm, year-round. Off season Monday-Saturday 10:00am-2:00pm. Please note that there are no tours offered before any afternoon or Sunday home game. Tours start at the top of each hour and last approximately one hour. No reservations are necessary. Educators: Educational tours of a ball field? Yes, they have tours for Social Studies, Math, Art, etc. for group discounted prices. Just ask.*

THE HALL OF FAME MUSEUM is the starting point of Turner Field Tours and traces the Braves History. The museum features memorabilia commemorating legends of the game and key moments in Braves history from Boston to Milwaukee to Atlanta. On display are artifacts including Hank Aaron's historic 715th home run bat and ball, more than 50 game jerseys, game bats, an actual railroad car from the B&O Railroad used to transport players in the 1950s, the knee brace worn by Sid Bream during his famous slide into home plate that captured the 1992 NLCS pennant for the Braves, and the 1995 World Series trophy and championship rings.

THE TURNER FIELD TOUR is probably the highlight of the visit. See Sky Field, a luxury suite, the press box & broadcast booth, the dugout, and the Plaza with the giant baseballs. But the real behind-the-scenes fun is a peek in the locker room. Look for the "putting green" and the 561 TVs throughout the stadium. They have more TVs here than trash cans! What young, little leaguer wouldn't love this tour?

Looking UP from field level was a real treat...

ATLANTA CYCLORAMA

***Atlanta** - 800 Cherokee Ave. SE (I-75 exit 246 or I-20 to exit 59a (Boulevard). Follow signs. Located next to Zoo Atlanta in Grant Park) 30315. Phone: (404) 658-7625. www.atlantacyclorama.org. Hours: Tuesday-Saturday 9:00am-4:30pm. Thanksgiving, Christmas, New Years Day and Martin Luther King's birthday. Admission: $10.00 adult, $8.00 senior (60+) & child (4-12). Parking free with admission. Tours: Tour guides conduct a 40-minute, two-part educational program on the Battle of Atlanta every hour on the half hour from 9:30am-4:30pm. The program includes special lighting, sound effects, music and narration. Educators: Scavenger Hunt Packages for 1st-8th grade students are available upon request.*

Did you know?
One of the dying soldiers in the diorama is a portrait of the actor Clark Gable.

Home of the world's largest oil painting, "The Battle of Atlanta". Through spectacular music, art and sound effects, history comes alive as you step back to July 22, 1864 and become part of the eight hour battle. Cycloramas place the spectator in the middle (standing or sitting) as you "follow" the sequence of events. Shows begin with a film, narrated by James Earl Jones, that covers the history of the Atlanta Campaign leading up to the battle. Tiered central seating is lit as you enter, then the house lights dim. Each section of the painting is viewed from the slowly rotating seating and a guide points out highlights of the painting. Look for General Sherman and Old Abe (the eagle). After the show you may visit a Civil War museum that includes The Texas, a Civil War era train that was engaged in an episode now commonly called "The Great Locomotive Chase."

ZOO ATLANTA

***Atlanta** - 800 Cherokee Avenue SE (I-75 exit 246 or I-20 exit 59A. Follow signs east or south.) 30315. Phone: (404) 624-5822. www.zooatlanta.org. Hours: Daily 9:30am-4:30pm (5:30pm on weekends). Grounds remain open 1 hour after admissions close. Closed on Thanksgiving, Christmas. Admission: $21.99 adult (12+), $17.99 senior (65+), military and college student; $16.99 child (3-11). Educators: Educator Loan Boxes are available to rent for classroom use.*

Located near downtown in historic Grant Park, the Zoo Atlanta is home to Giant Pandas, as well as many rare and endangered species, including Sumatran orangutans and tigers, black rhinos and African elephants. Don't miss the Giant Pandas of Chengdu and their cubs (what are their favorite scents? What do they like to eat?) in person or online on Panda Cam! See gorillas, lions, giraffes, birds & more in natural habitats. See more than 700 animals representing 200 species from all over the world.

PAPER MUSEUM AT IPST

Atlanta - ***500 10th Street N.W. (I-75/85 exit 250 to IPST Bldg. At Georgia Tech) 30332. Phone: (404) 894-7840. www.ipst.gatech.edu/amp/. Hours: Monday-Friday 9:00am-5:00pm. The Museum is closed on Georgia Tech holidays. Admission: FREE. Suggested donation $3.00 per person. Tours: By Reservation. Grades 3-12. Minimum 10, Maximum 30-40. Fee for tours (see below)***

Trace the history of paper from 4,000 BC to today. Learn how Asians started a fine art and how companies through the ages each developed a way to "watermark" their signature on their product. The gallery showcases the work of contemporary paper artists with special exhibits changing at least twice a year. The permanent exhibit space is FROM HAND TO MACHINE - Follow the path of papermaking that began in ancient China and leads to the advanced technology of today. (self-guided tour is a donation fee)

PAPER TRAVEL - This tour includes the museum as well as "Paper-The Video", a fun and lively video which highlights the history and the uses of paper. The charge for this tour is $5.50 per person. Weekdays at 10:00am. Allow 1 hour.

PAPERWORKS! - This includes a guided tour of the Museum of Papermaking and "Paper-The Video", as well as a hands-on papermaking workshop. Students will enjoy making their own sheets of paper from cotton pulp. The charge for this tour is $8.50 per person. Weekdays at 10:00am. Allow 1½ hours.

Making paper is somewhat of a lost art, so this museum may be one of the most unique you'll ever visit!

GEORGIA STATE CAPITOL & MUSEUM

Atlanta - ***2 Martin Luther King Dr. (I-75 exit 248A or B, look for the gold domed building, Capitol Hill at Washington Street) 30334. Phone: (404) 656-2846. www.sos.ga.gov/state_capitol. Hours: Monday-Friday 8:00am-5:00pm. Admission: FREE.***

Native Georgia gold tops the dome of this state capital, an 1889 building that houses a Hall of Flags, Hall of Fame, and a natural science museum. The fourth floor is where you'll spend most of your time on this self-guided tour. Here, you'll be able to peek in the gallery overlooking the Senate and House Chambers - they look serious, don't they? This floor is also host to many displays of the history of Georgia. We learned cotton used to be the cash crop here. When it faded, what three "P's" took over? - peaches, pecans and peanuts.

DOGWOOD FESTIVAL

Atlanta - *Piedmont Park. www.dogwood.org. Celebrate spring at Piedmont Park while the dogwoods are in bloom. The Kid's Village offers arts and crafts, bounce houses, and face-painting. Watch world-class Frisbee dogs compete in national championships and join a block party with live music and dozens of food vendors. Activity prices vary. (third weekend in April)*

EASTER EGGSTRAVAGANZA

Atlanta - *Callanwolde Fine Arts Center, 980 Briarcliff Road, N.E. (2 miles east of Midtown). Phone: (866) 633-5252. www.callanwolde.org. Callanwolde and Radio Disney present a giant Easter egg hunt, interactive games and activities, concessions, local personalities, music, Easter baskets, candy and prizes. (Saturday before Easter)*

ATLANTA GREEK FESTIVAL

Atlanta - *Greek Orthodox Cathedral, 2500 Clairmont Road, NE (I-85 exit 91. On Clairmont Rd. between Briarcliff Rd. and LaVista Rd). www.atlgoc.org/festival.htm. Celebrate Greek heritage with music, Greek tragedy theatre, dancing, singing and mouthwatering food. Admission. (first long weekend in October)*

PEACH DROP

Atlanta - *Underground Atlanta. Phone: (404) 523-2311. www.peachdrop.com. Beginning at noon on Thursday, December 31, Underground Atlanta will be bursting with activities for the entire family. Then, just before the clock strikes midnight, the New Year's Eve tradition will come alive when our 800-pound peach begins its descent! As the clock strikes 12 midnight, spectacular fireworks fill the air. FREE. (New Years Eve)*

SIX FLAGS OVER GEORGIA

Atlanta (Austell) - *275 Riverside Pkwy. SE (I-20 exit 47 or 46A) 30168. Phone: (770) 948-9290. www.sixflags.com/overgeorgia/ Hours: Daily (late May through mid-August). Weekends (April-May, late August-October). Admission: $59.99 regular, $39.99 senior and child (under 48" tall). Season passes and online discounts are worth the effort.*

Six Flags Over Georgia continues to make significant additions to its family offerings. Nine roller coasters, including the Georgia Scorcher, one of the Southeast's tallest and fastest stand-up coasters; as well as Acrophobia with a 200-foot rotating tower drop; will propel you and your family through enough twists and turns to last you for weeks. Five new kids' rides, including the Wile E. Coyote Canyon Blaster and the recent enlargement of the kids' area will entertain little ones and the rest of the family. Here's how to zero in on rides that are just your speed - Use Ride Ratings: MILD - When you want to go for a ride, not break the sound barrier. MODERATE - Fun and fast, but just enough to get the blood pumping. MAX - Better warm up your vocal chords because you're gonna scream. Step inside the Drive-In Theatre for the park's pop music show or meet-n-greet with Loony Tunes. Thomas Town joins the numerous other fun rides and entertainment.

DUNWOODY NATURE CENTER

Atlanta (Dunwoody) - ***5343 Roberts Drive (Rte. 400 north to exit 6) 30338. Phone: (740) 394-3322. www.dunwoodynature.org. Hours: Park is open sun-up to sundown, daily. Nature Center is open Monday-Friday 9:00am-5:00pm, and Saturdays by event. Admission: FREE. Programs and I-SPY rentals ($10.00) carry a fee. Note: Sign up to rent one of their I-SPY Packs and lead your own exploration through the park, any day of the week. Self-guided activities, games, learning tools and more will engage Pre-K through High School students in outdoor learning.***

The Park features wetland, two miles of woodland and streamside trails; display gardens; a picnic meadow; and a shaded playground. The Boardwalk meanders through part of the park and is where you'll learn about the great diversity of plant and animal life in the wetlands without damage to this fragile but hard-working ecosystem. You can even do all of this without getting your shoes dirty. The Nature Center includes a Compost Demonstration Site, How Worms Work, a Honeybee Observation Hive (under guidance, kids may even get to handle the Queen), and the Raptor Information Center (Learn about their habitat, food, habits, building nest boxes for owls, and wing span).

DUNWOODY NATURE CENTER - COCOA AND CANDLES / LIGHT UP DUNWOODY

Atlanta (Dunwoody) - *5343 Roberts Drive, 30338. www.dunwoodynature.org. Phone: (740) 394-3322. The Village is all a-twinkle with a fairyland of luminaries lining the trails and boardwalk. Make a holiday natural wreath and enjoy some cocoa. (Sunday before Thanksgiving)*

SWEETWATER CREEK STATE PARK

Atlanta (Lithia Springs) - ***1750 Mount Vernon Road (follow signs from I-20 exit 44, Thornton Road) 30122. http://gastateparks.org/info/sweetwater/. Phone: (770) 732-5871. Hours: Trails close at dark; other areas close at dark if not in use. Park opens at 7:00am, daily. Admission: $5.00 daily vehicle parking fee.***

Only minutes from bustling downtown Atlanta, nine miles of wooded trails follow the free-flowing stream to the ruins of the New Manchester Manufacturing Company, a textile mill burned during the Civil War. Beyond the mill, the trail climbs rocky bluffs to provide views of the beautiful shoals below. The 215-acre George Sparks Reservoir is popular for fishing, feeding ducks and canoeing. Fishing supplies & snacks are available in the park's bait shop, while maps & park information may be found in the Visitor Center.

REYNOLDS MEMORIAL NATURE PRESERVE

Atlanta (Morrow) - *5665 Reynolds Road (I-75 exit 233, left onto Jonesboro Road. Go 1.5 miles to Huie Road and turn left) 30260. Phone: (770) 603-4188. www.reynoldsnaturepreserve.org. Hours: The Nature Center is open Monday-Friday 8:00am-5:00pm, Admission: FREE.*

The preserve's primarily hardwood forest boasts ponds, wetlands, streams, designated picnic areas and four miles of well defined foot paths. The paths are laid out in convenient loops which bring visitors back to their starting point. The preserve's gardens include a heritage vegetable and herb garden featuring varieties from the late 1800's, a butterfly and hummingbird garden, and a native plants garden. The Georgia Native Plants Trail is wheelchair accessible. Inside the Nature Center you'll find a collection of native amphibians and reptiles as well as an observation honeybee hive and environmental education exhibits.

CHATTAHOOCHEE RIVER NATIONAL RECREATION AREA

Atlanta (Sandy Springs) - *1978 Island Ford Parkway (GA 400 exit 6, onto Dunwoody Place. Go 0.5 miles to Roberts Drive, turn right and go about a mile) 30350. Phone: (770) 538-1200. www.nps.gov/chat. Hours: Island Ford Visitor Center 9:00am-5:00pm daily. Park is open from dawn to dark all year long. Admission: $3.00 daily vehicle parking fee.*

An ancient river in a modern city. The word Chattahoochee means painted rock in the Cherokee language. The Cherokee made their homes along the Chattahoochee river for thousands of years until they were forced out in the early 19th century. Take a solitary walk to enjoy nature's display, raft leisurely through the rocky shoals with friends, fish the misty waters, or hike, bike and picnic along the trails. Most of the river flows at a very lazy pace, but portions can contain up to Class 2 rapids.

STONE MOUNTAIN PARK

Atlanta (Stone Mountain) - *(I-285 exit 39B, US 78 east to exit 8, follow signs-16 miles from downtown Atlanta) 30086. Phone: (770) 498-5690 or (800) 317-2006. www.stonemountainpark.com. Hours: Most open at 10:00am, closing between 5:00-8:00pm. Weather conditions may affect operating schedules. Admission:*

Entrance into Stone Mountain Park requires a $10.00 one day permit per vehicle. This permit gives you access to many of the Park's amenities including the public picnic areas, nature trails, children's playground, walk-up trail and the Lasershow Spectacular. Each attraction: $7.00-$13.00 extra or purchase combos for $22-$40 per person for basically all day passes. Note: Crossroads 1870s theme town, Gristmill picnic area, pedal boats, Paddleboat Cruises, fishing, hiking/nature trails, boat rentals, Beach & Waterslide complex, Geyser Towers waterplay, Several theme restaurants serving buffets and Southern-style sandwiches and chicken dishes. Snow Mountain play area (winter only).

Stone Mountain Park offers so much family fun and adventure, you may just want to get the most value for your money by following a few tips and tricks. Here's just some of the our favorite parts of the lineup of attractions:

The world's largest exposed mass of granite - this mountain ROCKS!

STONE MOUNTAIN: The world's largest exposed mass of granite has a Confederate Memorial carving that is larger than the size of a football field! When workers were carving, they would hide from the elements in the carved horses' mouths. Try doing this same thing at the photo op in the Stone Mountain Memorial Museum.

SUMMIT SKYRIDE: takes guests to the top (825 feet) in high-speed Swiss cable cars. Once on top, walk out onto the top and sides of the mountain! It looks like giant moon craters up there! A must do! Exhilarating! (bathrooms, snacks on top to refresh).

The 1.3 mile ***Walk Up Trail*** to the top of the mountain is esteemed and so worth the effort. Be sure to bring plenty of water. Remember to take pictures once you reach the top! Criss-cross diagonally if you start to become weary climbing and remember the walk back down is ALL downhill.

At the bottom, be sure to take time to wonder through Confederate Hall (free). Watch the Civil War movie and then take a journey through rock history - even walk underneath the mountain (simulated)!

We rode the cable cars to the top and then we walked to the top! Well worth the effort - be sure to do both !

LASERSHOW SPECTACULAR: a modern laser animation projection system transforms brilliant, colorful lights into dramatic stories, historic tales and all sorts of comical characters. With a state-of-the-art surround sound system, dazzling fireworks and a flame cannon shooting fireballs hundreds of feet into the air...this is a great way to end your day. Bring a blanket, grab a snack and lounge chairs and gaze at the evening mountainside. (Nightly each summer, Saturdays only in Spring and Fall).

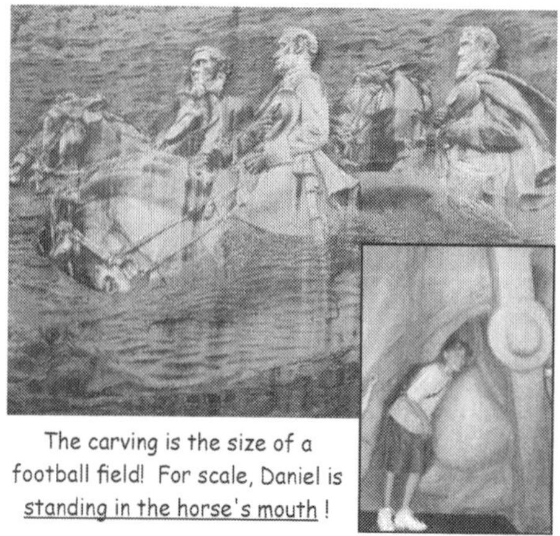

The carving is the size of a football field! For scale, Daniel is standing in the horse's mouth !

RIDE THE DUCKS ADVENTURE: Timed tours. The unique amphibious sightseeing experience takes visitors on a 20 minute tour, on land and water, through a portion of the park. The best part - the fast descent from trolley to boat into the water! Every kid that wants to gets to drive the boat. Along the way, you can't help but give in to the urge to blow your complimentary duck whistle along with the catchy tunes.

Part bus, part boat...sure is fun!

What a great thrill, yet, it was safe fun. Parents & Kids facing challenges together..

SKY HIKE & CAMP HIGHLAND OUTPOST: This treetop adventure is like trekking through the sky - the more you succeed, the higher you can go. It looks easier than it was and we really had to conquer some fears of being "suspended" between rope footholds. Even so, this was a highlight and the attraction is run very safely - parents and kids can face the challenge together while secured to a patented overhead safety system.

Most of these favorite attractions meet or exceed your expectations. The other attractions that are part of the Adventure Pass make for a well-rounded day: Crossroads Kids Shows, Mini-golf, Scenic Railroad rides, the Great Barn indoor playspace where kids collect points for completing tasks, and Tall Tales of the South (or some other theme) 4D Movie. Overnight at the park in a modern resort, the park Campground (largest in the state with 441 sites and high cleanliness ratings), or Stone Mountain Inn - right across the street from the Mountain. They have spacious rooms that are updated and comfortable with a nice courtyard and outdoor pool. Their modest pricing and convenient location add to the perks of special ticket offers only available by staying within the park.

STONE MOUNTAIN PARK - EASTER SUNRISE SERVICE

Atlanta (Stone Mountain) - *Top of Stone Mountain & Memorial Lawn. The Stone Mountain Ministerial Association will present two simultaneous, non-denominational Easter services at the top of Stone Mountain and at the base of the mountain on Memorial Lawn. (Easter Sunday early morning)*

STONE MOUNTAIN PARK - HIGHLAND GAMES

Atlanta (Stone Mountain) - *Experience two days of great fun with Highland athletic events, dancing, piping, drumming, and Scottish Harping. Join in for Scottish country dancing demonstrations, Kirking of the Tartans, Clan Challenge, and the Parade of the Tartans. See the Clan and Tartan information tents along with many colorful Scottish shops. (third weekend in October)*

STONE MOUNTAIN PARK - PUMPKIN FESTIVAL

Atlanta (Stone Mountain) - *The Pumpkin Pyramid – The South's Largest Talking Pumpkin Tree, a hay maze, fall treats and great live entertainment. Guests of all ages can participate in a variety of activities, arts & crafts and contests. (weekends in October)*

STONE MOUNTAIN PARK - POW WOW & INDIAN FESTIVAL

Atlanta (Stone Mountain) - *Native Americans from across the United States will gather to compete in dance and drum competitions. Primitive skills educators demonstrate fire making, basket weaving, hide tanning and prepare Native American foods. Native arts and crafts available for purchase and the kids will love the live buffalo, bear and other animals. (first weekend in November)*

STONE MOUNTAIN PARK - STONE MOUNTAIN CHRISTMAS

Atlanta (Stone Mountain) -*The 1870s town of Crossroads is filled with fascinating townsfolk, entertainers and skilled crafters. The town is decorated with millions of Christmas lights. Families enjoy the live entertainment, the 4D Christmas Movie – Polar Express, train ride with a live show and visiting Santa Claus. Special snowfalls every day. Reduced regular admission. (mid-November thru December)*

Calhoun

NEW ECHOTA HISTORIC SITE

Calhoun - ***1211 Chatsworth Highway NE (one mile east of I-75 exit 317 on GA 225) 30701. Phone: (706) 624-1321. http://gastateparks.org/info/echota/. Hours: Thursday-Sunday 9:00am-5:00pm. Closed Thanksgiving, Christmas and New Years. Admission: $2.50-$6.00 per person.***

The Cherokee National group established New Echota as its capital in 1825. This government seat became headquarters for the independent Indian nation that once covered northern Georgia and parts of four other southeastern states. This is the site of the first Native American newspaper office, the signing of a treaty which relinquished Cherokee claims to lands east of the Mississippi, and finally, the sad assembly of Cherokee Indians for the removal along the infamous Trail of Tears. Many artifacts from the original print shop and methods of archeological digs are on display. Today, the site has a museum where you can view a 17-minute video and then take a self-guided tour of historic buildings. The structures include: a print shop, a court house, Council House, a missionary home, Vann's tavern and several homes and farm buildings. Did you know the Cherokee were the most civilized Indian tribe? Learn some Cherokee language with Sequoyah: si-yo = Hello, ga-du = bread, a-ma = water.

An original printing press

NEW ECHOTA- CHRISTMAS CANDLELIGHT TOUR

Calhoun - *1211 Chatsworth Highway NE 30701. Phone: (706) 624-1321. Bring your candle lantern to kick off the holiday season. We'll celebrate Christmas New Echota-style with decorations, music and refreshments reminiscent of the 19th century Cherokee Nation Capital. Admission. (first Saturday evening in December)*

Canton

CAGLE'S DAIRY FARM

Canton - ***355 Stringer Road (I-75 north to I-575 north. Exit 14 at Holly Springs. Take the right as you come off the ramp at Hickory Road) 30115. Phone: (770) 345-5591. www.caglesfamilyfarm.com. Hours: they are a working farm, so public tour times vary. See online calendar each season. Admission: $7.00 per person. Tours: Tour lasts about 1 hour. They have grassy area to sit and have a picnic lunch.***

Their old-fashioned hayride takes students on a tour of the farm, and makes a great venue for staging the herding demonstrations! Watch Oak and Tib busy herding different groups of farm animals. Meet lots of characters in the Animal Barn.

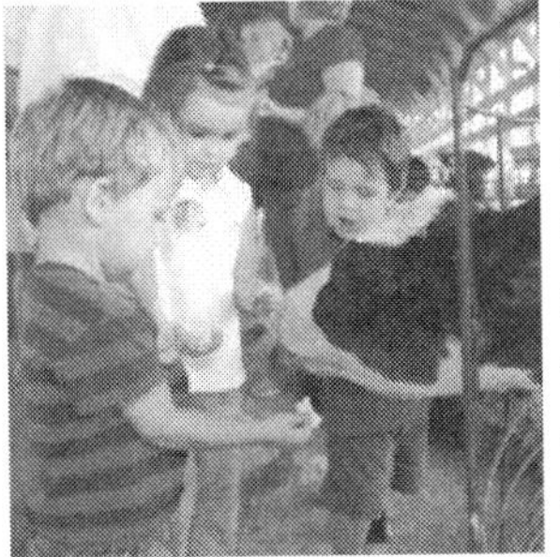

Fall field trips will include some pumpkin picking! A trip thru the corn maze is an additional $7 per person.

Cagle's Dairy was a full milk processing center until recent years, so they share some history on the farm tour with dairy cow milking demonstrations. See more at: http://caglesfamilyfarm.com/school-field-trips/.

CAGLE'S DAIRY FARM - MAIZE

Canton - *The Cagle family and a leading maze designer hope to challenge the wits of those seeking to find the one exit from their mind-boggling puzzle. Though the correct pathway can be walked in 45 minutes, most wanderers will require about one hour to travel more than three miles of twists, turns, and decision points. Enjoy the dairy tour, good farm food, and the option for small children to ride the Cow Wagon Train through the corn stalks. Admission $10. (weekends Labor Day through third weekend in November, Friday-Sunday)*

Carrollton

JOHN TANNER STATE PARK

Carrollton - ***354 Tanner's Beach Road (6 miles west of town off GA 16) 30117. Phone: (770) 830-2222. http://gastateparks.org/info/jtanner/. Hours: Daily 7:00am-10:00pm. Admission: $5.00 daily vehicle parking fee.***

This Georgia park is best known for having the largest sand swimming beach of any Georgia state park. Water lovers find a haven here looking for boating and fishing. Or, enjoy camping, mini-golf, volleyball, pedal boats and horseshoes. The small lodge near the beach has six units, each with fully equipped kitchens, dining area, living area and bedroom. There are two hiking/nature trails - one 1/4 mile and the other 1-mile lake loop trail. Boating is electric motors only.

Cartersville

BARTOW HISTORY CENTER

Cartersville - ***13 North Wall Street (downtown, follow signs from I-75 exit 288) 30120. Phone: (770) 382-3818. www.bartowhistorycenter.org. Hours: Monday-Saturday 10:00am-5:00pm, Sunday 1-5pm, plus Thursday evenings. Admission: $2.00-$3.00 (Students and adults). Educators: www.bartowhistorycenter.org/school.htm for lesson plans.***

Do you know anything about the Etowah Mounds or DeSoto, the Cherokee or General Sherman? Exhibits at the Bartow History Center focus on the settlement and development of Bartow County, Georgia, beginning with the early nineteenth century, when the Cherokee still inhabited the area. Pioneer life, Civil War strife, post-war recovery, the Great Depression era, early industry, and notable figures are depicted through interactive exhibits in the permanent gallery space. At the History Center, kids can practice penmanship on slate boards, recite lessons, and perform school chores to avoid wearing the dunce cap. Learn map skills with games and puzzles at the History Center. Sit down at the switchboard and explore the history of communication from tin can phones to old radio shows.

BOOTH WESTERN ART MUSEUM

Cartersville - ***501 Museum Drive (I-75 exit 288, Main St. Go west 2.2 miles, follow signs) 30120. Phone: (770) 387-1300. www.boothmuseum.org. Hours: Tuesday-Saturday 10:00am-5:00pm, Sunday 1:00-5:00pm. Open late on Thursday evenings. Admission: $10.00 adult, $8.00 senior, $7.00 student (over 12). Children 12 and under and active military get in free anytime but certain Thursday evenings and Saturday mornings, they have free family admission or themed crafts for $1.00. Note: Gift shop and café.***

Daniel rode into town to see some Western Art...

Explore the West without leaving the South! This place is spectacular! The artwork is certainly emotional, whether its a cowboy checking to see who is riding behind them, or a lifelike bull staring you in the face as you exit the elevator.

Start with an orientation film about the history of the West. Then, families are able to check out saddle bags filled with activity sheets and sample artifacts. This "scavenger hunt" method is very engaging and even has a beaded bracelet kit to take home (the rest of the bag's contents remain for the next child). Now, if that wasn't fun enough, head downstairs to Sagebrush Ranch hands-on area. Begin by dressing up as a cowgirl or boy (chaps and all). Take a ride in the rocking stagecoach, sit on a life-size horse or brand a cow. Draw, ride, cook, puzzle or read, too. It's authentic and it's a hoot! Not many art museums are this kid-friendly anywhere - and, such a fun theme - cowboys and Indians. Excellent!

Chuckwagon cookin' with Jenny...

ETOWAH INDIAN MOUNDS HISTORIC SITE

Cartersville - ***813 Indian Mounds Road SE (5 miles SW of I-75 exit 288, follow brown directional signs) 30120. http://gastateparks.org/info/etowah/. Phone: (770) 387-3747. Hours: Wednesday-Saturday 9:00am-5:00pm. Closed Thanksgiving, Christmas and New Years. Admission: $4.00-$5.50 per person. Note: at least once per month, the site holds special themed Indian events on Saturdays. Educators: Online links describe how to create authentic dugout canoes, thatched wattle & daub houses.***

These mounds were the ceremonial center of a town that was home to several thousand Mississippian Indians more that 400 years ago. All the mounds are flat-topped and made from earthen material (dirt). The largest stands 63 acres and appears to serve as the temple for the "Priest-Chief" and as burial sites for Indian nobility. You actually get to climb the 134 steps to walk along the top. In another mound, nobility were buried in elaborate costumes accompanied by items they would need in their after-lives. Many artifacts in the museum show how the natives of this political and religious center decorated themselves with shell beads, tattoos, paint, feathers and copper earrings. You'll see a sample burial site and fish traps. Well-preserved stone effigies and objects made of wood, sea shells and stone are also displayed. This is a mysterious site because these were prehistoric peoples and no one recorded history. The mounds are very well-preserved and fun (but aerobic) to climb.

RED TOP MOUNTAIN STATE PARK

Cartersville - ***50 Lodge Road SE (1.5 miles east of I-75 via exit 285) 30121. Phone: (770) 975-0055 lodge or (770) 975-4226 center. http://gastateparks.org/info/redtop/. Hours: Daily 7:00am-10:00pm. Admission: $3.00 daily vehicle parking fee. Note: July 4th - enjoy the lakeside beach or go on a guided hike. Nature programs, a bluegrass concert, fireworks & more. $2.00 parking.***

Named for the soil's rich red color caused by high iron-ore content, Red Top Mountain was once an important mining area for iron. Now, this park is on Lake Allatoona and is especially ideal for swimming (beach and pool), boating, and fishing. If you don't have a boat, rentals are available. Several hiking trails wind through the park (12 miles of trails, 3/4 mile paved trail behind the restaurant suitable for strollers). One hike spot is a reconstructed 1860s log cabin (open and staffed on Saturdays). The park's lodge and restaurant plus many cottages, offer overnight accommodations. There's also mini-golf and sport courts.

RED TOP MOUNTAIN - CHRISTMAS AT THE CABIN

Cartersville - *Join in an 1860's style Christmas celebration at the log cabin located behind the Lodge. Enjoy old-time Christmas music, open-hearth cooking, primitive toys, and chestnuts on the fire. Breakfast with Santa at the Mountain Cove Restaurant. Pictures available. Dinner at the lodge and enjoy holiday craft activities for children. Local artisans. $5 park pass. (first two Saturdays in December)*

TELLUS NORTHWEST GEORGIA SCIENCE MUSEUM

Cartersville - ***100 Tellus Drive, Hwy 411 (I-75 North to Exit 293 in town of White) 30184. Phone: (770) 606-5700. www.tellusmuseum.org. Hours: Daily 10:00am-5:00pm. Closed most national holidays. Admission: $14.00 adult, $12.00 senior (65+), $10.00 child (3-17) Note: Science In Motion (solar-powered) planetarium. Educators: www.tellusmuseum.org/education/pre-and-postactivities.***

Minerals or "rocks" are very important natural resources for this area. William Weinman, for whom the museum was originally named, was a Barite miner. Barite is used in the manufacture of rubber for tennis balls, golf balls, brake shoes, eye glasses & much more. The largest exhibit contains a fossil dig filled with real and replicated bones, shark teeth, trilobites, and more. Specimens in the museum are likely to generate questions and comments. When kids look at Okenite (from India), you'll hear comments like "cotton balls" and "fuzzy". Okenite is soft, and touching it will destroy its delicate fibers. Try to find the "fuzzy rock" on your visit to the museum!

In My Big Backyard gallery, students have the opportunity to match the life cycle of various insects, match animals to their habitats and to what they eat in the food cycle, and explore other interactive exhibits, complete with rain and snow simulation. "Play" with light, magnets and even an electrical "hair-raising" experiment. There's a Little Kids' Science Garden where they can dig for fossils, tromp through Mad Scientists backyard, and travel to the center of earth. The Great Hall features a full scale cast of an Apatosaurus. At nearly 80 feet, this was one of the largest dinosaurs to ever walk on North America.

BATTLE OF ALLATOONA PASS ENCAMPMENT

Cartersville - *Allatoona Battlefield (I-75 exit 283). www.notatlanta.org. Phone: (800) 733-2280. Visit with Civil War soldiers near the field hospital that still bears bullet holes (home open for tours). Fought on October 5, 1864, this battle was the inspiration for the familiar hymn "Hold the Fort," and is remembered for the summons to surrender message by a Confederate General, "in order to avoid a needless effusion of blood." (October weekend)*

ETOWAH VALLEY INDIAN FESTIVAL

Cartersville - *Sam Smith Park (I-75 exit 288, follow signs to Etowah Indian Mounds) Phone: (800) 733-2280. www.notatlanta.org. Celebrating Cartersville's rich Native American heritage with traditional dance, music, foods, storytelling and educators of traditional crafts and survival skills. Sponsored by the City of Cartersville, the festival is part of a month-long "Cowboys and Indians in Cartersville" extravaganza. FREE for kids, admission for age 16+. (second weekend in October)*

PUMPKIN FEST

Cartersville - *Pettit Creek Farms (I-75 exit 288). Phone: (770) 386-8688. www.pettitcreekfarms.com/pumpkinfest.shtml. Arts & crafts, demonstrations, live music, food court, petting zoo, hayrides, corn maize, pony or camel rides, animals, pumpkin pickin' patch. Admission. (monthlong in October)*

PETTIT CREEK CHRISTMAS HOLIDAY LIGHTS DISPLAY

Cartersville - *Pettit Creek Farms (I-75 exit 288 west). Phone: (770) 386-8688. www.pettitcreekfarms.com. Christmas light show extravaganza open nightly. Hayrides through the lights nightly – bring your lap blanket. Exotic animals, live nativity and Santa with live reindeer. Admission per vehicle (drive-thru) or per person for hayride. (end of November thru end of December, Thursday-Sunday)*

Cave Spring

CAVE SPRING AND ROLATER PARK

Cave Spring - *Cave Spring Square (southwest of Rome, on Hwy 411, South) 30124. Phone: (706) 777-3382. www.cityofcavespring.com/rolater.asp.*

Located in shady Rolater Park, just off the town square, are the natural limestone cave and spring which are the town's namesakes. Open to the public, the cave has impressive stalagmites and the legendary "Devil's Stool" formation. The spring water has won awards for purity and taste and is commercially bottled. Many visitors bring jugs to fill at the spring and take home for drinking. A favorite with locals is swimming in the 1.5 acre chlorine-free invigorating mineral water pool shaped like the state of Georgia. Open daily. FREE.

Chatsworth

CHIEF VANN HOUSE HISTORIC SITE

Chatsworth - *82 GA 225 North (outskirts of town at the intersection of GA 225 and GA 52A) 30705. Phone: (706) 695-2598. http://gastateparks.org/info/chiefvann/. Hours: Thursday-Saturday 9:00am-5:00pm, Sunday 2:00-5:30pm. Closed Monday (except holidays), Thanksgiving, Christmas and New Years. Closed Tuesday when open Monday. Admission: $2.00-$3.00 per person.*

Known as the "Showplace of the Cherokee Nation," the brick mansion was built in 1804 by Chief James Vann, a Cherokee political leader and wealthy plantation owner. "Feared by many and loved by few," Vann was both a hero and a brute. On tour, you'll even see where he fired a pistol at dinner guests through the floor of the upstairs bedroom.

The painted walls within the house represent colors of the earth, sky and harvest. Even President James Monroe stayed here. Their children played Cherokee stickball which is a smaller version of lacrosse. Chief Vann's greatest gift to the Cherokee Nation was the establishment of Springhouse Moravian Mission School. Although the missionaries were interested in bringing the gospel to the tribe, Vann saw an opportunity to educate Cherokee children. The Chief's son, Joseph, became an educated businessman and instrumental voice in the Cherokee legislature. However "Rich Joe" was forced off his property in 1835 at the beginning of the Cherokee removal process.

CHRISTMAS BY CANDLELIGHT CHEROKEE HOME TOUR

Chatsworth - *In 1805, Cherokee Chief James Vann opened his new brick mansion to the Moravian missionaries to hold one of the first Christmas celebrations in the Cherokee Nation. Experience an 1800s Christmas in one of America's best preserved Cherokee Indian homes. Admission. (second weekend in December)*

FORT MOUNTAIN STATE PARK

Chatsworth - ***181 Fort Mountain Park Road (I-75 Exit 333 toward GA 411 & GA 52) 30705. Phone: (706) 695-2621. http://gastateparks.org/info/fortmt/. Hours: Daily 7:00am-10:00pm. Admission: $5.00 daily vehicle parking fee.***

Fort Mountain derives its name from an ancient 855-foot-long rock wall which stands on the highest point of the mountain. The mysterious wall is thought to have been built by Indians as a fortification against other more hostile Indians. Hikers and mountain bikers (14-30 miles) will find beautiful trails that wind through hardwood forest and blueberry thickets, occasionally crossing streams and vistas. For horseback riders, there are horse rentals, stables and 18 miles of trails. During the summer, families can enjoy the sand beach located on a cool mountain lake. 15 Cottages and several campsites are available as well as fishing and pedal boat rental or mini-golf.

Dallas

PICKETT'S BATTLEFIELD HISTORIC PARK

Dallas - ***4432 Mt. Tabor Church Road (I-75 exit 263 west, off GA 381, accessed by Dallas-Acworth Rd. or Due West Road) 30157. http://gastateparks.org/info/picketts/. Phone: (770) 443-7850. Hours: Thursday-Saturday 9:00am-5:00pm. Closed Thanksgiving, Christmas and New Years. Admission: $3.00-$5.50 per person. Note: Hiking trails and picnic sites. Battle Living History Encampment, Homefront cooking and farming demos and Candle Lantern tours, annually.***

Pickett's Mill is one of the best preserved Civil War battlefields in the nation. The scene of this bloody conflict looks much the same today as it did in 1864. Visitors may travel roads used by Federal and Confederate troops, see earthworks constructed by these men, and walk through the same ravine where hundreds died. The Confederate victory resulted in a one-week delay of the Federal advance on Atlanta. The Visitor Center is full of artifacts and exhibits relating to the battle and shows a film.

Dalton

HAMPTON INN DALTON

Dalton - *1000 Market Street (I-75 exit 333) 30720. www.hamptoninn.hilton.com/dalton. Phone: (706) 226-4333. The hotel has a complimentary large hot/cold breakfast with new foods introduced each morning plus fresh fruits. There is also an outdoor pool and an indoor spa. It's located next to an outlet center, Cracker Barrel, Dairy Queen and many other restaurants and shopping within walking distance.*

DALTON CARPET MILL TOURS

Dalton - *(I-75 exit 333 west one block) 30722. Phone: (706) 270-9960 www.daltoncvb.com. Tours: Groups can schedule a tour of a carpet mill by calling the CVB. See some of Catherine's original hand-tufted spreads, as well as chenille made by machine, visit the HAMILTON HOUSE MUSEUM in town.*

A wedding gift started the carpet industry. Catherine Evans Whitener made an bedspread designed with a stitch that locked into the fabric when clipped and washed called a "tuft". The bedspread was so liked by those who saw it that, later she began a cottage industry of making them to sell. The Singer Sewing Machine Company in nearby Chattanooga, Tennessee, took an interest and produced a machine to perform the task more efficiently. The product produced by machine were called "Chenille", the French word for "caterpillar", because the rows of machine-tufted threads resembled the creature. Businessmen experimented with the machines as a way to produce carpet. Their ideas worked. Today carpet mills remain major area employers. See the giant carpet sewing machines that today produce modern carpet styles while on tour.

Dalton is home to the multi-billion dollar carpet industry, making it the "Carpet Capital of the World."

DALTON DEPOT RESTAURANT

Dalton - *110 Depot Street (I-75 exit 333, go east on Walnut to left on Thorton. Right on Crawford, left on Hamilton and then one block to Kings St) 30722. Phone: (706) 226-3160. www.daltondepot.net. The Western & Atlantic Depot of the 1850s served as a Confederate army ordinance depot during the war. It has been converted into a restaurant while maintaining its history. Surrounding the interior is a lengthy mini-railroad track with trains running. Kids can push button control the lobby display. Speaking of trains, you will likely hear a real one go by as you dine (maybe even 3-4 trains!). Upscale Casual. Children's Menu under $5.00, Dinners run $10.00-$16.00. Hours: Open for lunch and dinner, daily.*

BATTLE OF RESACA CIVIL WAR REENACTMENT

Dalton - *Resaca Confederate Cemetery (I-75 exit 333, Walnut Ave. east 2 miles, right on Thornton). Phone: (800) 331-3258. www.friendsofresaca.org. Following the Battle of Resaca, this site became the burial place of 450 Confederates moved from shallow graves around the plantation home of Col. John Green. (third weekend in May)*

BATTLE OF TUNNEL HILL REENACTMENT

Dalton - *Tunnel Hill behind Meadowlawn. Tunnel Hill Heritage Center. Phone: (800) 331-3258. www.tunnelhillheritagecenter.org. General William Sherman took over Meadowlawn while planning his Atlanta campaign. The battle is reenacted to memorialize the heritage and courage of those who fought in our country's most tragic war. (weekend after Labor Day)*

PRATER'S MILL COUNTRY FAIR

Dalton - *Prater's Mill, GA Hwy 2 (I-75 exit 341, north on Hwy 201 to Hwy 2, left 2.6 miles to the mill). Phone: (706) 694-6455. www.pratersmill.org. Self-guided tours of Prater's Mill, Shugart Cotton Gin, 1898 Prater's Store and Westbook Barn; Civil War living history; nature trail; canoeing; pony rides; and barn animals. The 1855 water-powered gristmill still grinds corn and wheat the old-fashioned way. This is also the site of Union and Confederate troops during the Civil War. Southern foods, mountain music, square dancing, and storytelling. Admission. (Columbus Day Weekend, each October)*

Ellijay

APPLE PICKIN' JUBILEE, HILLCREST ORCHARDS

Ellijay - *9696 Hwy 52 East (9 miles east of town). www.hillcrestorchards.net. Pick your own apples or buy some apples and apple products in Grandma's Kitchen. Large picture windows allow you to watch them cooking. The barn is bursting with baby farm animals and a winding trail leads you through the forest filled with scenes from Fairy Tales and Nursery Rhymes. Meet Barney the Talking Bull or the giant Man Eating Catfish aboard one the their tractor-drawn wagons as it travels the orchards laden with apples headed for the "Land of Oz". The wagon goes through the water and below Rainbow Mountain. There are honey bee demos, a pig race, pedal cart track racing & apple bobbing. Admission. (last two weekends in September)*

GEORGIA APPLE FESTIVAL

Ellijay - *Ellijay Lions Club Fairgrounds South of Ellijay, off Hwy. 5. Producing 500,000 bushels of apples each fall, Gilmer County is Georgia's Apple Capital. Great food, a children's section, live entertainment, a parade, and hand-made country products. www.geogiaapplefestival.org. Admission. (second and third weekend in October)*

Fairburn

GEORGIA RENAISSANCE FESTIVAL

Fairburn - *I-85 exit 61 @ Fairburn/Peachtree City. www.georgiarenaissancefestival.com. Enter the gates of elaborate 15th Century Kingdom and you'll be welcomed by over 1,000 colorfully costumed characters on twelve stages packed with great shows, a jousting tournament, a medieval amusement park, and Birds of Prey Show. Feast like a king on an enormous roasted turkey leg or other hand-held foods. Admission. (Mid-April thru early June weekends, including Memorial Day)*

Fort Oglethorpe

CHICKAMAUGA NATIONAL MILITARY PARK

Fort Oglethorpe - ***(I-75 exit 350, then west on Hwy 2, south on 27, follow signs) 30742. Phone: (706) 866-9241. www.nps.gov/chch/index.htm. Hours: Daily 8:00am-5:00pm. Park open till dusk. Closed Christmas Day. Admission: FREE battlefield admission.***

In 1863, Union and Confederate forces fought for control of Chattanooga, the gateway to the deep south. The Confederate's were victorious at nearby Chickamauga in September, but renewed fighting in Chattanooga in November gave Union troops final control. This is the site of the bloodiest two-day battle of the Civil War. In September, 1863, over 100,000 soldiers fought for control of Lafayette Road, resulting in 34,000 casualties. The Cherokee word "chickamauga" means "River of Death."

In the Visitor Center watch a multi-media presentation of the battle. Ranger "soldiers" (in costume) present historical talks near the exit to the visitors Center. They may give you some hints as to why this battle was so fierce (rifled muskets-accurate to 350 yards & could shoot every 20 seconds). The seven-mile tour route includes passing/stopping by: the Gordon-Lee Mansion (home headquarters to US General William Rosecrans - now open by appt. - it's a bed & breakfast); Lee and Gordon's Mill (station for General Braggs Confederate forces before the battle, stronghold station for General Rosecrans during the battle to prevent Confederates from crossing Chickamauga Creek).

CHICKAMAUGA NATIONAL MILITARY PARK - WAR BETWEEN THE STATES DAY

Fort Oglethorpe - *McLemore's Cove at Davis Crossroads (where the Battle was precipitated - 10 miles south of the Battlefield Park). 30742. Phone: (706) 866-9241. www.battleofchickamauga.net. Held during the 3rd weekend in September featuring Living History Demonstrations, Parades, and Arts & Crafts. Activities during the day will include re-enactors demonstrating refugee camp life, artillery firing, soldier camp life and period food. Refugee camps will represent life for area farm families affected by the battle. Ride a Steam Engine to the battle, wash your feet in the creek, period worship service, sutlers row for period wares. (third weekend in September)*

Hampton

ATLANTA MOTOR SPEEDWAY TOURS

Hampton - ***1500 Tara Place (I-75 South to Exit #218 and continue on Highway 20 and follow signs) 30228. Phone: (770) 707-7904 or (770) 707-7970 (tours). www.atlantamotorspeedway.com. Tours: daily and run every half hour during operating hours (Monday-Saturday 9:00am-4:30pm, Sunday 1:00-4:30pm). Tours are just $5.00 adult and $2.00 child. Ages 6 and under are free.***

Thrill to the excitement of NASCAR racing and special racing events watched around the world. Twice a year, Atlanta Motor Speedway is the bustling center of the NASCAR Cup world, filled with hundreds of thousands of fans from all over the country. But the rest of the year, this premier racing facility is open to the public for speedway tours and a behind-the-scenes look. TOURS: Official track tours include a brief track history, a visit to Petty Garden, a tour of one the track's luxury suites, a sneak peek at the garages and Victory Lane and two laps in the Speedway van around the same 1.54-mile track where stars like Jeff Gordon and Dale Earnhardt Jr. race.

Jonesboro

BATTLE OF JONESBORO REENACTMENT

Jonesboro - *Stately Oaks Plantation. Phone: (770) 473-0197. This 1839 planter's home, nestled among live oaks is the site for a day of costumed interpreters and battle re-enactments. Admission. (second weekend in October)*

Kennesaw

SOUTHERN MUSEUM OF CIVIL WAR AND LOCOMOTIVE HISTORY

Kennesaw - *2829 Cherokee Street NW (I-75 exit 273 west) 30144. Phone: (770) 427-2117 or (800) 742-6897. www.southernmuseum.org. Hours: Monday-Saturday 9:30am-5:00pm, Sunday 11:00am-6:00pm. Closed New Years, Easter, Thanksgiving and Christmas time. Admission: $7.50 adult, $6.50 senior (60+), $5.50 child (6-12). FREEBIES: ask for scavenger hunt.*

The true story behind the old Disney movie, "The Great Locomotive Chase," is what the Southern Museum is all about. The museum's star attraction is The General, a steam locomotive nabbed by Yankee raiders in 1862 just 100 yards from where it stands today. The daring band of 22 planned to drive The General north to Chattanooga and destroy Confederate supply lines along the way. Rebels manned a locomotive of their own and chased The General, full throttle, for 100 miles until the raiders were forced to abandon ship. Most were captured. Unfortunately for Kennesaw, a few thousand of their friends came back two years later. The Battle of Kennesaw Mountain that followed was one of the bloodiest conflicts fought during the 1864 Atlanta Campaign.

But the Museum doesn't end there. Peek into Glover Machine Works: An interactive presentation detailing the train building process, from metallurgy and patterns to casting and construction helps visitors experience life as a factory worker. Other kids interactives include tapping out Morse Code; driving a simulated train; or dressing up in the old-timey village.

KENNESAW MOUNTAIN NATIONAL BATTLEFIELD PARK

Kennesaw - *900 Kennesaw Mountain Drive (I-75 exit 269, Barrett Pkwy, follow signs) 30152. Phone: (770) 427-4686. www.nps.gov/kemo. Hours: Daily 8:30am-5:00pm. Admission: FREE admission. The mountain road is closed every weekend and on major holidays. They offer a shuttle bus that will provide transportation to the top of the mountain for $1.50-$3.00 per person fee vs. walking.*

The Confederate Army soundly defeated the Union Army here on June

27, 1864. This important battle brought General Sherman's march toward Atlanta to a halt for two weeks. The name Kennesaw is derived from the Cherokee Indian "Gah-nee-sah" meaning cemetery or burial ground. While walking some of the 17.3 miles of interpretive walking trails you will see historic earthworks, cannon emplacements and various interpretive signs. Atop Kennesaw Mountain is an observation platform and memorial to 14 Confederate generals. Inside the Visitor Center, view interpretive showcases and an 18-minute orientation film. Outside, original earthworks and Civil War artillery can be viewed along marked trails.

Marietta

GEORGIA BALLET

Marietta - *1255 Field Parkway (performances at Cobb County Civic Center's Anderson Theatre. I-75 exit 263 west) 30060. www.georgiaballet.org. Phone: (770) 425-0881.*

This Professional dance company provides a school-year season of many family-oriented ballets. Watch as toymakers or foreign people tell their story through dance. They perform renditions of the famous Nutcracker each year in December.

THE BIG CHICKEN

Marietta - *12 N. Cobb Parkway (I-75 exit 265 west to corner of Hwy 120 & US 41) 30062. Phone: (770) 422-4716.*

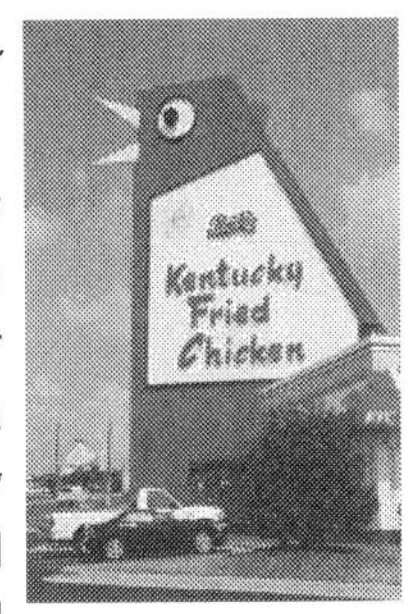

The Big Chicken is the extraordinary sign for a very ordinary KFC in Marietta. In 1963, the owner of a drive-in wanted to draw attention. And thus, Tubby Davis, owner of Johnny Reb's Restaurant, and an egghead Georgia Tech engineering student built the world's first and only post-modern cubist steel chicken. Using locally milled steel, it stands 50-feet tall. Three decades and several owners later, the Big Chicken still rises proudly above Cobb Parkway. Inside the building is a gift shop with all kinds of Big Chicken memorabilia. Its legacy has even spread to surrounding businesses, many using the nomenclature of "Big Chicken This"...

WHITEWATER PARK, SIX FLAGS

Marietta - *250 Cobb Parkway, North (off I-75 north exit 265) 30062. Phone: (770) 424-WAVE. www.whitewaterpark.com. Hours: Vary from 10:00am-6:00pm pre-season and post-season to 10:00am-8:00pm peak season. Park open weekends in*

May, daily Memorial Day- mid August, weekends though Labor Day. Admission: $30-$40 day tickets. Parking $15. Online discounts.

The South's largest water theme park with nearly 50 water play fun activities. A variety of thrilling water slides, rides, attractions, and special areas for small children are featured at this water park where you will find "The Ocean," a 750,000 gallon pool that whips up four foot waves and "The Cliffhanger," one of the tallest freefalls in the world where the rider is propelled 90 feet straight down at high-speed. Or, try the 735-foot-long Run-a-Way River, a vicious four-person tunnel raft ride. If that's not enough, try the "Tornado" (riders are set in motion down a 132-foot long tunnel and thrown into the giant open-ended funnel), Typhoon Twister, Gulf Coast Screamer or Banzai Pipeline.

For Little Kids (and Chickens): There are other ways to play—splash in Little Squirt's Island and Captain Kid's Cove, or just float down one of two lazy rivers. And everybody loves the 750,000 gallon wavepool, family raft rides and body flumes. For Everyone: The Pirate Invasion Dive Show brings Vegas-show glitz and high-diving heroics to the wavepool most weeknights, followed on summer Fridays by "Dive-In Movies." Float up to the big screen or find a seat on the deck for a family-friendly flick. Never was cinema more refreshing.

NORTH GEORGIA STATE FAIR

Marietta - *Jim Miller Park (I-75 exit 260 west). www.northgeorgiastatefair.com. Phone: (770) 423-1330. Start with fair food, amusement rides, to top entertainment concerts. Then add in animal shows and the Human Cannon Ball who is shot across the entire midway several times per day. Admission. (end of September for ten days)*

McDonough

SOUTHERN BELLE FARM

McDonough - ***1658 Turner Church Rd. (I-75 exit 218 take Hwy 81 east thru town, left onto GA 20, follow signs) 30252. www.southernbellefarm.com. Phone: (770) 898-0999. Hours: vary by season, generally Friday, Saturday and Sunday afternoons. Admission: Generally $8.00-$10.00 for 8-10 farm activities. Tours: pre-arranged group tours offer discounted packages and a treat to eat. Picnic at the farm is available, too. Note: Concession Stand. Country Market. We recommend casual attire, very comfy shoes, and maybe a hat for sunny days. FREEBIES: activity sheets on corn, cotton, pumpkin and dairy farming are downloadable online on***

the School Field Trips/Teaching Resources page.

Start your visit with a Hayride through an 80-acre portion of the farm where you can get the 'lay of the land'. Visit the Barnyard and enjoy the antics of silly farm animals. Kids can pet goats and Holstein calves. Try your hand at the Corn Cannon and see how far you can shoot an ear of corn or a tiny pumpkin! The newest attraction is Pig Races at Oinker Stadium. Watch these little squealers charge around the race track and you'll be howling with laughter! Another funny attraction is the Goat Walk skywalk that the resident goats enjoy climbing on. Experience farm life first hand by trying your hand at picking cotton. Visit the dairy barn to see how cows are milked, then ride on the cow train. Or just come out each Fall and enjoy the maze with all of the other folks who are getting lost and having fun!

SOUTHERN BELLE FARM - MAIZE

McDonough - *1658 Turner Church Rd. 30252. www.southernbellefarm.com. Phone: (770) 898-0999. Six acres of fun - twisty-turny paths cut through the corn stalks! It's where getting lost can be so much fun! After sundown, you'll want a flashlight to make your way through the rustling stalks of corn. Take an old-fashioned hayride through the fields to the pumpkin patch and pick your own! (Mid-September thru November 1st)*

Rising Fawn

CLOUDLAND CANYON STATE PARK

Rising Fawn ***- 122 Cloudland Canyon Park Road (on GA 136, 8 miles east of Trenton and I-59) 30738. http://gastateparks.org/info/cloudland/. Phone: (706) 657-4050. Hours: Daily 7:00am-10:00pm. Admission: $5.00 daily vehicle parking fee.***

Located on the western edge of Lookout Mountain, this scenic parks offers rugged geology and beautiful vistas. With elevation differing from 800 to 1,980 feet, the most spectacular views into the canyon are found near the picnic area parking lot. However, additional views can be found along the rim trail. (4.8-mile West Rim and Waterfalls Trail and 2-mile backcountry trail) Rugged hikers might want to walk to the bottom of the gorge to find two waterfalls cascading over layers of sandstone and shale. Cottages are located near the canyon edge, where the park's walk-in campsites provide privacy, too.

Rome

CHIEFTAINS MUSEUM

Rome - *501 Riverside Parkway (between GA 53 & US 27) 30161. Phone: (706) 291-9494. www.chieftainsmuseum.org. Hours: Wednesday-Saturday 10:00am-5:00pm. Closed all major holidays. Admission: $2.00-$5.00.*

The Museum tells the story of Major Ridge, the prominent Cherokee leader who struggles to adapt to the white man's culture while retaining his Cherokee heritage. Located on the banks of the Oostanaula River, Ridge and his family became ferryboat masters, store owners and slave-owning planters nearby. The white clapboard plantation home contains exhibits describing Ridge's life and the history of the Cherokee people.

CHIEFTAINS MUSEUM - CHRISTMAS AT CHIEFTAINS

Rome - *Visit Chieftains' special holiday exhibit. View Christmas trees decorated in the style of different eras: the Ridge Years, Civil War, Victorian, 1930s, 1940s and 1950s. Period toys and Christmas cards on view. Admission. (early Nov thru early January)*

Roswell

BULLOCH HALL

Roswell - ***180 Bulloch Avenue (Intersection of GA Hwy 120 and GA Hwy 9. Bulloch Hall is located just one block west of the Historic Square) 30075. Phone: (770) 992-1731 or (800) 776-7935. www.bullochhall.org. Admission: $8.00 adult, $6.00 student (6-12). Tours: Monday-Saturday 10:00am-3:00pm, Sunday 1:00-3:00pm. Tours on the hour. Educators: Check back often for updated games and pages to color on the For Children Only page, lesson plans for Parents & Educators and specially designed Tours for Children. Christmastime crafts & candy hunt.***

Mittie Bulloch Roosevelt was a Georgia lady who left a legacy that would impact a nation and the world. Her son, Theodore Roosevelt, served as the 26th President of the United States. Her granddaughter would marry Franklin Roosevelt, serve as our nation's First Lady, and change the role of women in the White House. Mittie's childhood home is open for docent-lead tours including the house, slave quarters, garden and grounds.

CHATTAHOOCHEE NATURE CENTER

Roswell - *9135 Willeo Road (I-285 exit US 19 north. Turn left on Azalea, then left on Willeo) 30075. Phone: (770) 992-2055. www.chattnaturecenter.com. Hours: Monday - Saturday 9:00am-5:00pm. Sunday Noon-5:00pm. Admission: $6-$10.00.*

An environmental education facility located on the banks of the Chattahoochee River, the Chattahoochee Nature Center is home to a variety of woodland and wetland critters—waterfowl, birds of prey, reptiles. You might even spot a beaver or otter rippling through a pond. Injured owls, hawks, raccoons, and other animals are brought here for rehabilitation and eventual return to the wild. Short interpretative hiking trails, canoe trips and a scenic river boardwalks let you spend as little as an hour or most of the day in the wilds of this natural habitat without really "roughing it." Live animal demonstrations are usually held in the exhibition center, where you can also watch honey bees at work or peek into "life in a log." Stop by for a morning bird walk, where you'll discover different birds around the park, or stop in for raptor mealtime and watch presentations on the nature center's animals, including every raptor indigenous to the state of Georgia. Among the center's other special programs is an overnight camping experience complete with a workshop on nocturnal animals.

The Creek Indians named the river, **Chatto-hoche**, "river of painted rock".

SMITH PLANTATION HOME

***Roswell** - 935 Alpharetta Street (GA 400/US 19 north exit 7B) 30075. Phone: (740) 641-3978. www.archibaldsmithplantation.org. Admission: $8.00 adult, $7.00 senior (65+), $6.00 child (6-12). Tours: Monday-Saturday 10:00am-3:00pm, Sunday 1:00-3:00pm. Tours leave on the hour. Last tour one hour before closing. Closed New Years, July 4th, Thanksgiving and Christmas. Note: Try to tour with other families, Camps, Fall Farm Days, or a school group - the "kids" version tour is best for grade-schoolers.*

Guides in period costume invite you to spend 45 minutes to one hour with the memories and artifacts of three generations of the Archibald Smith family. Built in 1845, the Smith's livelihood was cotton crops and they kept around 30 slaves to help with the work. In the main house, you will get a chance to touch cotton plants, figure out how long it took to make a simple turkey sandwich for lunch, see an unusual "fly swatter" centerpiece, or glance at family pictures (why aren't they smiling?). Look for the actual 1833 piano that was moved to southern Georgia when the family fled the Yankee invasion.

Outside, you'll peek in working outbuildings - the cook house, a spring house (used as a refrigerator) and a slave cabin.

ANDRETTI INDOOR KARTING

***Roswell** - 11000 Alpharetta Highway (I-75 south to I-285 east to Hwy 400 north to exit 8, left on Mansell, right on Hwy 9) 30076. www.andrettikarting.com. Phone:*

(770) 992-5688. Hours: Monday-Thurs 3:00pm-10:00pm, Friday/Saturday 11:00am-2:00am, Sunday 11:00am - 10:00pm. Admission: Varies, generally each activity $7.00-$12.00 for kids. Note: Andretti Grill restaurant. It's a party scene after dark so best bring kids daytime. You must wear closed-toe, closed-heel shoes.

Got the need for speed? The unique, indoor event center offers oval or road race track driving, rock climbing, high ropes course, and one of the largest arcade areas in the southeast (mostly "speed" oriented games and simulators). The Junior Karts (age 8+) are an indoor, miniature speedway course. Get suited up after you pass your drivers test. The orientation room is where techs (in white lab coats) teach you the basics before you get behind the wheel.

Summerville

JAMES H. "SLOPPY" FLOYD STATE PARK

Summerville - ***2800 Sloppy Floyd Lake Road (3 miles southeast of town via US 27) 30747. Phone: (706) 857-0826. http://gastateparks.org/info/sloppy/. Hours: Daily 7:00am-10:00pm. Admission: $5.00 daily vehicle parking fee.***

This quiet park in northwest Georgia offers outstanding fishing on two stocked lakes. Visitors can hike along three miles of lake loop trails and relax in swings. Children like the playground, feeding fish from the boardwalk and renting pedal boats. A small campground and a few cottages are nestled on tree-covered hillsides.

Waleska

FUNK HERITAGE CENTER

Waleska - ***7300 Reinhardt College Circle (on Reinhardt College campus) 30183. Phone: (770) 720-5970 or (770) 720-5971. www.reinhardt.edu/funkheritage/. Hours: Tuesday-Friday 9:00am-4:00pm, Saturday 10:00am-5:00pm, Sunday 1:00-5:00pm. Closed major holidays. Admission: $6.00 adult, $5.50 senior, $4.00 child. Educators: Pre-visit materials (craft, story, puzzle) online: School Field Trips.***

The museum interprets the story of the Southeastern Indians and the early Appalachian settlers through interactive touch screens, dioramas and exhibits of contemporary Native American art. The museum's giant Theater shows an award-winning film, "The Southeastern Indians", which gives visitors some background into the history of these native people. Outside, a recreated early 19th century settlers' village includes a settler's cabin, woodwright's cabin, blacksmith shop, syrup mill, grain crib, 'tater house, and threshing floor. Can you guess how each of the thousands of tools for craft and trade are used.

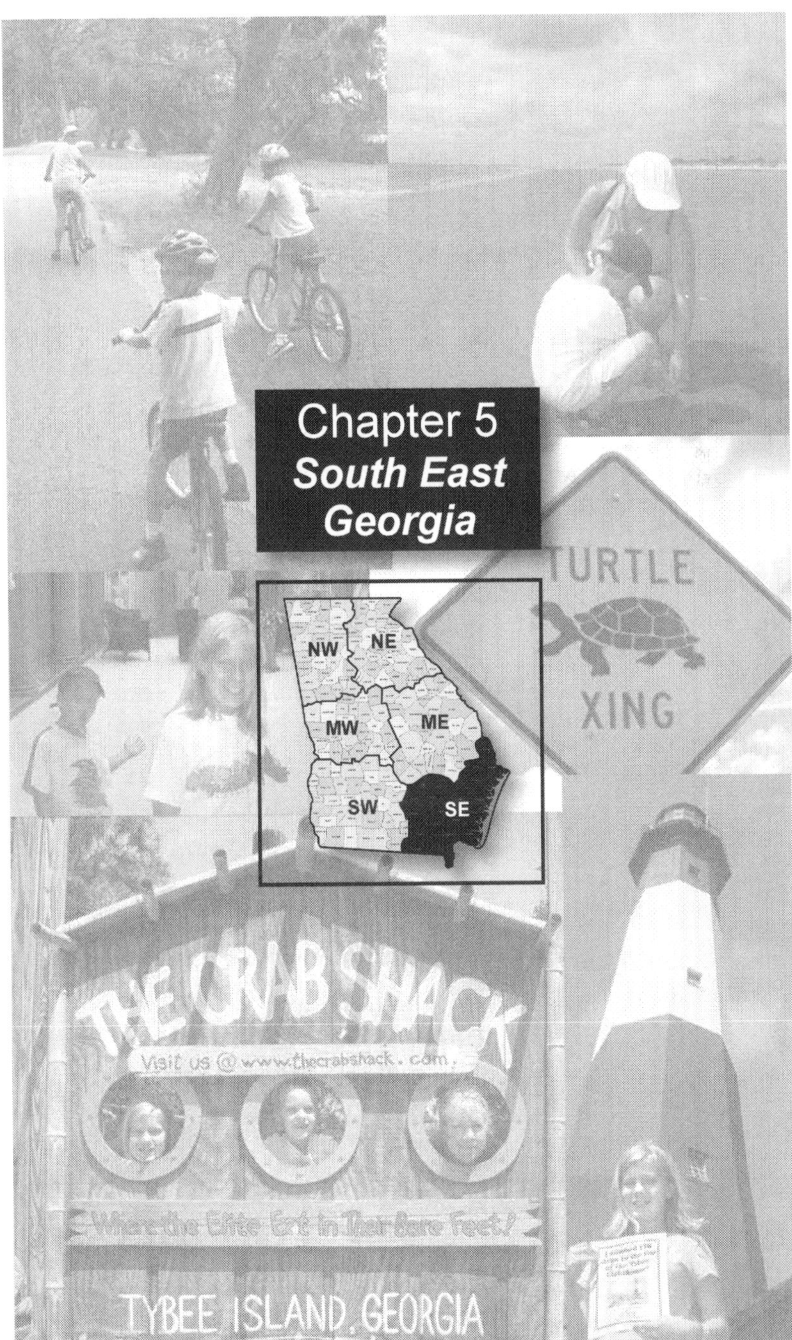
Chapter 5
South East
Georgia
NW
NE
MW
ME
SW
SE
TURTLE
XING
THE CRAB SHACK
Visit us @ www.thecrabshack.com
Where the Elite Eat in Their Bare Feet!
TYBEE ISLAND, GEORGIA

Brunswick

- Mary Ross Waterfront Park
- Mary Ross Waterfront Park - Brunswick Seafood Festival
- Hofwyl-Broadfield Plantation Historic Site
- Hofwyl-Broadfield Plantation Historic Site - Christmas On The Old Plantation

Darien

- Fort King George Historic Site
- Fort King George Historic Site - Scottish Heritage Days
- Fort King George Historic Site - Cannons Across The Marsh

Darien (Sapelo Island)

- Sapelo Island Reserve - Geechee Community Tour

Fargo

- Stephen C. Foster State Park

Folkston

- Folkston Funnel Train Watching
- Okefenokee National Wildlife Refuge

Jekyll Island

- Georgia Sea Turtle Center
- Jekyll Island Biking
- Jekyll Island Museum & Historic District
- Jekyll Island Museum & Historic District - Fireworks Extravaganza
- Jekyll Island Museum & Historic District - Holiday Island
- Summer Waves Water Park
- Tidelands Nature Center
- Villas By The Sea Resort Hotel

Meridian

- Blue Heron Bed & Breakfast

Midway

- Fort Morris State Historic Site
- Seabrook Village

Nicholls

- General Coffee State Park

Odum

- The Maize

Richmond Hill

- Fort McAllister Historic Park
- Fort McAllister Historic Park - Winter Muster & Battle

Savannah

- Comfort Suites Historic District
- Juliette Gordon Low Birthplace
- Juliette Gordon Low Birthplace - Christmas 1886 With The Gordons
- Massie Heritage Center
- Roundhouse Railroad Museum
- Savannah History Museum
- Savannah Trolley Tours, Gray Line
- Whistle Stop Café
- Old Fort Jackson National Historic Park
- Wormsloe Historic Site
- Wormsloe Historic Site - Colonial Faire And Muster
- Wormsloe Historic Site - Colonial Christmas At Wormsloe
- Oatland Island Education Center
- Skidaway Island State Park
- Uga Marine Education Center And Aquarium
- River Street Riverboat Company
- Bamboo Farm And Coastal Garden
- Savannah Ogeechee Canal Museum And Nature Center
- Scottish Games Festival
- 4th Of July At Battlefield Park
- Savannah Southern Lights

Savannah (Pooler)

- Mighty Eighth Air Force Museum
- Oglethorpe Speedway Park

St. Marys

- Crooked River State Park
- Cumberland Island National Seashore
- St. Marys Family Aquatic Center
- St. Marys Submarine Museum
- St. Marys Toonerville Trolley

St. Simons Island

- Barbara Jean's Restaurant
- Best Western Island Inn
- Dolphin Tours - St. Simons Transit Company
- Fort Frederica / Bloody Marsh Battle Site
- Mullet Bay Restaurant
- St. Simons Island Kayak And Canoe Trips
- St. Simons Island Lighthouse
- St. Simons Island Maritime Center
- St. Simons Trolley Tour

Tybee Island

- Captain Mike's Dolphin Tours
- Fannie's On The Beach Restaurant
- Fort Pulaski National Monument
- Fort Pulaski National Monument - Candlelantern Tours Of Fort Pulaski

Tybee Island (cont.)

- Oceanfront Cottage Rentals On Tybee Island
- The Crab Shack
- Tybee Island Marine Science Center
- Tybee Lighthouse
- Sand Arts Festival, Scad

Waycross

- Okefenokee Swamp Park
- Okefenokee Swamp Park - Enchanted Wilderness Light Show
- Obediah's Okefenok
- Laura S. Walker State Park
- Okefenokee Heritage Center
- Southern Forest World

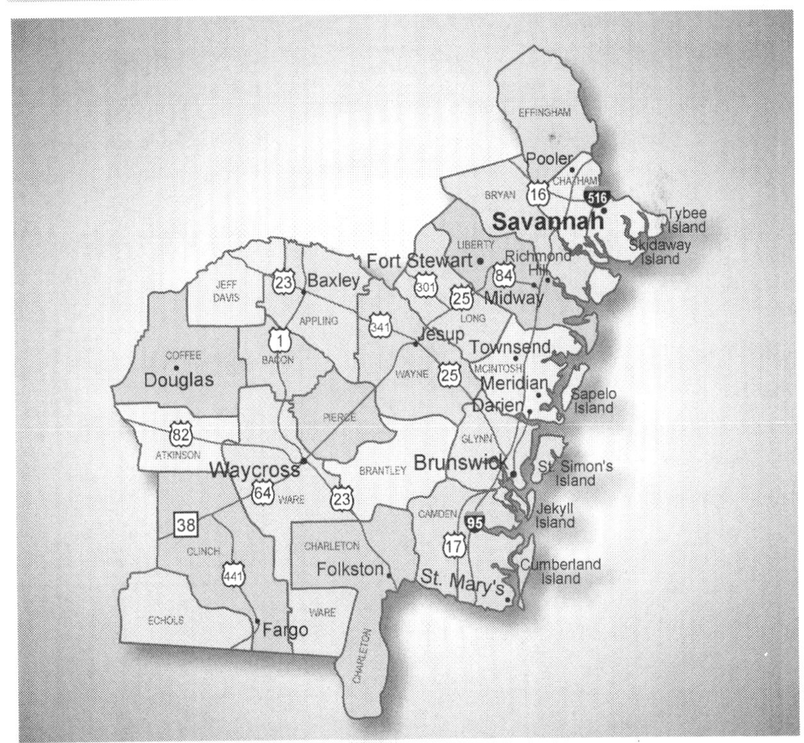

A Quick Tour of our Hand-Picked Favorites Around...

South East Georgia

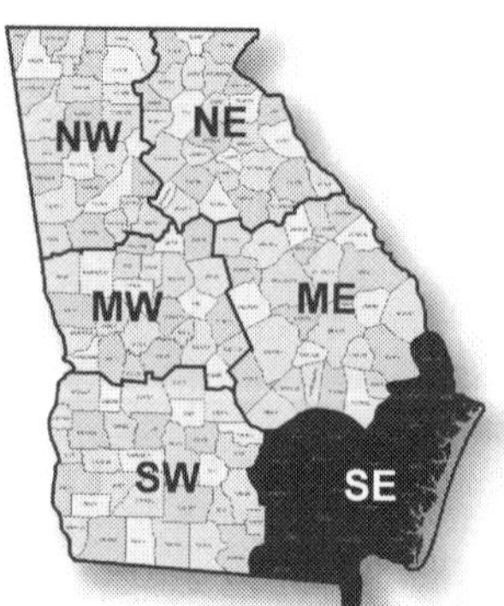

Georgia's five lighthouses, each set on a pristine barrier island, once served as beacons in the night to traveling ships. They now serve as beautiful museums that challenge you to climb their steep steps and take in their spectacular views. There are three climbable beacons, Tybee Light Station, Saint Simons Island Lighthouse and the Sapelo Island Lighthouse. All three islands are famous for their family fun but for very different reasons. **Tybee Island** has an ocean city boardwalk charm with attractions and a big city nearby. **St. Simons** is more laid back in the marshes and **Sapelo Island** is as remote as you can get and still be inhabited – by native Geechee no less! Descendents of plantation workers survive on the island and authentic locals give you the grand tour.

On a bluff overlooking what is now the Savannah River, Oglethorpe founded the state and then helped create the nation's first planned city - **Savannah**. Like St. Simons Island, Savannah is best to get an overview of by **trolley tour**. On tour, they'll point out many points of interest but a girl's favorite may just be the **Juliette Gordon Low Birthplace** – the founder of Girl Scouts. Even boys like to hear the stories of how a spunky rich girl liked to be active, artsy and get into mischief.

Like nature? You can watch dolphins dance on various coastal Island **Dolphin Sightseeing tours**, sea turtles crawl while exploring Jekyll Island on bicycle at the **Georgia Sea Turtle Center**, or encounter live alligator at **Okefenokee Swamp Park** in Waycross.

Sites and attractions are listed in order by City, Zip Code, and Name. Symbols indicated represent: Restaurants Lodging

Brunswick

MARY ROSS WATERFRONT PARK

Brunswick - ***(Brunswick Harbor Market at the end of Gloucester Street) 31520. Hours: Daylight Admission: FREE.***

A scaled-down replica of the WWII workhorse ship, the Liberty Ship is docked here. The park also has outdoor musical playscape (make music on the playground equipment), staged pavilion, farmers market and amphitheater. Brunswick is one of the shrimp capitals of the world. The shrimp fleet may be seen from Bay Street (US 341) between Gloucester and Prince Streets - best late afternoon when the ships come in.

BRUNSWICK SEAFOOD FESTIVAL

Brunswick - *(Brunswick Harbor Market at the end of Gloucester Street) 31520. Phone: (912) 265-4032. www.brunswickgeorgia.net. Fresh seafood prepared in every conceivable way, live entertainment, games for the kids, The Scrapyard Navy Boat Race (for kids at heart), The Brunswick Rotary Club Rubber Duck Race, art and crafts vendors, historic home tours, car, boat and industry displays, and special sales in the Historic Old Town National Register Historic District across the street from the park. (Mothers Day weekend in May)*

HOFWYL-BROADFIELD PLANTATION HISTORIC SITE

Brunswick - ***US Hwy 17 North (I-95 exit 42 east on US 17) 31525. Phone: (912) 264-7333. http://gastateparks.org/info/hofwyl/. Hours: Tuesday-Saturday 9:00am-5:00pm, Sunday 2:00-5:30pm. Last main house tour 1 hour before closing. Closed Monday except holidays. Admission: $2.50-$5.00.***

Around 1807, what was once a vast cypress swamp gave way to a man named Brailsford who carved from the terrain a rice plantation along the banks of the Altamaha River. Some 350 slaves worked the highly productive venture until war, hurricanes and the abolition of slavery caused its decline. Visitors today can see a model of a busy rice plantation, furnishings, and a brief film on the plantation's history before walking a short trail to the antebellum home. The site also includes a nature trail that leads back to the Visitor Center along the edge of the marsh where rice once flourished.

HOFWYL-BROADFIELD PLANTATION - CHRISTMAS ON THE PLANTATION

Brunswick - *This magical experience will demonstrate how Christmas was celebrated on a Southern rice plantation during the 1850s. Take a candlelit stroll down the old carriage road to the owner's home, then get an exclusive peek into domestic life on the plantation during the antebellum period. Admission. (first weekend in December)*

Darien

FORT KING GEORGE HISTORIC SITE

Darien - ***1600 Wayne Street (I-95 exit 49 east) 31305. Phone: (912) 437-4770. http://gastateparks.org/info/ftkinggeorge/. Hours: Tuesday-Sunday 9:00am-5:00pm, Closed Mondays (except holidays) and winter holidays. Admission: $4-$7.00. Educators: There's a link to School Programs and it has some thorough lesson plans for teachers and worksheets for students.***

From 1721 until 1736, Fort King George was the southern outpost of the British Empire in North America. His Majesty's Independent Company garrisoned the fort. They endured incredible hardships from disease, threats from the Spanish and Indian nations, and the harsh, unfamiliar coastal environment. After the fort was abandoned, General James Oglethorpe brought Scottish Highlanders to the site in 1736. The settlement eventually became the town of Darien and saw milling became a major industry. A museum and film cover the Scots of Darien and 19th century sawmilling when Darien became a major seaport. Walk around a fort replica as well as remains of three sawmills and tabby ruins.

FORT KING GEORGE HISTORIC SITE - SCOTTISH HERITAGE DAYS

Darien - *In 1736, General James Oglethorpe brought a group of Scottish Highlanders to Georgia. In this event, they pay tribute to those brave Scots who settled Darien. A reenactment of the Battle of Bloody Marsh will be conducted along with other festivities related to Scottish culture and lifestyle. Admission. (last weekend in March)*

FORT KING GEORGE HISTORIC SITE - CANNONS ACROSS THE MARSH

Darien - *Celebrate America's birthday at this coastal fort with cannon firings, living history tours, demonstrations and free watermelon. Admission. (Saturday after July 4th)*

SAPELO ISLAND RESERVE - GEECHEE COMMUNITY TOUR

Darien (Sapelo Island) - *Sapelo Island Visitors Center (35 minutes north of Brunswick, US 17 to Darien, go east on GA 99 to Meridian, follow signs to ferry and Reserve) 31305. http://gastateparks.org/info/sapelo/ or www.sapelonerr.org. Phone: (912) 437-3224. Hours: Center: Tuesday-Friday 7:30am-5:30pm, Saturday 8:00am - 5:30pm, Sunday 1:30-5:00pm. Admission: 1/2 day tours: $10.00 adult, $6.00 child (6-12). Tours: Half- and full-day tours Wednesday 8:30am-12:30pm (mansion and Island) and Saturday 9:00am-1:00pm (lighthouse and island). An additional tour is offered Friday 8:30am-12:30pm (lighthouse and island) - summer only Extended tour offered the last Tuesday of the Month (March-October), 8:30am-3:00pm (lighthouse, mansion and island). Reservations are required. Miscellaneous: Check in at the Visitors Center where you can orient to the area via displays on the history and culture of this remote island. Pack a backpack with snacks and water or purchase food at the small café on the island (a stop on the tour). Bicycles aren't allowed on DNR ferry rides, but you may rent bikes on the island. Campgrounds and group lodging.*

The lighthouse before and after

This unique, undeveloped barrier island is one of the last places where the Geechee culture is lovingly maintained by residents, many of whom are the descendants of slaves. The similarities that link the cultures of Georgia's sea islands and the Windward Rice Coast of West Africa are generally referred to as the "Gullah Connection." Geechee distinguishes the language and slaves of Coastal Georgia. Gullah dialects, which combine English with the languages of African tribes, is still somewhat spoken here. During the guided tour of the island you will visit the antebellum mansion or the restored lighthouse, depending on the day that you visit. You'll see virtually every facet of a barrier island's natural community, from the forested uplands, to the vast salt marsh, and the complex beach and dunes systems. We learned and saw: ruins of a sugar mill; sampling leaves from a Toothache Tree (Prickly Ash) - we bit them and then rubbed it on our tongue or gums - it numbs it!; talked with natives, especially chatting with

A peaceful solitude here for sure...

Geechee woman, Cornelia for a story or two; casting a net and examining your catch; and stop at the Post Office and mail yourself a postcard from the Island. Explore the Reynolds Mansion (highlights were the solarium, gameroom and circus ballroom). Want

Jenny tries her hand at "cast-net" fishing...seems like a natural...

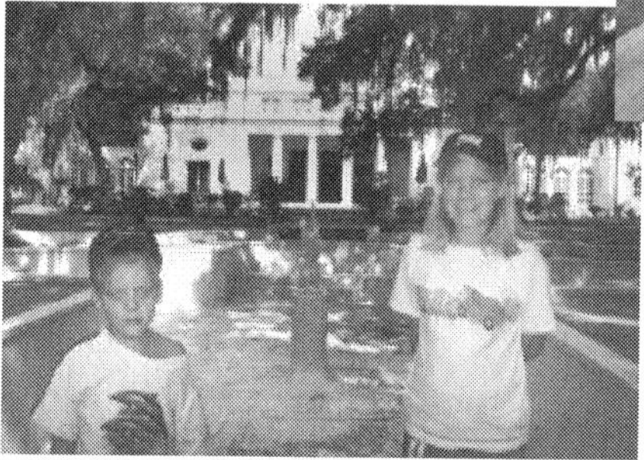

The Reynolds Mansion was an interesting surprise. Feel "rich for a day"...

to spend a couple of nights? You can – group rates are available! Climb the winding stairs of the lighthouse and explore the beach or wade in the water. Like sand dollars and starfish? You can collect gobs of them as a souvenirs!

Fargo

STEPHEN C. FOSTER STATE PARK

Fargo - ***(18 miles northeast of town via GA 177) 31631. Phone: (912) 637-5274. http://gastateparks.org/StephenCFoster Hours: Daily 7:00am- dark. Admission: $5.00 daily vehicle parking fee.***

Named after songwriter Stephen Foster, this remote park is a primary entrance to the famed Okefenokee Swamp. Moss-laced cypress trees reflect off the black swamp waters and visitors can look for alligators, turtles, raccoon, black bear, deer and hundreds of species of birds while on the park's elevated boardwalk. Take the guided boat trip or (for the more adventurous), rent motorized boats or canoes for further exploration of the swamp, including a trip to historic Billy's Island.

Visitors learn not only about alligators and cypress trees, but also how buildings can be made from recycled car parts and plastics in the Visitors Center. The center overlooks a bend in the black water river where people can fish and launch boats. Inside, visitors learn that tannic acid produced by decaying vegetation is what gives the river its tea color, and that unlike other reptiles, mother alligators actively care for their babies. Animal displays include a black bear, bobcat, fox squirrel, otter, snakes, alligator snapping turtle, carnivorous plants, tree frogs, fish and numerous birds, including an endangered wood stork. A short film takes visitors on a leisurely trip through the river and swamp, highlighting flowers, insects, misty morning fog and the many creatures that call the waters home. The center also includes exhibits on the timber industry and local history. The park contains cottages and modern campgrounds.

Folkston

FOLKSTON FUNNEL TRAIN WATCHING PLATFORM

Folkston - *103 N. First Street 31537. www.folkston.com/trains/trains.htm. Phone: (912) 496-2536. Hours: More than 60 trains pass through this spot each day.*

The "Folkston Funnel" is a double track which serves as the main artery for railroad traffic into and out of Florida. From the viewing platform in Folkston, visitors can see trains passing on their way to and from Florida in the south, and a split north of town where trains go west and north. The trains traveling through Folkston carry automobiles, coal, gravel, phosphate, grain, molten sulphur, and orange juice. Several Amtrak trains pass daily, including the Autotrain. The lighted platform features a scanner to listen in to radio traffic between trains. Adjacent to the platform are picnic tables, a grill, and a new restroom facility. Trains can also be enjoyed from the grounds of the restored Folkston depot, just diagonally across the tracks from the platform. Most folks who have visited this site claim it's one of the best viewing areas anywhere.

OKEFENOKEE NATIONAL WILDLIFE REFUGE

Folkston - *Okefenokee Parkway (8 miles southwest of town on SR 121/23, then 4 miles west of main entrance) 31537. http://okefenokee.fws.gov. Phone: (912) 496-7836. Hours: Daily sunrise to sunset. Admission: General Admission Fee is $5.00 per vehicle. Visitors Center open Thursday-Monday 9am-5pm.*

This swamp remains one of the oldest and most well preserved freshwater areas in America. Okefenokee is a vast bog inside a huge, saucer-shaped depression that was once part of the ocean floor. Okefenokee is the derivative of the Indian words meaning "Land of the Trembling Earth". Peat deposits, up to 15 feet thick, cover much of the swamp floor. These deposits are so unstable in spots that one can cause trees and surrounding bushes to tremble by stomping the surface! Why are some swamp waters tea-colored?

Jekyll Island

DOLPHIN TOURS - ST. SIMONS TRANSIT COMPANY

St. Simons Island - *(departs from Historic Jekyll Island Wharf marina) 31527. Phone: (912) 635-3152. www.captainphillips.com Admission: $24.00 adult, $12.00 child (10 and under) Tours: 90 minutes long. Departures Monday-Saturday at 11:00am & 1:30pm. Off season (Labor Day-February) are only Tuesday and Saturday at 11:00am. Note: Boats are fully sun-covered with bathrooms on board.*

See dolphin frolicking in their natural habitat as you explore the marshes, the sound and tidal rivers. Comfortable, shaded tour boats offer plenty of move-about room to get a great view of the dolphins. Cruise the inland waters, so it is never rough. You will also enjoy marvelous views of shrimp boats, local birds and wildlife. Adequate and comfortable seating allows a maximum of 40 passengers. The captain and crew share a relaxed overview of the coastal environment.

GEORGIA SEA TURTLE CENTER

Jekyll Island - *214 Stable Road 31527. Phone: (912) 635-2284 or 912-635-4036 Center. www.georgiaseaturtlecenter.org. Hours: Daily 10:00am-5:00pm. Closed winter Mondays. Admission: $5.00-$7.00 age 4+. Tours: 8:30 and 9:30pm (June thru mid-August). Any age is welcome with a parent; children over age 12 can participate unattended with parental permission. Note: Video presentation and exhibits detail the history of the island from the native inhabitants to the present.*

Be especially careful during the turtle "rush hour"...

TURTLE WALKS: Under a cover of darkness, female Loggerhead sea turtles swim ashore, make their way across the sand, dig their nests and lay their eggs. Designated a threatened species by state and federal law, loggerhead sea turtles have found safe haven on Jekyll Island. Their nests, tucked among the dunes of Island beaches are the treasure find of the tours. Following a description of sea turtles and their habitat, local wildlife guides conduct shoreline walks in search of turtle tracks and nesting mothers. From a safe distance, participants view the fascinating pageant of life as 80-100 eggs are deposited in the nest.

CENTER: The old Power Plant is now used as a combination of exhibit space, hospital, classroom, office, and gift shop, all rolled into one. The Georgia Sea Turtle Center has had a wide variety of patients come through its doors since opening in June 2007. Visitors to the Georgia Sea Turtle Center explore exhibits on sea turtle conservation, rehabilitation, and their amazing journey from egg to adulthood. Daily programs include patient updates and dinnertime feeding.

JEKYLL ISLAND BIKING

Jekyll Island - ***Beachview Drive (begins at mini golf) 31527. Phone: (912) 635-2648 or (877) 4-JEKYLL. www.jekyllisland.com/ biking/. Hours: Daily 9:00am to 5:00 to 7:00pm. Admission: Rentals: $5.00-$7.50 per hour or $13 per day per bike. Helmets and child seats or baskets available. Georgia law requires children 13 and under to wear bike helmets. FREE if you bring own bikes. Note: Mini-golf $5.00 per game. Two courses.***

Over 20 miles of trails...what fun!

More than 20 miles of paved paths circle the island, providing a scenic ride for both the serious cyclist and pleasure biker. Starting from the rentals by mini-golf, travel two miles along the beach with ocean views and dunes. Continue on the North Loop past canopies of live oaks. To extend the ride, take the path to your right by the gate past Villas by the Sea to meander through the Clam Creek area. You'll be right in the middle of a marsh. Loop around the fishing piers, down more canopies of oaks draped in Spanish Moss towards the Historic District. Once in the Historic District, continue straight toward Jekyll Island Club on road ahead. Pass behind the hotel, by Faith Chapel and Villa Marianna. Continue down Old Plantation Road and stop at the Island Museum. Want more forest environs? Head to South Loop near Tidelands Nature Center. Once through the forest, head out towards the Beach again and see "Glory" Beach, where the movie was filmed.

JEKYLL ISLAND MUSEUM & HISTORIC DISTRICT

Jekyll Island - ***100 Stable Road (west end of island directly across from entrance to Island Club) 31527. Phone: (912) 635-4036. www.jekyllisland.com. Hours: Daily 9:00am-5:00pm, except holidays. Tours: For more information on pricing and***

tour availability or to make reservations, please call the Jekyll Island Museum.

Take a brief walk through the American Indian history, past the Millionaire's era up to the present at the island. Simulate the first intercontinental phone call made using two old-fashioned pay phones. Or, light up the Archeological Mystery boxes and see what glows.

JEKYLL ISLAND - FIREWORKS EXTRAVAGANZA

Jekyll Island - *(west end of island across from entrance to Island Club). Fireworks Extravaganza at the beach. Fun Zone. FREE. (July 4th)*

JEKYLL ISLAND - HOLIDAY ISLAND

Jekyll Island - *(west end of island directly across from entrance to Island Club). Christmas Light Tours - Guides take you on an one-hour evening tram tour through the Historic District in all its holiday splendor. Magical Night of Christmas Stories – Museum guides weave Christmas stories the first Saturday in December. Professional storytellers and refreshments. Bingo with Santa – Hot cocoa, punch and cupcakes. Santa calls the numbers for bingo at Villas by the Sea Resort. Admission. (weekends in December)*

SUMMER WAVES WATER PARK

Jekyll Island - ***210 South Riverview Drive (next to the marsh on Riverview Drive) 31527. Phone: (912) 635-2074. www.jekyllisland.com/summerwaves/index.asp. Hours: Vary by season. Daily from Memorial Day to Labor Day and on select weekends in May and September. Monday-Thursday 10:00am-6:00pm, Friday-Saturday 10:00am-8:00pm, Sunday 11:00am-7:00pm. Admission: $16.00-$20.00 (age 4+). $11.00 senior (60+) and Night Splash. Note: Changing areas, restrooms and eateries are available.***

More than one million gallons of splashing water fun and 11 acres of rides. Gather your courage for the Pirates Passage, a totally enclosed speed flume that jets riders over three humps in total darkness or the Force 3 inner tube flume. Or, catch a wave in the Frantic Atlantic wave pool and enjoy a lazy inner tube ride on Turtle Creek. For kids under 48" tall, Summer Waves kiddie pool offers carefully supervised water playgrounds complete with slides and waterfalls in just 12 inches of bubbling water. (inner tubes and life vests are provided throughout the park at no charge).

TIDELANDS NATURE CENTER

Jekyll Island - ***100 Riverview Drive (next to Summer Waves Water Park) 31527. Phone: (912) 635-5032. www.tidelands4h.org. Hours: Monday-Saturday 9:00am-4:00pm, Sunday 10:00am-2:00pm. Admission: $4.00 (age 4+). Boat rentals - $15.00/hour.***

Have you ever touched a live seashell? Now you can. Stop by and visit a young sea turtle, corn snake, fish, alligators and other species native to Georgia's coast. Aquariums and touch tanks on site specialize in the local ecosystems. Touch a starfish and many crabs - even pet turtles. The touch box room is a stop for kids (near the end so they can apply what they've learned). Our favorite part has to be the hatchling loggerhead turtles that are being raised here. You'll be mesmerized as they watch you and show off their giraffe-like legs, thick "log" neck and pretty yellow, orange and brown color. (Note: if you can't go out looking for turtle nests - they have a great diorama of a mother nesting that shows the instinctive habit they have every summer). There is also a self-guide nature trail. Sign up for nature walks to the beach or marsh. Maybe even go seining - kick off your shoes and learn to use a seine net to capture creatures in the surf.

VILLAS BY THE SEA RESORT HOTEL

Jekyll Island - *1175 N Beachview Drive 31527. Phone: (912) 635-2521 or (800) 841-6262. www.villasbythesearesort.com. Lovely villas with fully equipped kitchens, private living room/dining areas full baths, separate bedroom(s) and private patio or balcony. 1,2, or 3-bedroom villas nestled among 17 acres of stately oaks with a partially shaded large pool area and 2,000 feet of oceanside beach. Restaurant with early bird specials and a Kids Menu. Other amenities include bicycle rentals for Jekyll's 20 miles of scenic paved trails, playground, volleyball, badminton, and basketball. $100.00-$200.00 per night. Lower rates available for mid-week and weekly stays.*

Meridian

BLUE HERON BED & BREAKFAST

Meridian - *1 Blue Heron Lane (I-95 exit 58, GA 99 southeast towards Sapelo Island ferry, 1 1/2 mile before ferry, left on Sea Breeze Drive) 31319. Phone: (912) 437-4304. www.blueheroninngacoast.com. Wanna spend the overnight on a real marsh (teaming with shrimp, blue crab, blue heron, egrets and maybe an alligator or snake)? Most all the rooms are facing the marsh, with private balconies. A luscious freshly prepared gourmet breakfast (their signature lime French toast - or plain for the kids) is part of your stay. Bill and Jan are gracious hosts and the modern home is minutes away from the ferry over to Sapelo Island where you can tour the remote island (see separate listing). Have a boat? The owners say families can stay for days if they bring water transportation. Nice combo for adventuresome families. Great comfy hospitality inside, yet wildlife galore outside. Rates around $125-200.00/night.*

Midway

FORT MORRIS STATE HISTORIC SITE

Midway - *2559 Fort Morris Road (I-95 exit 76 via Islands Highway and Fort Morris Road) 31320. Phone: (912) 884-5999. http://gastateparks.org/info/ftmorris/. Hours: Thursday-Saturday 9:00am-5:00pm. Admission: $1.00-$4.50.*

When the Continental Congress convened in 1776, the delegates recognized the importance of a fort to protect their growing seaport from the British. When the British demanded the fort's surrender in 1778, the defiant Col. John McIntosh replied, "Come and take it!" The British refused and withdrew back to Florida. This Revolutionary War fort was eventually captured by the British in 1779, then used again by Americans during the war of 1812. Today, visitors can stand within the earthwork remains and view scenic Saint Catherine's Sound. A museum and film describe the colonial port of Sunbury and the site's history. There is a one mile nature trail on the premises. Reenactments occur seasonally.

SEABROOK VILLAGE

Midway - *660 Trade Hill Road (east on US 84, four miles east of I-95, turn left on Trade Hill Road) 31320. Phone: (912) 884-7008. www.seabrookvillage.org. Hours: Tuesday-Saturday 10:00am-4:00pm and by special arrangement. Admission: $1.50-$3.00 for walking tours. Fees vary for groups. Tours: Interactive tours available for groups of 15 or more. Note: Special events include story-telling, hay rides, cane grinding, clay chimney building, Country Christmas and more.*

Seabrook Village features eight turn-of-the-century buildings on a developing 104-acre site. Visit the one-room Seabrook School where "reading and writing and arithmetic were taught to the tune of a hick'ry stick." Next, visit the homesteads and try your hand at grinding corn into meal and grits or washing clothes on a scrub board. Exhibits include the Material Culture Collection of hand-made items from a peanut roaster to twig furniture. Planned group visits (our recommendation to get the full effect) are fully interactive as costumed interpreters engage visitors in all aspects of old time village life.

Nicholls

GENERAL COFFEE STATE PARK

Nicholls - *46 John Coffee Road (6 miles east of Douglas on GA 32) 31554. Phone: (912) 384-7082. http://gastateparks.org/info/gencoffee/. Hours: Daily 7:00am-10:00pm. Admission: $5.00 daily vehicle parking fee. Note: look for monthly*

Pioneer Skills Day or seasonal hayrides and refreshments.

This park is known for interpretation of agricultural history at its Heritage Farm, with log cabins, a corn crib, cane mill, barnyard animals, tobacco barn and others. A 17-mile river winds through a cypress swamp where the park harbors rare and endangered plants. The threatened gopher tortoise make their homes in this longleaf pine/wiregrass natural area. Overnight accommodations include camping and cottages. Their 4 mile hiking trails include nature trails and a boardwalk. The river dock rents canoe and pedal boats.

Odum

THE MAIZE

Odum - *1765 Hyma Poppell Loop (Hwy 341 north, look for signs). www.poppellfarms.com. Hayrides to the pumpkin patch (includes pumpkin), petting farm, games, catfish pond, duck race pond, and bounce house included with regular admission. Add on the Corn Maze with a different "current events" theme each year. Evening flashlight thru maze. Admission. (October thru the first weekend in November)*

Richmond Hill

FORT MCALLISTER HISTORIC PARK

Richmond Hill ***- 3894 Fort McAllister Road (10 miles east of I-95 on GA Spur 144, exit 90) 31324. Phone: (912) 727-2339. http://gastateparks.org/info/ftmcallister/. Hours: 8:00am-5:00pm (museum). Park open 7:00am-10:00pm. Admission: $4.50-$6.50 per person. Educators: link to detailed information about the fort and the short battle that ended Sherman's March to the Sea.***

The sand and mud earthworks were attacked seven times by Union ironclads, but did not fall until captured in 1864 by General Sherman during his infamous "March to the Sea". The museum interprets the best-preserved earthwork fortification of the Civil War using numerous themed displays. The interior design of the museum resembles a bombproof shelter and also contains a gift shop and shows a video on the history of the site regularly. This park is a quiet location for camping, hiking, fishing and picnicking. There are 4.3 miles of hiking and biking trails.

FORT MCALLISTER HISTORIC PARK - WINTER MUSTER & BATTLE

Richmond Hill - *Enjoy a day of fort activities leading up the 15-minute battle that captured Fort McAllister. Witness and smell the battle that ended Sherman's March to the Sea. Admission. (second Saturday in December)*

Savannah

COMFORT SUITES HISTORIC DISTRICT

Savannah - *630 West Bay Street (under bridge). 31401. www.comfortsuites.com. Phone: (912) 629-2001. Located within walking distance of the historic area including River Street and City Market, each spacious suite has a microwave and frig. There is also a heated indoor pool, spa and complimentary deluxe continental breakfast. Off season rates start at $89.*

JULIETTE GORDON LOW BIRTHPLACE

Savannah - ***10 East Oglethorpe Avenue (corner of Bull Street and Oglethorpe Avenue) 31401. Phone: (912) 233-4501. www.juliettegordonlowbirthplace.org/. Hours: Monday-Saturday 10:00am-4:00pm, Sunday 11:00am-4:00pm. Closed winter Wednesday, major holidays. Admission: $9.00 adult, $8.00 student (5-21), $25.00 family (up to 2 adults/4 children). Girl Scout adult chaperone $8.00, Girl Scout $7.00. Note: Ask for the special visit Girl Scout pin at the Museum shop (about $3.50 to purchase). Guided tours begin every so often.***

Juliette Gordon Low, founder of the Girl Scouts, is one of the most famous women in American history. She was born in Savannah, and her home serves as a Historic Landmark. Begin on a guided tour and hear firsthand about the Gordons, a great American family. From William Washington Gordon I, founder of the Central of Georgia Railroad, to his world famous granddaughter. Enjoy funny stories of the spirited "Nelly" Gordon (loved to slide down the curved staircase) and "Daisy" Low (Juliette, a creative artist - look for her sculpture and paintings throughout the house). Juliette Gordon Low, multi-talented and quirky but severely hearing impaired, founded the organization of productive fun for young ladies. Why is the Boy Scout founder very connected to the founding of Girl Guides? "Come right over! I've got something for the girls of Savannah and all America and all the world and we're going to start it tonight!" - Juliette's famous words that started the Girl Scouts in 1912 to become one of the most significant organizations of the time. She gave the girls of America the career opportunities, outdoor activities and the fun they so desperately wanted.

JULIETTE GORDON LOW BIRTHPLACE - CHRISTMAS 1886 WITH THE GORDONS

Savannah - *Step back in time at the Juliette Low Birthplace, beautifully decorated for the holidays. Explore customs during the Victorian era. The table is set for Christmas dinner, the stockings are ready in Mama's bedroom, and the vintage "Game of Merry Christmas" is out. Come for a taste of Christmas 1886. Admission. (end of November to end of December)*

MASSIE HERITAGE CENTER

Savannah - ***207 East Gordon Street (Calhoun Square) 31401. Phone: (912) 201-5070. www.massieschool.com. Hours: Monday-Saturday 10:00am-4:00pm, Sunday Noon-4pm. Simply ring the bell to the right of the front doors. Admission: $7.00 adult, $5.00 child (5-17). FREEBIE: Savannah Coloring & Activity History Guide - a wonderful print-off booklet to complete as you traverse this famous city and state on your sidetrips on the Georgia coast. Educators: a Kids Page covers more activities-even a cookie recipe and word search.***

The old school house provides group participation including the:

- HERITAGE CLASSROOM - You can experience lessons just like those of students a hundred or more years ago... sit up straight and place your folded hands on top of your desk. Lessons include oral recitation and even penmanship using real quill pens. Do your arithmetic and take your spelling test using a slate board.
- SAVANNAH'S CITY PLAN - It is the old city of Savannah as it developed according to James Edward Oglethorpe's plan from 1733 to 1856 when all of the publicly owned land was used up.
- THE DEBATABLE LANDS - Over a span of 12,000 years, Native Americans built villages and forts, burial grounds and playgrounds, and summer and winter camps. When Europeans finally arrived, they built their towns on or near these earlier inhabited sites. The space informs visitors about the history of Chatham County and Coastal Georgia prior to Oglethorpe's arrival in 1733.

Also, displays on the Victorian Era and Classical architecture are covered.

SAVANNAH HISTORY MUSEUM

Savannah - ***303 Martin Luther King Jr. (adjacent to the Savannah Info Center) 31401. Phone: (912) 238-1779. www.chsgeorgia.org/shm/home.htm. Hours: Daily 9:00am-5:00pm. Opens at 8:30am weekdays. Admission: $4-$7.00 (age 2+). Note: nearby (41 MLKing Blvd) is the Ships of the Sea collection (miniature ship models) displayed within the Scarbrough House (www.shipsofthesea.org).***

This museum is housed in the old railroad passenger train shed. Inside, you can see rare dugout canoes and 1800s fashion. Highlighted exhibits include an 1800 cotton gin, Central of Georgia steam locomotive Baldwin #403, Juliette

The Forest Gump park bench from the movie "Forest Gump"

Gordon Low's family carriage and Forrest Gump's bench (with pics from the movie and even his little suitcase). An 18-minute video overview of Savannah explains the founding of the city from founding father, Oglethorpe's point of view (excellent start to tour) and a diorama depicts the siege of attacks on the city.

SAVANNAH TROLLEY TOURS

Savannah - *Visitors Center pickup (we suggest starting from the Visitors Center located on MLK Blvd) 31401. www.trolleytours.com/savannah. Phone: (912) 284-Tour or (800) 426-2318. **Admission: HOP ON/HOP OFF Trolley: $24.95 adult, $10.95 child (5-11) for fully narrated tour and unlimited on/off privileges at 13 convenient stops until 5:30pm. FREE parking.** Tours: Daily 9:00am-4:00pm (leave every 20 minutes). Tour 75-minutes long.*

The official daily tours of the Historic Foundation have more than 20 departures daily through the Historic district and Low Country. You'll see and hear about: The film "Glory" production site in old Revolutionary War ruins; The Mary Ghost of Telfair - she doesn't permit food or beverage in the Telfair Art Museum; "Forrest Gump" famous bench site (the bench can be seen in the History center); Sherman's Headquarters where he promised not to burn Savannah; A 400 year old live oak tree; A Real Pirate's House Inn (you might want to avoid this place if you lived in the 1800s - you might have ended up on a pirate boat as a slave); and, pass the founder of the Girl Scouts birthplace. This is absolutely the best way to survey Savannah's numerous historic sites and squares and shops. Start your stay in the city on tour.

WHISTLE STOP CAFÉ

Savannah - *303 Martin Luther King, 31401. Phone: (912) 651-3656. At the far end of the Visitors Center station building, it serves breakfast and lunch in a railroad car setting. Average menu pricing $4.00-$6.00. Kiddies Caboose Menu has choices of Freightliner Fish, Southbound Spaghetti, Central Georgia Chicken Fingers, or Hobo Beef Stew.*

GEORGIA STATE RAILROAD MUSEUM

Savannah - ***655 Louisville Road, 31401 (next to History Museum). Phone: (912) 651-6823. www.chsgeorgia.org/railroad-museum.html. Hours: Daily 9:00am-5:00pm Admission: $10.00 adult, $6.00 child (2-12). Train Rides: Diesel rides 11am, 1pm and 2pm. Steam rides 11am, 1pm, 2pm and 3pm. All Sunday rides at 1pm and 2pm only. Schedule and locomotives subject to change, please call ahead.***

Originally designed to transport valuable Georgia cotton, the 190 miles of rail line between Savannah and Macon formed the longest continuous railroad in the world. As a tribute to the Industrial Revolution, the site includes a massive roundhouse with operational turntable, the oldest portable steam engine int he U.S., and an HO scale model of Savannah. From guided tours of the Museum's office cars and rolling stock to nostalgic train rides, and occasional turntable and blacksmithing demonstrations, there is always something exciting to do and see! Download the Train Ride Schedule for more information about dates and times.

SAVANNAH CHILDREN'S MUSEUM

Savannah - ***655 Louisville Road, 31401 (next to GA State Railroad Museum). www.savannahchildrensmuseum.org. Hours: Tuesday-Saturday 10:00am-4:00pm , Sunday 11am-4pm. Admission: $7.50 per person (age 1+).***

Originally designed to transport valuable Georgia cotton, the 190 miles of rail line between Savannah and Macon formed the longest continuous railroad in the world. As a tribute to the Industrial Revolution, the site includes a massive roundhouse with operational turntable, the oldest portable steam engine int he U.S., and an HO scale model of Savannah. From guided tours of the Museum's office cars and rolling stock to nostalgic train rides, and occasional turntable and blacksmithing demonstrations, there is always something exciting to do and see! Download the Train Ride Schedule for more information about dates and times.

OLD FORT JACKSON NATIONAL HISTORIC PARK

Savannah - ***1 Fort Jackson Road (2 miles east of downtown) 31404. Phone: (912) 232-3945. www.chsgeorgia.org/old-fort-jackson.html. Hours: Daily 9:00am-5:00pm Admission: $4.00-$7.00 age 2+.***

This fort is the oldest remaining brickwork fort. The fort first saw service in the War of 1812 and then again during the Civil War. This fort guards Five Fathom Hole, the 18th century deep-water port in the Savannah River. The fort displays artifacts depicting the history of town and Coastal Georgia. Seasonal demonstrations and exhibits are scheduled for the second weekend of each month.

WORMSLOE HISTORIC SITE

Savannah - ***7601 Skidaway Road (10 miles southeast of Savannah's historic district) 31406. Phone: (912) 353-3023. http://gastateparks.org/info/wormsloe/. Hours: Tuesday-Saturday 9:00am-5:00pm, Sunday 2:00-5:30pm. Closed Mondays except holidays. Admission: $4.50-$10.00 per person. Educators: click on the fact sheet details online.***

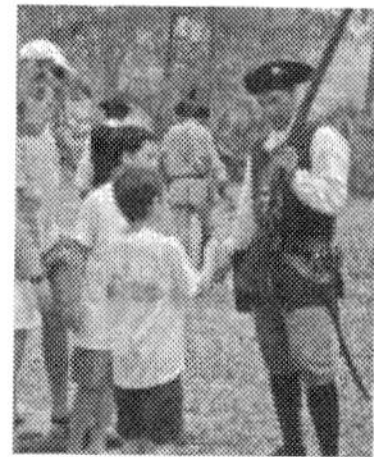

An avenue lined with live oaks leads to the tabby ruins of Wormsloe, the colonial estate constructed by Noble Jones, one of Georgia's first settlers. Jones was an English physician and carpenter who carved out an even wider career in the colonial wilderness. He came to Savannah with James Oglethorpe in 1733 and commanded a company of Marines, served as constable, Indian agent, surveyor and a member of the Royal Council. He was also one of the few original settlers to survive hunger, Indians and Spaniards in this new wilderness. Today, visitors can view artifacts excavated at the site and watch a film about the founding of the 13th colony. A scenic nature trail leads to the living history area where, during special programs, costumed staff show skills and crafts necessary to early settlers. The living history programs are the best time to visit as a family.

WORMSLOE HISTORIC SITE - COLONIAL FAIRE AND MUSTER

Savannah - *Military encampment, a Sutler's Row. crafts, demonstrations, and Colonial music. Admission. (February)*

WORMSLOE HISTORIC SITE - COLONIAL CHRISTMAS AT WORMSLOE

Savannah - *Join in a Christmas celebration 18th century style, with caroling and dance, the burning of the Yule Log, holiday observances of the Colonial period, games and refreshments. Admission. (second Sunday in December)*

OATLAND ISLAND EDUCATION CENTER

***Savannah** - 711 Sandtown Road (5 miles east of Savannah off Island Expressway) 31410. Phone: (912) 898-3980. www.oatlandisland.org. Hours: Daily 10:00am-4:00pm. Guests can remain on grounds until 5:00pm. Admission: $5.00 adult, $3.00 child (4-17). Educators: Their school programs and home school programs meet several of the science standards and provide worksheets at visit.*

Located on a marsh island, the Center features a 2 mile "Native Animal Nature Trail" that winds through maritime forest, salt marsh, and freshwater wetlands. Along the way, visitors can observe native animals such as Florida panthers, Eastern timber wolves, alligators, bison and bears in their natural habitat. It is not unusual to see blue tailed (five-lined) skinks, neotropical birds, herons, hawks, raccoon tracks, or otter scat. Your kids might actually like finding the bat, snake, lizard and tarantula who live here...

SKIDAWAY ISLAND STATE PARK

***Savannah** - 52 Diamond Causeway (I-16 to exit I-516 (#164A). Turn right on Waters Avenue and go straight ahead to Diamond Causeway) 31411. Phone: (912) 598-2300. http://gastateparks.org/info/skidaway/. Hours: Daily 7:00am-10:00pm. Admission: $5.00 daily vehicle parking fee.*

With Savannah at one end and Tybee Island beaches nearby, this barrier island has both salt and fresh water due to estuaries and marshes that flow through the area. The park borders Skidaway Narrows, a part of the intracoastal waterway, and provides scenic camping and picnicking. Two nature trails wind through marshes, live oaks, cabbage-palmettos and longleaf pines. Watch for deer, raccoon and migrating birds. Observation towers provide another chance to search for wildlife. The interpretive center has a bird-viewing station and a giant Ground Sloth fossil replica.

UGA AQUARIUM

***Savannah** - 30 Ocean Science Circle (I-516 to town as it becomes DeRenne Ave. Right on Waters, changing to Whitfield, then Diamond Cseway. Go past State Pk, left on McWhorter 4 miles) 31411. http://marex.uga.edu/aquarium/ Phone: (912) 598-FISH. Hours: Monday-Friday 9:00am-4:00pm, Saturday 10am-5:00pm. Admission: $3.00-$6.00 (age 3+).*

The University of Georgia's public saltwater aquarium exhibits display organisms typical of the various habitats that are found along the coast: the tidal creeks of the salt marshes, the ocean beaches, and the open waters of the continental shelf including "live bottom" areas such as Gray's Reef National Marine Sanctuary. Renovated in 2007, fourteen exhibit tanks hold

200 live animals that represent approximately 50 species of fish, turtles, and invertebrates found along the Georgia coast. Look for sharks, whales, mastodons and mammoths dredged from the Skidaway River. Native American artifacts dating back to the "Guale" era of Georgia's prehistory are also on exhibit, as are sea island grass baskets crafted by the Gullah residents of Sapelo Island. Outside, hike on the wheelchair accessible Nature Trail & Boardwalk.

SAVANNAH RIVERBOAT COMPANY

Savannah - *9 E River Street (departing from Savannah's Historic River Street directly behind City Hall) 31412. www.savannahriverboat.com. Phone: (912) 232-6404 or (800) 786-6404. Admission: Sightseeing Tours: $21.95 adult, $12.95 child (under 12). Luncheon: $10-$16 more. Dinner cruises more. Tours: One Hour Sightseeing: Daily once or twice an afternoon (March-November). Winter, weekends only at 2:00pm. Noon Luncheon cruises: Weekends at Noon (1 1/2 hrs.) Miscellaneous: Riverboat Snack Shop onboard.*

Savannah is a river town, so what better way to get an overview of her harbor and port than to cruise. The 600 passenger Savannah River Queen and the 600 passenger Georgia Queen are triple-decker, red, white and blue, vessels that offer a variety of different tours all through the harbor. Relive a bygone era on board one of the replica paddle wheelers for a view of the sites from the water. Hear the Captain's intriguing tales and historic facts as you travel a river once used by industrialists and war maneuvers. Sit back and enjoy the view. Some examples of Holiday Cruises they offer: Thanksgiving, Boat Parade of Lights, Santa Cruise, Easter Cruise and Fantastic Fourth Fireworks Cruise.

COASTAL GEORGIA BOTANICAL GARDENS

Savannah - *2 Canebrake Road (I-95 exit 94. Go east on GA 204 to Hwy 17 south exit. Travel for one mile) 31419. Phone: (912) 921-5460. www.coastalgeorgiabg.org Hours: Monday-Friday 8:00am-5:00pm, Saturday 10:00am-5:00pm, Sunday Noon-*

5:00pm. Admission: FREE (donations accepted).

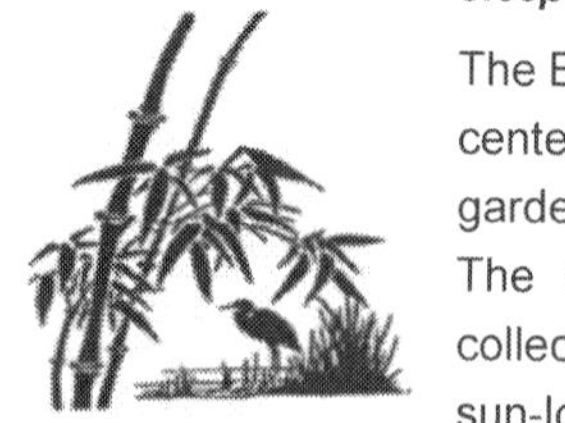

The Bamboo Farm serves as a research and education center and houses a number of plant collections, gardens and research plots maintained by UGA staff. The Bamboo Farm is perhaps best known for its collection of more than 140 varieties of shade- and sun-loving bamboos. The oldest grove of bamboo on the property, the Giant Japanese Bamboo, was planted more than 100 years ago. The farm is the largest collection of bamboo available for public viewing in the U.S. Two display gardens, the Cottage Garden and the Xeriscape Garden, are housed at the Bamboo Farm. The Cottage Garden serves as a trial garden where old and new varieties of perennials, annuals and bulbs can be evaluated for their adaptability to the southeastern coastal climate and soil. The Xeriscape Garden demonstrates the seven principles of water-wise landscaping and is used to teach water conservation practices to local gardeners and landscapers.

SAVANNAH OGEECHEE CANAL MUSEUM AND NATURE CENTER

Savannah - ***681 Fort Argyle Road (located off GA 204, only 2.3 miles west of I-95 at exit 94) 31419. www.savannahogeecheecanalsociety.org. Phone: (912) 748-8068. Hours: Mondays & Fridays 10am-4pm, Saturday 9am-5pm, Sunday 1-5pm. Admission: $1.00-$3.00 per person.***

Discover the history of the Savannah Ogeechee Canal at this Museum. Visitors are able to view the remnants of Canal Locks 5 and 6 and see a replica gate and lock model. The Nature Center consists of 184 acres of river swamp, pine flatwoods, and sandhill habitat with low-impact walking trails (something we look for when hiking miles at a time) throughout the area. The Nature Center supports a diverse group of stationary and migratory birds as well as reptiles and other animal life. Kids especially love the gopher tortoise habitat. Studying State History? The Museum and Nature Center is home to Georgia's state tree, the live oak; Georgia's state flower, the Cherokee rose; Georgia's state wildflower, the wild azalea; and Georgia's state reptile, the gopher tortoise. The state bird, the brown thrasher, can also be seen around the Nature Center.

SCOTTISH GAMES FESTIVAL

Savannah - *Bethesda Home for Boys, 9520 Ferguson Avenue (south of Wormsloe Historic Site, near Montgomery). www.savannahscottishgames.com. A traditional-style Scottish Games festival featuring competitions, clan displays and booths, food and drink, music of the bagpipes & other Scottish music. (first Saturday in May)*

4TH OF JULY AT BATTLEFIELD PARK

Savannah - *Battlefield Park. Phone: (912) 651-6895. www.chsgeorgia.org. Family-friendly historical activities at the 1779 Battlefield Memorial, site of the 1779 Battle of Savannah. Will include musket fire and military demonstrations, plus free copies of the Declaration of Independence. (Independence Day weekend)*

SAVANNAH SOUTHERN LIGHTS

Savannah - *Downtown and Riverfront locations. www.savannahsouthernlights.com. Experience holiday activities with appearances by old St. Nick, local artisans and holiday music at their annual lighted boat AND light float parades, and the ceremonial lighting of the community Christmas Tree as Southern Lights celebrates the holidays. Skating under the stars, concerts, ballets and free activities for the kids (cookie decorating, ornament making, petting zoo, storytelling, face painting) add to the variety of spectacular events. Admission for performances, most community outdoor activities are FREE. (from Thanksgiving to New Year's, most major events occur on weekend Saturdays)*

MIGHTY EIGHTH AIR FORCE MUSEUM

Savannah (Pooler) - ***147 Bourne Avenue (I-95 exit 102, just 2 miles south of the Savannah International Airport) 31322. www.mightyeighth.org. Phone: (912) 748-8888. Hours: Daily 9:00am-5:00pm Admission: $10.00 adult, $9.00 senior and $6.00 child (6-12). Educators: pre-visit and post visit materials will be made available to teachers once the program is booked.***

The museum honors the courage, character and patriotism embodied by the men and women of the Eighth Air Force from WWII to the present. You will be moved by the inspiring stories of heroism, courage, and sacrifice as well as be reminded of the price that was paid for our freedom. Fly a bombing mission with a B-17 crew, take a gunner's position aboard a B-17 in defense, or view historic aircraft in this modern and well lit indoor museum.

OGLETHORPE SPEEDWAY PARK

Savannah (Pooler) - ***200 Jesup Road (I-95, use exit 102 (US Highway 80) and go east three miles) 31322. Phone: (912) 964-RACE. www.ospracing.net.***

This NASCAR sanctioned park entertains thousands every weekend with stock car and go-cart racing. RV campground on site. View website for schedule and fees for each event.

St. Marys

CROOKED RIVER STATE PARK

St. Marys - ***6222 Charlie Smith St. Highway (7 miles north of St. Mary's on GA 40 or 8 miles east of I-95 exit 3) 31558. http://gastateparks.org/info/crookriv/. Phone: (912) 882-5256. Hours: Daily 7:00am-10:00pm. Admission: $5.00 daily vehicle parking fee.***

This park offers cozy facilities with views of salt marshes and Spanish moss-draped oaks. Campsites are surrounded by oaks, while cottages overlook the river. Hikers can explore the nature trails (4 miles), which winds through maritime forest and salt marsh. Visitors may venture to the nearby ruins of the tabby "McIntosh Sugar Works" mill, built around 1825 and later used as a starch factory during the Civil War. Just down the road is the ferry to famous Cumberland Island National Seashore known for secluded beaches. The park also has an Olympic-size pool and bathhouse and a miniature golf course.

CUMBERLAND ISLAND NATIONAL SEASHORE

St. Marys - ***(Visitors Ctr. is located at the Dungeness Dock on the Island. The inland museum is just blocks from the water) 31558. Phone: (912) 882-4335 or (888) 817-3421. www.nps.gov/cuis/. Hours: Ice House Museum: 8:00am-4:00pm daily. Mainland Museum: 1:00-4:00pm. Generally, two ferry departures per day operating. Admission: Day Use Fee: $4.00 per person/visit (age 16+). Ferry Price (round trip): $20.00 adult, $18.00 senior (65+), and $14.00 child (12 and under). Note: The ferry does not transport pets, bicycles, kayaks, or cars. Boating, camping, fishing and hiking are activities available on the island. Educators: ask for Scavenger Hunt or activity sheets at visitors center.***

Once home to several of the Carnegie family's splendid estates, Cumberland Island is now home to hundreds of wild horses, a resort inn and some of the most beautiful camping on the East Coast. It is Georgia's largest and southernmost barrier island, with pristine maritime forests, undeveloped beaches and wide marshes. It is well known for its sea turtles, wild turkeys, wild horses, armadillos, abundant shore birds, dune fields, maritime forests, salt marshes, and historic structures. Special Programs conducted by rangers (on the island) are at 4:00pm dockside each afternoon when the ferry is operating. The Mainland Museum is located on Osborne Street, two blocks from the waterfront. The museum houses a collection of artifacts from Cumberland Island to highlight the people of the island. The lives of Native Americans, African Americans, the Carnegie family as well as others who lived on the island in the 19th and 20th centuries are seen in the island environment. This is the first major effort to bring the island story to mainland facilities. Another portion of the total collection is still on display on the island.

ST. MARYS FAMILY AQUATIC CENTER

St. Marys - *301 Herb Bauer Drive 31558. Phone: (912) 673-8118. www.funatsmac.com Hours: Monday-Friday 11:00am-6:00pm, Saturday 10:00am-6:00pm, Sunday 1:00-6:00pm (June - mid-August). Weekends only (late April, May, late August, September). Admission: Generally $7-$10 per person..*

This brand new 7 acre water play area has something for the whole family. Adults can relax in a tube as you float around the park in the endless river or get in some exercise swimming in the lap pool. There is also a two story tall slide full of twists and turns that is sure to be exciting. Kids over four feet tall can ride the big slide, but the big attraction for the little ones is the play pool with dozens of ways to squirt, spray and splatter your friends with gallons of water.

ST. MARYS SUBMARINE MUSEUM

St. Marys - *102 St. Marys Street West, waterfront 31558. Phone: (912) 882-ASUB. http://stmaryssubmuseum.com. Hours: Tuesday-Saturday 10:00am-4:00pm, Sunday 1:00-5:00pm. Admission: $3.00-$5.00 (age 6+).*

Get ready to see firsthand a working periscope, models of torpedoes, and many displays made from actual submarines. See a deep-sea diving suit & submarine uniforms, command plaques, photographs and models of submarines, an area for watching movies on submarines, working sonar panels, and a gift shop. Walls and walls of memorabilia track the history of the submarine.

ST. MARYS TOONERVILLE TROLLEY

St. Marys - *406 Osborne Road 31558. Phone: (866) 386-8729. www.stmaryswelcome.com/toontrolleyV2.html. Tours meet at flag pole on waterfront.*

Toonerville Trolley - "See You In The Funny Papers!" This saying originated by Roy Crane in his 1935 "Wash Tubbs & Easy" comic strip. The strip featured the many local personalities who used this railcar to commute from St. Marys to Kingsland in the late 1920s. Take a Historic ride through St. Mary's including historic 1800s churches. Call for Tram tours price and reservations.

St. Simons Island

BARBARA JEAN'S RESTAURANT

St. Simons Island - *214 Mallery Street (Village) 31522. Phone: (912) 634-6500. www.barbarajeans.com. Famous for "Eastern shore" crab cakes (best ever) and home-style entrees (like meatloaf) with southern style sides (greens, squash casserole). Open Breakfast, Lunch & Dinner daily. Kids Menu under $5.00.*

ISLAND INN

St. Simons Island - *301 Main Street Plantation Village (follow causeway straight on Demere, left into complex) 31522. www.islandinnstsimons.com. Phone: (912) 638-7805. Enjoy the sub-tropical landscaping around the outdoor pool or unwind in the bubbling hot tub beneath the gazebo. They have a complimentary deluxe continental breakfast bar and bike rentals on site.*

FORT FREDERICA / BLOODY MARSH BATTLE SITE

St. Simons Island - ***6515 Frederica Road (off Sea Island Road on Rte. 9, Battle site is 5 miles south of Fort) 31522. Phone: (912) 638-3639. www.nps.gov/fofr/. Hours: Gates open at 8:00am. Museum: Daily 9:00am-5:00pm. Closed Christmas Day. Admission: $3.00 per person on foot, bike, or bus (age 16+). Note: "Fort Frederica: History Uncovered". The film is shown in the visitor center every 30 minutes from 9:00am-4:00pm. Educators: thorough lesson plans are online under For Teachers/Curriculum Materials.***

When General James Oglethorpe claimed Georgia territory for England, it was important to build settlements within forts. He found this site on the river bank and named it Frederica. By the 1740s, Frederica was a thriving village of about 500 citizens. When Spanish troops sought to capture St. Simons Island in 1742, Oglethorpe's men won a decisive victory in what is now called The Battle of Bloody Marsh. In July of 1742, an outnumbered force of British troops ambushed and defeated Spanish troops, halting an attack aimed at Fort Frederica. The battle proved to be the turning point in the Spanish invasion of Georgia. By the late 1740s the fort was not needed and disbanded. Today, you can visit the site of Fort Frederica and see the ruins of the fortifications, barracks and homes. A museum, film, dioramas, tours, and demonstrations bring the settlement vividly to life.

MULLET BAY RESTAURANT

St. Simons Island - *512 Ocean Boulevard 31522. www.mulletbayrestaurant.com. Phone: (912) 638-0703. Seafood, steaks, sandwiches, chicken, burgers, po-boys. Kids (and parents) can crayon on the table cloth. Kids menu (avg $4, served with oreos). Casual dining, moderate prices, dining indoors and outdoors. L, D daily.*

ST. SIMONS ISLAND KAYAK / CANOE TRIPS

St. Simons Island - *www.explorestsimonsisland.com/st_simons_canoeing.html*

Kayaks and canoes are great ways to explore the creeks and marshes of the Golden Isles. Many local outfitters offer instruction and can tailor customer outings to fit family needs and interests. Offered spring through fall.

- OCEAN MOTION, St. Simons Island, (912) 638-5225. www.oceanmotion.biz
- SOUTHEAST ADVENTURE OUTFITTERS, St. Simons Island (912) 638-6732. www.southeastadventure.com.

ST. SIMONS ISLAND LIGHTHOUSE

St. Simons Island - *101 12th Street (Causeway to St. Simons - Beachview Drive, oceanfront) 31522. Phone: (912) 638-4666. www.saintsimonslighthouse.org. Hours: Monday-Saturday 10:00am-5:00pm, Sunday 1:30-5:00pm. Last climb to top is at 4:30pm. Admission: $10.00 adult, $5.00 child (age 6-11). Includes admission to the Maritime Center.*

The last time it snowed on St. Simons Island was in 1989.

Inside the giant lens that projects the light

This lighthouse is the oldest brick structure in the area and is still maintained as an operational light by the US Coast Guard. The 104-foot-tall lighthouse has 129 interior steps. It sits behind the lightkeeper's dwelling which now houses the Museum. The second floor of the lightkeepers building is set up just as it would be in 1800s. The best part of the site for families is the climb up the six flights of stairs to the top of the light for a look around. Great view! Notice that most lighthouses are made of brick but this one is mostly locally made tabby mixture.

ST. SIMONS ISLAND MARITIME CENTER

St. Simons Island - *4201 1st Street (on East Beach) 31522. Phone: (912) 638-4666. www.saintsimonslighthouse.org/site/maritime.html. Hours: Monday-Saturday 10:00am-5:00pm, Sunday 1:30-5:00pm. Admission: $6.00 adult, $3.00 child (6-12). Combo discount tickets with Lighthouse Museum.*

Learning Nautical Knots

Located in the former U.S. Coast Guard Station, the Maritime Center offers an exciting look at coastal Georgia natural assets, while highlighting some of the area's maritime and military history. Visitors are guided through the museum by "Ollie", a fictional character based on journal entries and historical accounts by various Coast Guard personnel stationed at St. Simons Island during World War II. Seven galleries feature a variety of hands-on exhibits and activities (like learning how to tie knots like sailors).

ST. SIMONS TROLLEY TOUR

St. Simons Island - ***530 Beachview Drive (The Village/Pier area, between Lighthouse and Visitors Center) 31522. www.stsimonstours.com. Phone: (912) 638-8954. Admission: $23.00 adult, $10.00 child (4-12). Tours: 11:00am and 1:00pm (April, June & July), 11:00pm only (all other months). Reservations or tickets in advance are not required, but arrive early for scheduled departures. Tours are 1.5 hours long.***

See one of the largest live oak trees in the area...

Tour historic St. Simons Island on an antique trolley. Start with this tour to orient the family and give clues to sites you'll want to visit during your stay. The humorous and delightful drive-by tour includes the lighthouse, Bloody Marsh, Fort Frederica, Retreat Plantation (where relics from slavery days still exist), and a walking tour of Christ Church (what famous Presidents have attended church here?) Hear stories about the slave family that owns the best property on the Island (Neptune). What is tabby? Do you hear footsteps from Frederic the Friendly ghost when walking up the lighthouse stairs? What is the #1 food produced by the marshes? Why is Spanish moss not Spanish? Nor, is it something you would want to bag up and take home. It's possible, when looking closely at certain of the oak trees that cover the island, to find one actually looking back at you. These are the Tree Spirits-lovingly carved faces emerging from the trees. Your tour guide will point some out to you. The images portray the sailors who lost their lives at sea aboard the sailing ships that were once made from St. Simons Island oak. Their sad, sorrowful expressions seem to reflect the grieving appearance of the trees themselves with their drooping branches and moss.

Tybee Island

CAPTAIN MIKE'S DOLPHIN TOURS

Tybee Island - *1 Old US 80 East (Lazaretto Creek Marina just before or after the Lazaretto Bridge, follow Marina signs) 31328. Phone: (912) 786-5848 or (800) 242-0166. www.tybeedolphins.com. Admission: $15.00 adult, $8.00 child (12 and under). Tours: Call for daily, seasonal schedule. Usually twice daily during warm weather. 1.5 hours long. Reservations recommended. Note: The boat used is a working fishing boat, too. Metal seat ledges are around the perimeter of the boat and it is mostly covered by a canopy. However, because it is not a pontoon boat, you may experience sea sickness if you're prone to that. Just avoid moving to the front of the boat and you should be fine.*

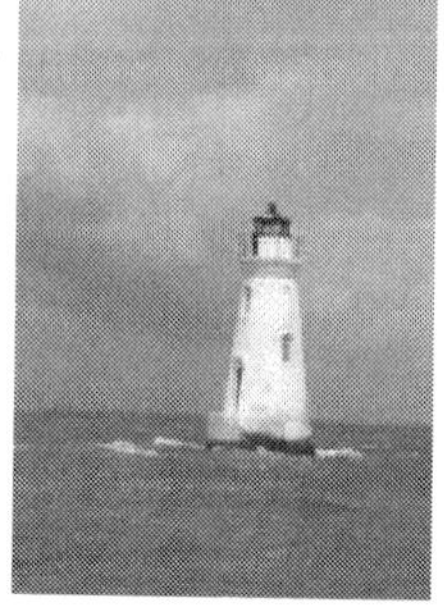

Looking for dolphin is just part of this cruise (you'll see dozens). Spot their blow holes (don't you love the "snorts") and then you'll see each special mammal fin (every dolphin's is different). Kids yell at the sight of every one, especially the ones closest to the boat! Do you know how long a baby dolphin (calf) stays with its mother? How do dolphins sleep? Besides the great exposure to dolphins, you'll learn lots about the lighthouse, Fort, shrimp boats and pelicans. If you love a narrated, learning tour about dolphins and their environment, this is an excellent tour.

Shrimp boats resting after a hard night's work...

FANNIE'S ON THE BEACH RESTAURANT

Tybee Island - *(on the Strand near 17th Street oceanside) 31328. Phone: (912) 786-6109. www.fanniesonthebeach.com. Right near our favorite spot (left or right of the pier) on our favorite Georgia beach, Tybee Beach, is a fun beach restaurant. Look for the sign near the pavilion that says "Time to Eat". Order anything with shrimp or a pizza and you will be happy. Try to sit upstairs on the deck or the real boat! Live music most nights - specializing in "Marsh-grass" musical blend of blues, bluegrass and low country. Casual attire, moderate seafood pricing.*

FORT PULASKI NATIONAL MONUMENT

Tybee Island - ***(US 80 east, 2 miles before reaching Tybee, cross over Cockspur Island Bridge to entrance) 31328. Phone: (912) 786-5787. www.nps.gov/fopu. Hours: Daily 9:00am-5:00pm. Admission: $5.00 per adult (age 16+). Children are FREE. Note: Guided Fort Tours held twice daily plus look for schedule of musket & soldier demos/ cannon firings several times daily. Educators: click online under: For Teachers/curriculum materials for Scavenger Hunt sheets and a web-based War for Freedom lesson.***

A wall of the fort after facing heavy Union bombardment in 1862

This fort was built between 1829 on Cockspur Island to guard the sea approach to Savannah. Future Confederate General Robert E. Lee was assigned to the fort as an engineer. The entrance to Fort Pulaski is known as the sallyport, a term dating back to when knights would sally or go forth from a castle. This area was heavily defended with iron gates and heavy doors. When the Confederates seized Fort Pulaski in 1861, they thought the brick fort would be an impregnable blockade. However, the use of new rifled cannons forced their surrender in just over one day's bombardment. After this, forts of this type were obsolete. Scenic marshlands and uplands, towering walls, artillery tunnels, two moats and a wide drawbridge are special features. As you cross the drawbridge, look for the jumping mullet fish (too cool!). Later, the fort was used as part of the Underground Railroad. It was even the site of baseball games. As you visit, be mindful of safety. Recommended activities include self-guided tours, fishing, hiking, picnicking and birding. Their hiking trails are fairly short and offer the best views of the Savannah River, Tybee Island, the marshes and the lighthouse.

An estimated 25 million bricks were used to construct Fort Pulaski.

FORT PULASKI NATIONAL MONUMENT - CANDLELANTERN TOURS OF FORT PULASKI

Tybee Island - *Fort Pulaski staff and volunteers conduct the annual Candlelantern tours which re-create the confederate Nog party of 1861. Come relive a Savannah tradition for over a decade and join in the celebration and share in the Christmas season with cookies and hot cider, music and merrymaking. Admission for adults. (second weekend in December, evenings)*

OCEANFRONT COTTAGE RENTALS ON TYBEE ISLAND

Tybee Island - *31328. Phone: (800) 786-5889. www.oceanfrontcottage.com. This is the only way to DO Tybee. Depending on the size of your party, rent a very comfortable, fully furnished and decorated condo, cottage or home, most right on the beach! Many homes provide grills and picnic tables and often beachside hot tubs. We were impressed with the cleanliness inside and out. If your family would like to bike around the island (highly suggested), you can pick up bikes from their office (as well as beach chairs) to use during your stay at no charge. The bike trails on the island are clearly marked and give you a "behind the main street" view of odd and pretty homes around every corner. Stop at the convenience store and pick up groceries for a light meal prepared and served tableside on your deck.*

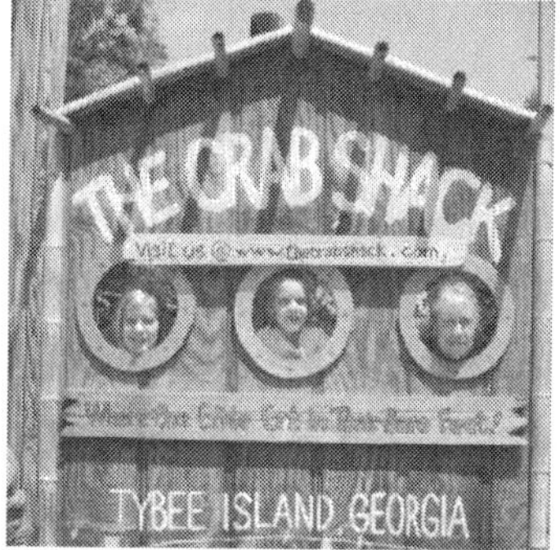

THE CRAB SHACK

Tybee Island - *40 Estill Hammock Rd (US 80/ SR 26. Right on Catalina Dr., then left onto Dav Rd.) 31328. Phone: (912) 786-9857. www.thecrabshack.com. Another very themed eatery is the CRAB SHACK (lunch & dinner daily). This is a very popular eatery on the island that is great for families. As well as having wonderful seafood, an outdoor deck, funny seafood "hole" tables and a kids menu, they feature live swampy environments with 78 live alligators and colorful talking macaw birds! Lunch specials feature a great potpourri of specialties for only $6.99. The motif is cute and great photo ops abound. Try ANYTHING CRAB or their BBQ. This place is so fun! Where the elite eat in their bare feet!*

TYBEE ISLAND MARINE SCIENCE CENTER

Tybee Island - ***1510 Strand Avenue (by Tybee Island pier and pavilion) 31328. www.tybeemarinescience.org. Phone: (912) 786-5917. Hours: Daily 10:00am-5:00pm. Admission: $4.00 (age 4+) Add $6.00 for beach walks with guides. Educators: Their indoor and/or outdoor classes are really quick (30 min. to one hour) and cover things you may not have access to in the classroom (ex. Dissect a squid).***

The museum consists of aquariums and a touch tank containing specimens indigenous to the coast of Georgia. It's Where Science Meets the Sea! Exhibits provide information on shells, sharks, sea turtles, marine mammals, marine pollution, the salt marsh, a cross-section of the beach, and maritime forest. Discovery beach walks and seinings are conducted daily. All ages are welcome to join in for shoreline discoveries. Learn about shells, sand dunes, geology, tides, and beach creatures of a barrier island.

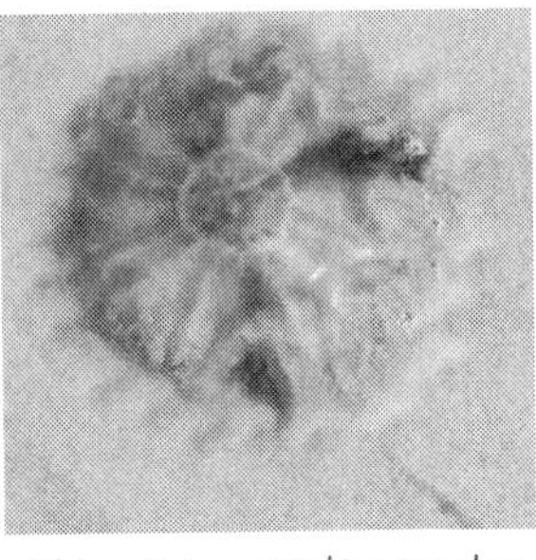

This critter wasn't a regular resident - we're so glad !!

Participants will sift the wetsand to find creatures that live beneath their feet and pull a seine net (weather dependent) to see what lives in the surf. If you're lucky, maybe you'll catch a glimpse of a jellyfish or make the different varieties of tide formations in the sand. Besides the interesting beach walks, our favorite part was the touch tank. Baby crabs, stingrays and living sand dollars were all there to touch. We were afraid to touch some of them so we asked a guide to help. They take the fear out of being "tickled" by sea creatures. It's surprising how much you can use all of your senses inside and outside the facility.

The beach was a great classroom - full of interesting critters....

Jenny with her climb certificate... 178 steps to the top!

TYBEE LIGHTHOUSE

Tybee Island - ***30 Meddin Ave. (US Hwy 80 at Fort Screven, follow signs) 31328. www.tybeelighthouse.org. Phone: (912) 786-5801. Hours: Daily 9:00am-5:30pm. Closed Tuesdays. Admission: $6.00, $5.00 senior (62+) & child (6-17). Educators: a Lighthouse and a Museum Education manual are downloadable on the Education page.***

Visitors can climb 178 steps to the top of America's third oldest and Georgia's oldest lighthouse that is still working today and recently restored. Enjoy a spectacular view of the entire island, then visit the keeper's cottage. The cottage appears as if the keeper and family have just left for a moment. After climbing all those stairs in the lighthouse, catch your breath in the **FORT SCREVEN MUSEUM** on the beach. Their Tybee Attic room (actually in the basement) has some interesting stuff. The museum features exhibits of early life on the Island, Indian and Civil War weaponry and dolls. By the way, when you finish climbing up and down the 178 steps, you are awarded a certificate saying so!

SAND ARTS FESTIVAL, SCAD

Tybee Island - *North Beach. Phone: (912) 525-5225. www.scad.edu/event/sand-arts-festival This annual event invites sand-loving SCAD students to create forms in the sand on the beach. Four contests are available for viewing: sand castle, sand sculpture, sand relief and wind sculpture. (first Saturday in May)*

Waycross

OKEFENOKEE SWAMP PARK

Waycross - ***US 1 South (7 miles south of town, off US 1, off US 82, follow signs) 31501. Phone: (912) 283-4056. www.okeswamp.com. Hours: Daily 9:00am-5:30pm. Closed major winter holidays. Admission: $15.00 adult, $14.00 senior (62+), Military or child (3-11). Add $6.00-$10.00 for boat tour (1/2 hour long). Internet discount coupons. Note: Please allow 3 1/2 to 4 hours to see and do it all. Online word search under: Field trips. Three Pigs BBQ snack bar serves grilled food for lunch. New Adventure Walk (right on top of swamp) to Observation Tower.***

Often perceived as a deep, dark, scary place, this wonder world of the Okefenokee is a preserved segment of what was here when America began. Boat tours are offered on original Indian waterways. See Pioneer Island and native animals in their own habitat or Pioneer Homestead, Honey Bee Farm, Turpentine Site or Seminole Indian Village. Enjoy productions and concerts in the amphitheater. The Wildlife Show, scheduled for different times during the day, is a huge hit with the kids. The host will bring out baby alligators, snakes and other wildlife, and give a short lecture on wildlife at this park. The train ride is also a delight. Learn about the natives - both human and plant or animal. They actually name the alligators here and you'll meet some that come along out of the water over towards the train to say hello! You'll come even closer to the gators in the boat tour. Stop at Pioneer Island and

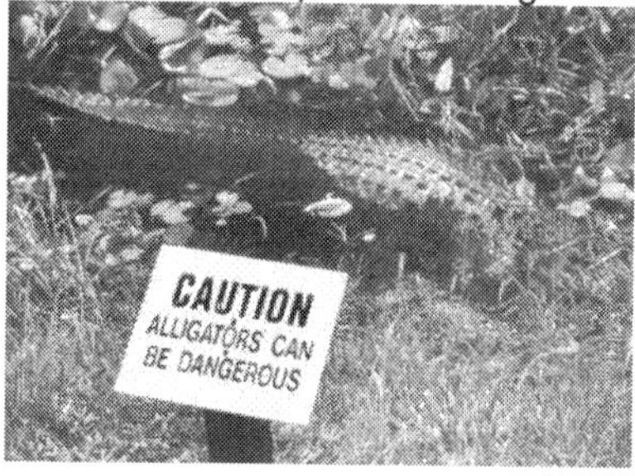

As if we really needed to read the sign...

A trainer calling his gator friend...

walk around a typical homestead and general store. This entire site is unique and cute - and, we promise - there will be lots of gators!

OKEFENOKEE SWAMP PARK - ENCHANTED WILDERNESS LIGHT SHOW

Waycross - *Get aboard the Lady Suwannee Train and be dazzled by the thousands of lights and displays along the Okefenokee Railroad and throughout the Swamp Park. See SANTA every Friday & Saturday night before Christmas. Special Indian camp fire program nightly. This is a rare opportunity to Explore Georgia's Natural Wonder at Night. Reduced park Admission. (every Friday & Saturday night in December)*

OBEDIAH'S OKEFENOK

Obediah's was everything we expected a swamp could be...and then some...

Waycross - ***5115 Swamp Road (US 82 onto Gilmore Street, follow signs about 8.5 miles south of town) 31502. Phone: (912) 287-0090. Hours: Daily 10:00am-5:00pm. Admission: $5.00-$6.50 (age 6+). www.okefenokeeswamp.com. Self-guided touring.***

Mr. Barber was born in July of 1825, married three times and fathered twenty children. In the mid-1800s, Obediah constructed a one-story cabin with wooded pegged walls and puncheon floors on the northern border of the Okefenokee Swamp. He and his father Isaac were said to be the first white settlers in the area. Legend has it that Obediah killed a large black bear with a fat knot tree branch. A colorful character and man of great honor and integrity, along with a physical structure of over 6 1/2 feet, Obediah was also called the "Southeast Paul Bunyan." Take the elevated boardwalk and trails past the cabins and wildlife. Meet an alligator, python, giant ostrich, black bear, cougar and an assortment of unusual spiders. See dioramas of action scenes from the

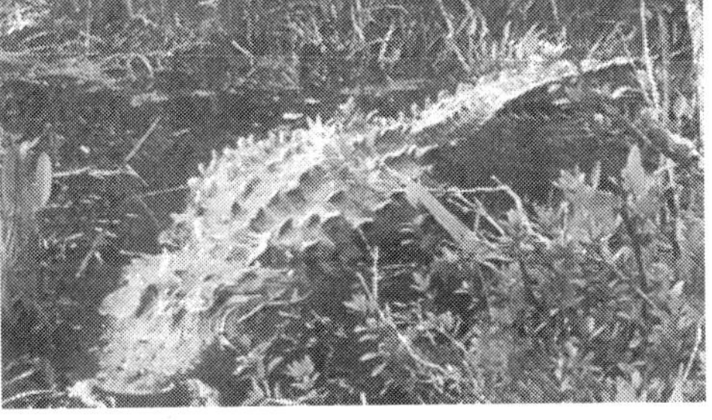
This gator was bigger than a small boat...yikes!

swamp. The Homestead consists of buildings and exhibits that have been restored as an example of the lifestyle in the area in the 1800s.

LAURA S. WALKER STATE PARK

Waycross - *5653 Laura Walker Road (9 miles southeast of Waycross on GA 177) 31503. Phone: (912) 287-4900. http://gastateparks.org/info/lwalker/. Hours: Daily 7:00am-10:00pm. Admission: $5.00 daily vehicle parking fee.*

This 63-acre park is one of the few state parks ever named for a woman, and richly deserved. Laura Walker was a Georgia writer, teacher, civic leader and naturalist who was a great lover of trees and worked for their preservation. Located near the Okefenokee Swamp, the park is home to many fascinating creatures and plants, including alligators. Walking along the lake shore and nature trail, visitors may see carnivorous pitcher plants, the shy gopher tortoise, numerous oak varieties, owls and great blue herons. Facilities at the park include tent and trailer sites, picnic shelters, a swimming pool, group camping, fishing, boating, canoeing, water-skiing and swimming.

OKEFENOKEE HERITAGE CENTER

Waycross - *1460 N. Augusta Avenue 31503. www.okefenokeeheritagecenter.org. Phone: (912) 285-4260. Hours: Tuesday-Saturday 10:00am-4:30pm. Summers 9am-2pm. Admission: $5-$7.00 per person (age 6+).*

The story of the heritage and life of people who lived in and around the Okefenokee Swamp and Native American life in South Georgia are documented through artifacts and exhibits. Outdoor exhibits to explore include a 1911 Baldwin Steam Locomotive and tender with additional cars, the Waycross Journal (a 1900s print shop) and the General Thomas Hilliard house, an 1840s farmhouse and outbuildings and varying art exhibits.

SOUTHERN FOREST WORLD

Waycross - *1440 N. Augusta Ave. 31503. www.okefenokeeswamp.com/Forest.htm. Phone: (912) 285-4056. Hours: Mon-Sat 10:00am-5:00pm, Sun 1:00-5:00pm. Admission: $2.00 per person.*

Adjacent to the Okefenokee Heritage Center, Southern Forest World features forestry exhibits documenting the importance of the development of forestry in the South. Fun and educational with hands-on exhibits, trees to climb, a collection of logging tools and a nature trail to explore. Indoor exhibits include a Talking Tree and a replica of a Loblolly Tree you can climb in. Stuckie the Dog, a canine that got caught in a hollow tree and mummified over 40 years ago, is here too.

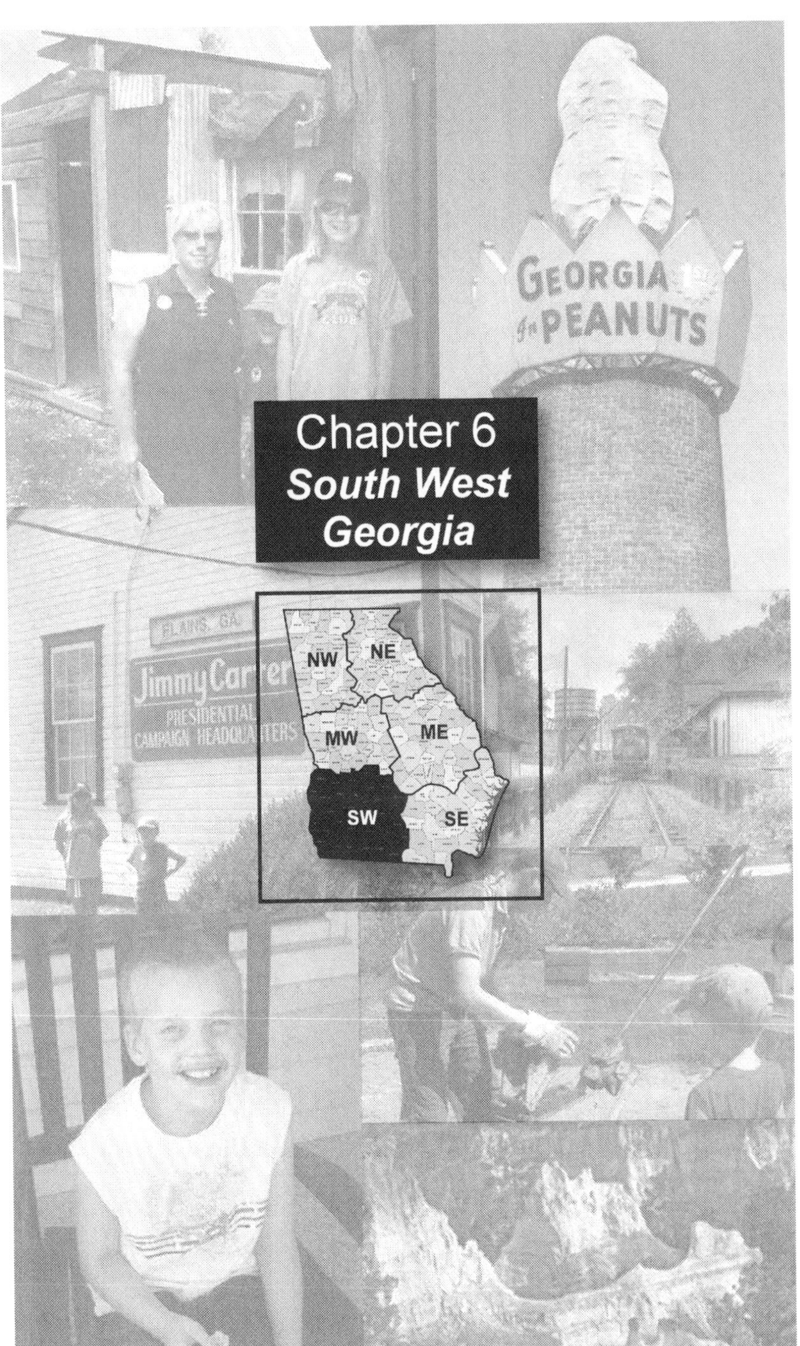
GEORGIA 1st
in PEANUTS
Chapter 6
South West
Georgia
PLAINS, GA.
JimmyCarter
PRESIDENTIAL
CAMPAIGN HEADQUARTERS
NW
NE
MW
ME
SW
SE

Adel

- Reed Bingham State Park
- Reed Bingham State Park - Christmas With Friends

Albany

- Parks At Chehaw
- Thronateeska Heritage Center
- Flint Riverquarium
- Albany Museum Of Art

Americus

- Habitat For Humanity Global Village & Discovery Center

Ashburn

- Crime And Punishment Museum & Last Meal Café
- World's Largest Peanut
- Fire Ant Festival

Blakely

- Kolomoki Mounds Historic Park

Colquitt

- Swamp Gravy

Cordele

- Georgia Veterans State Park
- Georgia Veterans State Park - July 4th Celebration
- Lake Blackshear Resort
- S A M Shortline Excursion Train
- S A M Shortline Excursion Train - Day Out With Thomas
- S A M Shortline Excursion Train - Sleigh Bells & Rails
- Watermelon Days Festival

Donalsonville

- Seminole State Park

Fitzgerald

- Blue And Gray Museum
- Bowens Mill Fish Hatchery
- Jefferson Davis Historic Site

Fort Gaines

- George T. Bagby State Park And Lodge

Lumpkin

- Providence Canyon State Park
- Westville
- Westville - Spring Festival
- Westville - Fourth Of July Celebration
- Westville - Harvest Festival
- Westville - Yuletide Season

Parrott

- Sound Play

Perry

- Georgia National Fair

Plains

- Jimmy Carter National Historic Site
- Plains Peanut Festival

Thomasville

- Children's Christmas Sampler @ Pebble Hill
- Fall Family Sampler @ Pebble Hill

Tifton

- Agrirama
- Agrirama - Spring Folk Life Festival
- Agrirama - Victorian Christmas Celebration
- Nespal Coastal Plain Experiment Station

Valdosta

- Wild Adventures Theme Park
- Wild Adventures Theme Park - Festival Of Lights

Vienna

- Ellis Brothers Pecan Packing Company
- Georgia Cotton Museum

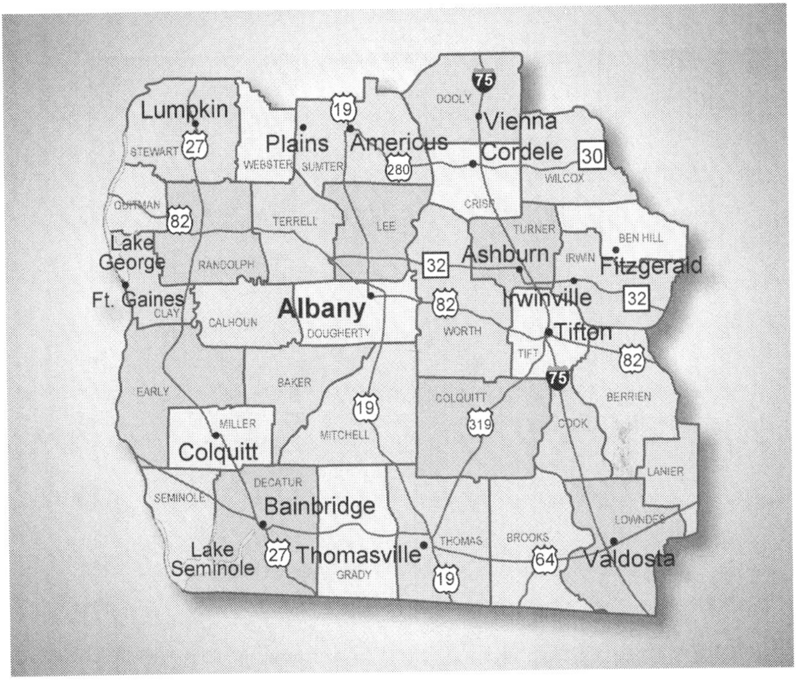

A Quick Tour of our Hand-Picked Favorites Around...

South West Georgia

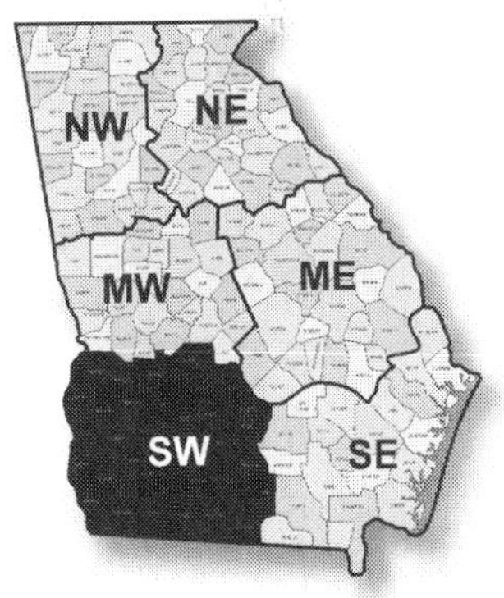

"All Aboard!" Georgia's rolling park. The **SAM Shortline** Train's 1949 railcars travel past pecan groves and country farms with stops in towns along the way. Step off the train at any stop, catching it back as it returns. You can pick the train up at **Georgia Veterans State Park** & the Lake Blackshear Resort in Cordele (pronounced Core-Deal). Rent a overnight room or condo to base from this well-maintained and active property that offers many family deals.

First stop off the train: Americus & **Habitat for Humanities Global Village**. With your Global Village Passport in hand, begin walking through the "Living in Poverty" houses. These are re-created structures normally found in severely poor areas of the world. Next, on to more hopeful settings: the Global Village of 35 houses built to provide better housing. At each house, review your passport and place a stamp in your book before you leave. Then, try your hand at making compressed-earth blocks or roof tile. This site so touched us and educated us that we recommend it to every family as a "must see" attraction!

The baton of peace was handed to a Georgia native, Jimmy Carter, a man who'd be president and devote his post-presidential life to creating peace and harmony wherever there was conflict. Visit his hometown routes by train or car in Plains, Georgia (**Jimmy Carter NHS**). Have a pack of peanuts and soda pop while browsing the general store.

Further south you will find **The Riverquarium**, located in Albany. The Flint RiverQuarium tells the fascinating story of the Flint River and the mysterious blue-hole springs that help create it. The 175,000 gallon, 22 foot deep, open-air Blue Hole is filled with the fish, reptiles and plants found in the Flint River's ecosystem in South Georgia.

Sites and attractions are listed in order by City, Zip Code, and Name. Symbols indicated represent: Restaurants Lodging

REED BINGHAM STATE PARK

***Adel** - 542 Reed Bingham Road (6 miles west of town on GA 37 via I-75 exit 39 and 14 miles east of US 319 in Moultrie) 31620. http://gastateparks.org/info/reedbing/. Phone: (229) 896-3551. Hours: Daily 7:00am-10:00pm. Admission: $5.00 daily vehicle parking fee.*

The park has become a major boating and waterskiing attraction in south Georgia. The Coastal Plain Nature Trail and Gopher Tortoise Nature Trail wind through a cypress swamp, sandhill area and other habitats representative of southern Georgia. Watchful visitors may see waterfowl, the threatened gopher turtles and indigo snake, and other creatures. However, the park's most famous residents are the thousands of black vultures and turkey vultures that arrive in late November and stay through early April. Other recreation opportunities include a swimming beach and mini-golf.

REED BINGHAM STATE PARK - CHRISTMAS WITH FRIENDS

Adel - *Celebrate Christmas with carols, games, hayrides and bonfires on the beach. Make s'mores, toast marshmallows and enjoy the sights and sounds of the season. Santa visits with children after arriving in a parade of lighted boats on the lake. Admission. (first Saturday in December)*

Albany

PARKS AT CHEHAW

Albany - ***105 Chehaw Park Road (I-75 exit 62 head west) 31701. Phone: (229) 430-5277. www.parksatchehaw.org. Hours: Daily 9:00am-5:00pm. Closed Thanksgiving, Christmas and New Years. Admission: $4.00-$8.00 (age 3+) for zoo and park. Note: Play park and nature trails.***

Walk through Georgia's flourishing forests inhabited by its native creatures. Travel down the creeks, streams, and trails that were traveled by the Native Americans of this area. Watch the white-tailed deer, raccoons, squirrels, and birds of all kinds as they play in their natural habitat. A basic zoo adds flare with Free Ranging Lemurs, Ben's Barnyard & Children's Farm, Giant Tortoises, American Bison, and a Swampland with alligators. A train takes visitors on a 20-minute ride through the park and the adjacent natural restoration area (extra $3.00 fee).

THRONATEESKA HERITAGE CENTER

Albany - ***100 W. Roosevelt Avenue (Heritage Plaza) 31701. Phone: (229) 432-6955. www.heritagecenter.org. Hours: Thursday-Saturday 10am-4:00pm. Planetarium Showtimes and Discovery Center Thursday-Friday 2:45pm, Saturdays 12:30pm, 1:30pm, 2:30pm. Admission: FREE except group tours are $3 a piece.***

The Discovery Center is a place to find out about science with your hands, ears and eyes. At Imagination Stations, visitors learn about light and electricity, magnetism and sound, nature and history. It's a hands-on experience to awaken scientific curiosity about your world. The Model Train Exhibit is located directly behind steam locomotive Georgia Northern 107 (you can't miss it) and housed in an actual railroad baggage car (Southern Railway 518). This detailed exhibit depicts a train journey from the city to the country. In the Wetherbee Planetarium it's always a starry, starry night. With a wide variety of programs from Diamonds in the Sky to a Report from Venus. Good facility for locals to share hands-on science and history with students.

FLINT RIVERQUARIUM

Albany - *101 Pine Avenue, downtown (near junction of US 82 & SR 300) 31702. Phone: (229) 639-2650. www.flintriverquarium.com. Hours: Tuesday-Saturday 10:00am-5:00pm, Sunday 1:00-5:00pm. Closed on Thanksgiving and Christmas Day. Admission: $9.00 adult, $8.00 senior (62+), $6.50 child (4-12). Add $4.50-$6.00 for Theater. Combo rates are discounted. Note: Aviary with feathered friends is a new space. Imagination Theater is a 3 story high, 40-feet wide theater screen showing educational water animal oriented films. Educators: Fun Scavenger hunts and Activity sheets are found on the link: Teachers & Kids/teacher resources online. Flint Nature Packs are only $1.50 each.*

The Flint RiverQuarium tells the fascinating story of the Flint River and the mysterious blue-hole springs that help create it. The 175,000 gallon, 22 foot deep, open-air Blue Hole is filled with the fish, reptiles and plants found in the Flint River's ecosystem in South Georgia. See more than 100 kinds of fish, turtles, alligators, snapping turtles and other creatures that make the Blue Hole their home. The Flint River Gallery features both freshwater and saltwater tanks, plus a live fish hatchery, to give you a first-hand look at life all along the river's path. Follow the Flint River's amazing 350-mile journey and learn about the vital role the river plays in sustaining life for thousands of curious creatures. Discovery Caverns puts you in control of nature with fun games and eye-opening exhibits. Control the weather. Change the way a river flows. Explore an underground cave to uncover mysterious subterranean creatures. The World of Water gives you an insider's view of other rivers around the globe that share similar features and challenges with the Flint. Dive Shows each afternoon.

ALBANY MUSEUM OF ART

Albany - *311 Meadowlark Drive (I-75 south, right on GA 300. GA 234 west and finally north on Meadowlark) 31707. Phone: (229) 439-8400. www.albanymuseum.com. Hours: Tuesday-Saturday 10:00am-5:00pm. Admission: $4.00 adult, $2.00 senior and child. Free admission to everyone on Thursdays.*

Join them for Family Days- a child friendly guided tour of one of the current exhibitions. Then spend time working together to create your own masterpiece based on the artwork you have seen. Before you leave, don't forget to explore AMAzing Spaces, an interactive hands-on gallery designed with children in mind. There are five sections to AMAzing Spaces which are based on the Permanent Collection of African, American and European art. Every visit, be sure to check out the latest in the Learning Curve gallery displaying the artwork of children and adults who are current students of art classes and schoolrooms.

Americus

HABITAT FOR HUMANITY GLOBAL VILLAGE & DISCOVERY CENTER

Americus - *721 West Church Street (I-75 to US 280 heading west, follow signs) 31709. www.habitat.org/gvdc/. Phone: (800) 422-4828. (229) 410-7663. Hours: Monday-Friday 9:00am-5:00pm. Also Saturday 10:00am-2:00pm. (March-Nov) Closed Sundays, most holidays & winter Saturdays. Admission: $3.00-$4.00 per person.*

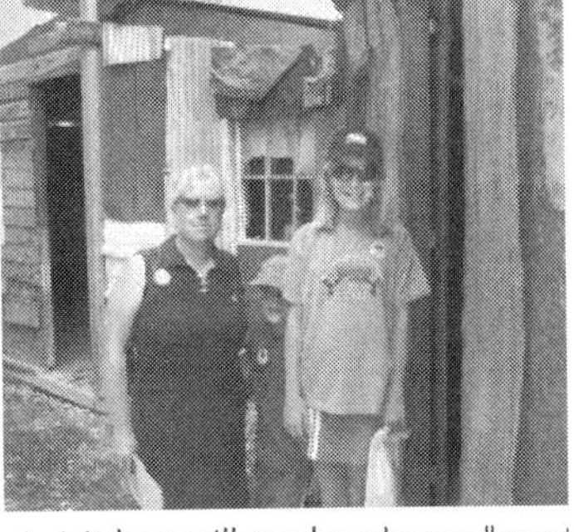

A visit here will surely make you "count your blessings" - A great life lesson!

Habitat for Humanity International is a Christian ministry dedicated to eliminating poverty housing. Founded in 1976 by Millard & Linda Fuller, Habitat for Humanity International and its affiliates in more than 3,000 communities and in 92 nations, have built and sold more than 150,000 homes to partner families with no-profit, zero-interest mortgages. With your Global Village Passport in hand, begin walking through the "Living in Poverty" houses. These are re-created structures normally found in severely poor areas of the world. Why do some dwellings have a single light bulb hanging from the ceiling when they don't even have electricity? Most Americans will never leave our country and visit third world countries...this may be their only exposure. Now, on to more hopeful settings: the Global Village of 35 houses built to provide better environmentally and culturally appropriate housing. At each house, review your passport for info on the building materials used and the style

A single light bulb symbolizes a dream here..

Learning to make a single brick with the most simple tools can build a village...

of life of the inhabitants. Kids engage by placing a stamp in their passport as proof they have visited each home. While touring houses, stop at one of the demonstration centers and learn how bricks, tile and other building materials are made and used in construction. Then, try your hand at making compressed-earth blocks or roof tile. This site so touched us and educated us that we recommend it to every family as a "must see" attraction!

Ashburn

CRIME AND PUNISHMENT MUSEUM & LAST MEAL CAFÉ

Ashburn - *241 East College Avenue (I-75 exit 82 west. Follow signs to downtown) 31714. Phone: (800) 471-9696. www.jailmuseum.com. Hours: Tuesday-Saturday 10:00am-5:00pm. Café open 11:00am-1:00pm. Admission: $1.00-$3.00. Built in 1906, the Turner County Jail resembles a castle outside, but not inside. The original jail cells remain upstairs, the sheriff's family quarters downstairs. Although mature for children, you can see the death cell, Old Sparky electrocution chair, and trap door for hangings. Combine this with heart wrenching stories about infamous criminals, murders, hangings, ghosts and even a love story. Check out the striped prisoner clothes. After the tour, stop in for dessert "to die for" at the Last Meal Café. There is a long standing tradition of death row inmates requesting their last meal with a lavish dessert. Enjoy Southern cobbler, pie, cake or ice cream or full meals are available for groups with advance reservations. Clever theme.*

WORLD'S LARGEST PEANUT

Ashburn - ***(off I-75 near exit 82) 31714. Phone: (229) 567-9696.***

Clearly seen beside Interstate 75, this monument is the largest of its kind in the nation. It is a daily reminder of the fact that Georgia's number one cash crop is peanuts. The peanut is approximately 20 feet tall!

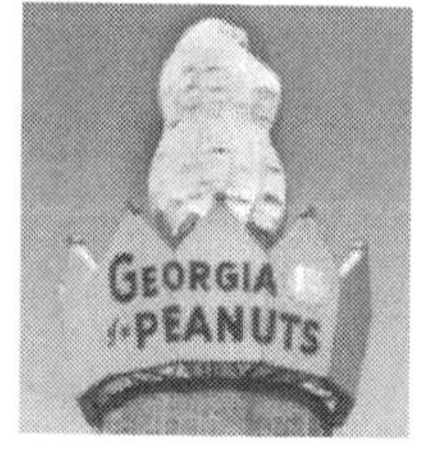

The Georgia State Crop is the Peanut.

FIRE ANT FESTIVAL

Ashburn - *Downtown (I-75 exit 82). www.fireantfestival.com. Known for its wacky and off the wall activities, the Festival offers family fun as they watch or participate in the fire ant calling contest, the fire ant fling, the giant fire ant maze and the fire ant surprise. Also, a drive-in movie, fireworks, bands, carnival and cooking contests with food. (fourth weekend in March)*

Blakely

KOLOMOKI MOUNDS HISTORIC PARK

Blakely - ***205 Indian Mounds Road (6 miles north of town off US 27). 39823. Phone: (229) 724-2150. http://gastateparks.org/info/kolomoki/. Hours: Park, Daily 7:00am-10:00pm. Museum, Daily 8:00am-5:00pm. Admission: $5.00 parking. $4.00-$5.00 admission.***

This unusual park is an important archaeological site as well as a scenic recreational area. Seven earthen mounds within the park were built over 1000 -2000 years ago by the Swift Creek and Weeden Island Indians. The mounds include the oldest state great temple mound, two burial mounds and four ceremonial mounds. When you walk into the museum, you're walking inside a partially excavated mound, providing an unusual setting for viewing artifacts and a film. Outdoor activities include camping, fishing, pedal boat and canoe rental, swimming pool, mini-golf, and 5 miles of hiking trails.

Colquitt

SWAMP GRAVY

Colquitt - ***166 East Main Street (Cotton Hall) 39817. Phone: (229) 758-5450. www.swampgravy.com. Shows: Fridays 7:30pm, Saturday 2pm & 5:30pm (October and March) Admission: $27.00. Note: The town's visual narrative, We've Got a Story to Tell," showcases nine murals in Town Square and throughout town. Not recommended for children under 4. May Haw and Christmas productions vary during other months.***

If you want to delve into the true character of a region and area inhabitants, there is no better way than to experience the Folk Life plays found in Georgia. Swamp Gravy, Georgia's Official Folk Life Play, will delight and entertain you with real life stories from rural south Georgia. Each performance is a blend of comedy, drama, and music featuring a cast of more than 100 volunteers. All of Swamp Gravy's plays are based on real life stories, taken from taped interviews and adapted for the stage. The state's general assembly designated Swamp Gravy as the "Official Folk Life Play of Georgia". Located inside a 60-year-old renovated cotton warehouse now aptly known as Cotton Hall, the hall itself is a tourist attraction. In addition to its theater, Cotton Hall houses a gift shop, the Museum of Southern Cultures, and a Commons area. Experience the play that "...united a town and moved a nation."

Cordele

GEORGIA VETERANS STATE PARK

Cordele - *2459A US 280 West (I-75 exit 101, west to Cordele on US 280) 31015. Phone: (229) 276-2371. http://gastateparks.org/info/georgiavet/ Hours: Daily 7:00am-10:00pm. Admission: $5.00 daily vehicle parking fee.*

Established as a memorial to U.S. veterans, this park features a museum with aircraft, armored vehicles, uniforms, weapons, medals and other items from the Revolutionary War through the Gulf War. Kids gravitate to the outdoor exhibit of real-life wartime tanks and aircraft. We even found a floating tank. They all seem so large to kids. The SAM Shortline Excursion Train runs through the park on its way from Cordele to Plains. Modern camping sites, rental cottages, R/C Model Airplane Flying Field, a seasonal swimming pool and beach, a marina and one-mile Nature Trail add to the site. An 18-hole golf course and pro shop, along with 8,600-acre Lake Blackshear, make this one of Georgia's most popular state parks.

GEORGIA VETERANS STATE PARK - JULY 4TH CELEBRATION

Cordele - *A fireworks show kicks off Friday and old-fashioned games held on Saturday. Whole weekend features hayrides, historical tours and nature crafts. (July 4th weekend)*

LAKE BLACKSHEAR RESORT

Cordele - *2459-H US Highway 280 West (I-75 exit 101, west on Hwy 280) 31015. Phone: (229) 276-1004. www.lakeblackshearresort.com*

The resort is a privately operated resort within Georgia Veterans State Park with 14 hotel rooms, 64 villa rooms, 10 cottages, indoor/outdoor pools and a restaurant. The sunsets are beautiful from your screened-in porch and folks around the pool tell us the boating is excellent, with friendly stations along the way to gas up or dock and grab some chow. Besides the nice pool area, the resort offers bicycle, paddle boat, canoe and kayak rentals. The golf course offers Jr. golf camps. This is a modern oasis in a natural setting. Average Bed & Breakfast package is $130-$140.00 per room/cabin (refrigerator in each room). Resort internet rates start at $89.00. Pets welcome.

S A M SHORTLINE EXCURSION TRAIN

Cordele - *105 East 9th Avenue (I-75 exit 101/Hwy 280 west to Hwy 41. You may also board the train at any of the stops) 31015. Phone: (229) 276-2715 or (877) 427-2457. www.samshortline.com. Admission: Coach Class - Seats are not assigned: $29.99 adult, $19.99 child (2-12). Premium - has tables and chairs, ceiling fans and carpet (add $6.00-$8.00). Tours: Reservations: 800-864-7275. Walk-ups: first come, first serve. All departures from Cordele at 9:30am, returning around 5:00pm. See online schedule or brochure for Thursday, Friday, Saturday departures (March - December). Note: FLIPS FLOPS and sandals without backs are not allowed on the train for safety purposes. Rain gear is suggested since most depots are not covered and the train runs rain-or-shine. Sandwiches and snacks are ready for you to purchase in the Leslie Car aboard the train. Some towns have restaurants, but riders with special dietary needs may want to pack a picnic lunch.*

Climb aboard the air-conditioned vintage train traveling past pecan groves and scenic country farms, stopping in four towns filled with historic attractions, restaurants and shopping. Most tours stop for 45 minutes to 75 minutes at each town. While you can board the Southwest Georgia's Excursion Train at any of its stops, the official beginning is at Cordele. The first stop on the route is Georgia Veterans State Park, one of Georgia's most-visited state parks, featuring sparkling Lake Blackshear and fascinating military exhibits (see separate listing). Your next stop may be Leslie, home of the Rural Telephone Museum that showcases antiques, switchboards, classic cars, colorful murals – and, of course, antique telephones ($3.00 adults and $1.00 students). The Victorian town of Americus is your next stop. Tour Habitat for Humanity's Global Village (see separate listing). The small Georgia town made famous by President Jimmy Carter is next. While in Plains, browse President Carter's campaign museum, then buy a bag of peanuts from local merchants. A bit further down the tracks is the community of Archery, featuring the president's boyhood home. The train will stop just steps from his old front porch, and you'll have plenty of time to explore the farm before the SAM Shortline returns to Cordele. Because this all day trip makes so many stops and allows you to tour the highlights of the area - it is the idea way to tour with kids. This is one of the best overall train rides we've ever experienced! All aboard!

TRAIN time is QUALITY family time...

S A M SHORTLINE EXCURSION TRAIN - DAY OUT WITH THOMAS

Cordele - *105 East 9th Avenue 31015. Phone: (229) 276-2715 or (877) 427-2457. www.samshortline.com. The All Aboard Tour Classic Storybook Engine Chugs Into Georgia Veterans State Park. 25-Minute Ride With Thomas, Meet Sir Topham Hatt, Enjoy Storytelling, Live Music & Much More! Eight, 25-minute excursions per day beginning at 9:00am on the hour until 4:00pm. www.thomasandfriends.com. Advance purchase is recommended. Ticket sales are final. Events are rain or shine. (October weekends)*

S A M SHORTLINE EXCURSION TRAIN - SLEIGH BELLS & RAILS

Cordele - *All train rides in December are Sleigh Bells and Rails. Come with the excitement of Christmas in your PJ's just as the passengers did in the Polar Express movie. The train is decorated with all types of bells. All children receives a complimentary candy cane and of course, all receive a collectable bell from SAM Shortline. Admission (reservations suggested). (month-long in December)*

WATERMELON DAYS FESTIVAL

Cordele - *Downtown (I-75 exit 101). As the "Watermelon Capital of the World," Cordele naturally celebrates the quality and abundance of this locally grown fruit. Dancing, singing, parade, eat tons of watermelon, and competitions in seed-spitting contests. (two weeks in July)*

Donalsonville

SEMINOLE STATE PARK

Donalsonville - ***7870 State Park Road (16 miles south of town via GA 39 or 23 miles west of Bainbridge on GA 253) 39845. http://gastateparks.org/info/seminole/. Phone: (229) 861-3137. Hours: Daily 7:00am-10:00pm. Admission: $5.00 daily vehicle parking fee.***

Lake Seminole, a 37,500-acre reservoir known for excellent sport fishing and boating. The lake is shallow, but natural lime sink ponds have left areas of cool, clear water with a variety of fish. The threatened gopher tortoise, Georgia's state reptile, makes its home along the nature trail (2.2 miles long) designed to interpret the wiregrass community habitat. Cottages and many campsites are situated on the water's edge, offering excellent lake views. The park offers bicycle and canoe rentals.

BLUE AND GRAY MUSEUM

Fitzgerald - *116 N. Johnston Street (I-75 exit 82 east on Hwy 107 for 22 miles) 31750. Phone: (229) 426-5069. http://fitzgeraldga.org/. Hours: Tuesday-Saturday 10:00am-4:00pm, Sunday 1:00-5:00pm. Admission: $2.00-$5.00 per person.*

There's a remarkable harmony story in Fitzgerald. Experience the history yourself in this town created by Yanks and Rebs, former enemies, working together after the Civil War. See the story revealed in the museum. Watch the "Marching as One" video documentary - the whole story of how an attorney created a plan to carve a city out of the woods for aging Union Veterans - and how enemies finally became friends. Housed in a historic depot, the site is full of rare Civil War artifacts from both sides of the conflict - each telling a story. See reunion caps worn by Republic and Confederates and the stories behind each soldier. Who received the Congressional Medal of Honor and who received the Southern Cross of Honor? Extend your visit by walking around town. Visit Evergreen Cemetery and find Yanks and Rebs "resting side by side". How did one man from Indiana truly create a peaceful community?

BOWENS MILL FISH HATCHERY

Fitzgerald - *1773 Bowens Mill Hwy (US 129 north of town) 31750. Phone: (229) 426-5035. www.georgiawildlife.com/Hatcheries/BowensMill. Hours: Monday-Friday 8:00am-4:30pm. Admission: FREE. Tours: 45 minute tour of operations.*

Tours of this state fish hatchery include largemouth bass, catfish, bluegill and red-ear sunfish. Fish are raised from "babies" here and released to state lakes and ponds for abundant fishing in Georgia. Call ahead for tours.

JEFFERSON DAVIS HISTORIC SITE

Fitzgerald - *338 Jeff Davis Park Road (I-75 exit 78 east on GA 32 to Irwinville. Turn left into park) 31750. Phone: (229) 831-2335. http://gastateparks.org/jeffersondavis. Hours: Wednesday-Sunday 9:00am-5:00pm. Admission: $2.75-$4.00 per person. Educators: download coloring sheets.*

When Confederate President Jefferson Davis and a few remaining staff members crossed the Savannah River into Georgia, they didn't know that pursuit was so close behind. At dawn, they were surrounded by two groups of Union cavalry who were unaware of each other's presence. Davis was taken prisoner and held in Virginia for two years until released. Today, a monument marks the sport where he was arrested. Visitors can tour the historic site that includes a museum, a brief film, 1/3 mile short trail and picnic facilities.

Fort Gaines

GEORGE T. BAGBY STATE PARK AND LODGE

Fort Gaines - ***(4 miles north of Fort Gaines off GA 39) 39851. Phone: (229) 768-2571. http://georgetbagby.com. Hours: Daily 7:00am-10:00pm. Admission: $5.00 daily vehicle parking fee.***

This resort park features a 60-room lodge, restaurant, swimming pool, cottages and golf course. The park's marina and boat ramp offer easy access to the lake for fishing and boating. A three-mile nature trail winds through hardwoods and pines. There are also canoe, fishing boat & pontoon boat rentals.

Lumpkin

PROVIDENCE CANYON STATE PARK

Lumpkin - ***(7 miles west of Lumpkin on GA 39C) 31815. Phone: (229) 838-6202. www.gastateparks.org/info/providence/. Hours: Daily 7:00am - dark. Admission: $5.00 daily vehicle parking fee.***

This is Georgia's "Little Grand Canyon" where rare Plumleaf Azalea and other wildflowers (and pink, orange, red an purple hues of canyon soil) make a beautiful natural full-color picture. See the massive gullies which are up to 150 feet deep. Visitors can enjoy views of the canyons from the rim trail. Camping is available. An interpretive center explains how the massive gullies were caused by erosion due to poor farming practices in the 1800s.

WESTVILLE

Lumpkin - ***1 MLK Drive (US 27 & SR 27) 31815. www.westville.org. Phone: (229) 838-6410. Hours: Thursday-Saturday 10:00am-5:00pm. Closed major winter holidays. Admission: $10.00 adult, $8.00 senior and military, $5.00 child (K-12). Online discount coupon. Note: Like lots of action going on? Check out their seasonal events (see listings following).***

The hard-working townspeople here have replicated a working village of year 1850, complete with appropriate gardens, furnishings, and dirt streets. They make cotton cloth at Westville just as they did in 1850. Some of the houses at Westville have curtains and quilts made from cloth right here in the town.

A girl usually learned to quilt by the time she was eight or nine. Cloth wasn't plentiful, so quilts were fashioned from bits and pieces of scrap cloth sewn together. In rural 1850 Georgia, very few families owned wood stoves. Meals were cooked over open fires. Sample their homemade gingerbread cooked on a wood stove. They dip wax candles (made from beeswax or animal fat) at Westville, weather permitting. You'll find the shops of a blacksmith, potter, boot maker and cabinet maker, as well as a general store and doctor's office. Step inside an old church and sit on the handmade pews. The volunteers at the schoolhouse will be glad to tell you all about learning before the Civil War.

WESTVILLE - SPRING FESTIVAL

Lumpkin - *View crop plantings with mules, as well as musicians playing traditional instruments and school children in period dress attending 1850s style classes complete with slate boards and pencils. Admission. (first two weeks of April)*

WESTVILLE - FOURTH OF JULY CELEBRATION

Lumpkin - *Fourth of July celebration. The Independence Day celebration includes a barbeque, games such as the grease-pole climb, and blowing-sky-high-of the blacksmith's buried anvil. Admission. (July 4th)*

WESTVILLE - HARVEST FESTIVAL

Lumpkin - *When the leaves change color, this town celebrates harvest time with music and crafts. Among a variety of activities, visitors can watch sugar can being ground into syrup and cotton being separated from seed by Westville's mule-powered cotton gin believed to be the only in operation in the United States. Admission. (early October thru early November)*

WESTVILLE - YULETIDE SEASON

Lumpkin - *Christmas Decorating Workshop, Yule Log Ceremony, Christmas Tree Lightings, and the Burning of the Greens Ceremony. Admission. (Saturdays in December)*

Parrott

SOUND PLAY

Parrott - ***108 Railroad Street 31777. Phone: (229) 623-5545. www.soundplay.com. Hours: Weekdays 10:00am-6:00pm and some weekend hours. Informal visitors are always welcome. Admission: FREE. Tours: They are happy to have visitors and can accommodate tours or mini-workshops/demos if given enough notice.***

Visitors are encouraged to tour the workshop and play drums shaped like box turtles or alligators, metallophones, and other unusual outdoor musical instruments that are made on-site. Using recycled and "tuned" wood and metal materials, Bond Anderson creates and operates a busy commercial enterprise here. They usually have a variety of instruments waiting to be installed for visitors to play as a "test run". Look for their works of musical art at outdoor science centers and gardens for kids. This idea is a great way to expose your family to the art of physics and music interplay.

Perry

GEORGIA NATIONAL FAIR

Perry - *Georgia National Fairgrounds & Agricenter (I-75 exit 134 & 135) 99910. Phone: (478) 987-3247. www.gnfa.com. A celebration of Georgia's youth, agriculture, and heritage with competitive exhibits, food, midway rides and games, vendors, street entertainers, free family entertainment, free circus, nightly fireworks, and major concerts. The Georgia National Schoolhouse attracts pre-K through high school students to tour the educational exhibits with students admitted free. Admission for adults. Kids FREE. (nine days in early October)*

Plains

JIMMY CARTER NATIONAL HISTORIC SITE

Plains - ***300 North Bond Street (I-75 exit 112 taking GA27 all the way into town. Places are throughout downtown and along railroad tracks) 31780. www.nps.gov/jica. Phone: (229) 824-4104. Hours: Most buildings open at 9:00am or 10:00am, closing at 4:30-5:00pm. Admission: FREE. Educators: go to www.jimmycarter.info/justforkids_1.html for games, puzzles and help with a report on our 39th president. Miscellaneous: An orientation film is shown in the visitor center auditorium and a self-guided tour book is available for purchase at the visitor center. Daily each June-October: Exhibits outside and inside the buildings give the visitor and idea of what life was like for Jimmy Carter on the farm.***

When Jimmy Carter was in office, the only soft drink allowed to be served in the White House was Coca-Cola.

Dedicated to the 39th President of the United States, this national park site includes President Jimmy Carter's residence, boyhood farm, the railroad depot which served as his campaign headquarters during the 1976 election, and the Plains High School Museum & Welcome Center filled with Carter memorabilia. Few U.S. Presidents have had such close ties with where they were born and raised. The rural southern culture of Plains, Georgia that revolves around farming, church and school, had a large influence in molding the character and in shaping the political policies of the 39th President of the United States. The town slogan "Plains, Peanuts and A President" is personified here. PLAINS DEPOT (Main Street and M.L. Hudson Street) - This building was restored as Jimmy Carter's 1976 campaign headquarters. Visitors may view different exhibits and films on Carter's 1976 presidential campaign. CARTER BOYHOOD HOME - Old Plains Highway, Archery - Exhibits outside and inside the buildings give the visitor an idea of what life was like for Jimmy Carter on the farm. Listen to Jimmy talking about each room. Why couldn't the family ever finish a meal without interruption? What were some of young Jimmy's favorite boyhood treasures?

Where it all started...

Jimmy's bedroom in his Boyhood Home

PLAINS PEANUT FESTIVAL

Plains - *Downtown. www.plainsgeorgia.com/peanut_festival.html. Continuous free entertainment, historical and educational displays, recipe contests, and food. In the past, President Carter and the Secret Service battle the Plains High School alumni at their annual softball game on Sunday (see who's playing this year). The SAM Shortline Excursion Train with vintage cars, runs shuttles all afternoon. At the Recipe Contest, a pro chef prepares the winning recipes and offer samples of the peanut dishes. The Plains musical folk play " If the Sidewalks Could Talk," is performed at the high school in the evening. The focus is on the agriculture that still thrives in this area and its importance. (last weekend in September)*

Tifton

GEORGIA MUSEUM OF AGRICULTURE (AGRIRAMA)

Tifton - ***1392 Whiddon Mill Road (I-75, Exit 63B) 31793. Phone: (229) 386-3344 or (800) 767-1875. www.abac.edu/museum. Hours: Tuesday-Saturday 9:00am-4:30pm. Also closed on New Year's Day, Thanksgiving Day, three days prior to Christmas and Christmas Day. Admission: $7.00 adult, $6.00 senior (55+), $4.00 child (5-16). Note: Enjoy the Wiregrass Opry on selected Saturday nights.***

The State's living history museum consists of four distinct areas: traditional farm community of the 1870s, progressive farmstead of the 1890s, industrial sites complex, and a rural town. Costumed interpreters are on location daily to explain and demonstrate the lifestyle and activities of the period. See bacon and ham curing in the smoke-house and veggies preserved in the canning shed. Ride a logging train into the woods, walk down to the sawmill and turpentine still, see the cooper's shed and the blacksmith's shop before crossing the street to the working print shop. At the Feed and Seed Store and Drug Store, order your favorite refreshments from a working marble top soda fountain. Kids especially love Agrirama's barnyard animals. Because there are over 35 structures relocated to the site, you can meet many different tradesmen and crafters performing different chores. Be careful, they may ask you to help them.

AGRIRAMA - SPRING FOLK LIFE FESTIVAL

Tifton - *Special demonstrations of the labors, including sheep shearing, rail spitting, log rolling, textile arts, quilting, workshops and more, plus enjoy music at the Wiregrass Opry. Special Antique Show & Turpentine Stilling. Admission. (Saturday of second weekend in April)*

AGRIRAMA - VICTORIAN CHRISTMAS CELEBRATION

Tifton - *Enjoy Christmas in an 1890's rural south village with historic decorations, Christmas carolers, a live nativity scene & the famous dessert sampler. Children can visit with Santa and shop at the Secret Santa Shop. Cane grinding party, corn popping, bon fires, candy pulling and live music. Fee for hayrides. FREE. (second Saturday in*

December)

Valdosta

WILD ADVENTURES THEME PARK

Valdosta - ***3766 Old Clyattville Road (I-75 exit 13) 31601. Phone: (229) 219-7080. www.wildadventures.com. Hours: Open practically year-round at 10:00am (peaks April-August). Closing time varies with season (6:00-10:00pm). Admission: $40.00-$45.00 per person. Parking $7.00. Educators: online lesson plans are under: Groups/School Field Trips/Teacher Resources (science/physics orientation).***

They boast five parks in one place. Through one gate there are wild rides, wild animals and wild entertainment...all with a safari animal theme. The park has 9 roller coasters, 5 water rides, go-karts, over 500 wild animals placed in natural habitats scattered throughout the park, and daily shows plus 50 big-name concerts and special events. Slide into something refreshing at Splash Island Water Park - ride Catchawave Bay or the Double Dip Zip, mist in the Rain Fortress or float Paradise River (seasonal weather-dependent hours). Entertaining shows feature animals, costumed characters, song, dance, magic and music. Board their safari train where you'll take a cross-continent ride through the open grasslands of Africa and Asia encountering elephants, antelope, zebra, giraffe and more. Walk through the Rain Forest on a journey through a natural wetland featuring birds, monkeys, reptiles and bears. Pet animals in the Wild West Petting Zoo. Evenings provide many eateries, a 3D laser and fireworks show and shopping along with numerous concerts.

WILD ADVENTURES THEME PARK - FESTIVAL OF LIGHTS

Valdosta - *3766 Old Clyattville Road (I-75 exit 13) 31601. Phone: (229) 219-7080. www.wildadventures.net. The south's largest Christmas celebration, it features millions of beautiful lights, displays, sounds, and wonderful holiday shows including an ice skating spectacular "Christmas on Ice." Admission. (mid-November thru December)*

Vienna

ELLIS BROTHERS PECAN PACKING COMPANY

Vienna - ***1315 Tippettville Road (I-75 exit 109 east) 31092. Phone: (229) 268-9041 or (800) 635-0616. www.werenuts.com. Hours: Retail Store open 8:00am-8:00pm (including holidays). Tours: Guided tours by appointment.***

Ellis Bros. Pecans is a family owned and operated wholesale and retail business. The original pecan grove was started in 1944 by Marvin and Irene

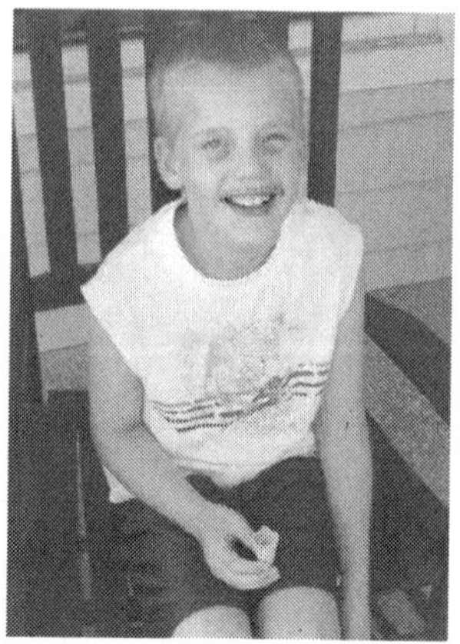
We LOVE stopping here - and yummy ice cream, too!

Ellis. The shelling plant and retail store are located adjacent to the original pecan grove. Elliott Ellis and his sons manage the operation today. Ms. Irene continues to oversee her candy kitchen. Visitors can view the pecan- and peanut-packing process firsthand by a pre-arranged tour or just watch thru a viewing window (seasonal). Our favorite part - sampling! (and then buying a variety of products made on-site). If you like to stop here for a restroom and ice cream and candied nuts break - try their pecan pie or peach ice cream. Sit a spell on the front porch rocking chairs or take it to go on your travels along I-75.

GEORGIA COTTON MUSEUM

Vienna - ***1321 E. Union Street (I-75 exit 109 west) 31092. Phone: (229) 268-2045. www.cityofvienna.org. Hours: Thursday-Friday 9:00am-4:00pm, Saturday 10:00am-2:00pm. Admission: FREE.***

The history of cotton is told with the aid of farm tools, cotton bolls, a cotton bale, scale and planters desk that kept accurate records of the harvest. It includes the slave issues and how their participation in the production of cotton contributed to the economy. How did farmers deal with insects and poor weather? Ride through the county in the fall to see the beauty of "snow in the south" harvest. The cotton is so thick and so white that it appears to be snow on the ground.

AMUSEMENTS

ANIMALS & FARMS

HISTORY

HISTORY *(cont.)*

MUSEUMS

OUTDOOR EXPLORING

SEASONAL & SPECIAL EVENTS

SEASONAL & SPECIAL EVENTS *(cont.)*

SEASONAL & SPECIAL EVENTS *(cont.)*

SCIENCE

SPORTS

SUGGESTED LODGING & DINING

THE ARTS

TOURS

30728211R00123

Made in the USA
Charleston, SC
25 June 2014